THE WAY HOME

AY

Reality

CROSSWAY BOOKS • WESTCHESTER, ILLINOIS
A DIVISION OF GOOD NEWS PUBLISHERS

The Way Home. Copyright © 1985 by Mary Pride. Published by Crossway Books, a division of Good News Publishers, Westchester, Illinois 60153.

Cover design by Sarah Cioni/The Cioni Artworks

Second printing 1985

Printed in the United States of America

Library of Congress Catalog Card Number 84-73078

ISBN 0-89107-345-0

To my husband Bill
    a Christian gentleman;

to our two good helpers
    Theodore and Joseph
    who are learning to be Christian gentlemen
        "just like Daddy";

and to Sarah Elizabeth
    who is not yet old enough to help
    or to want to be like Mommy
    but who makes our lives sing
        just by being there.

Contents

Acknowledgments

Three years of struggle would not have been enough to finish this book without the help of the following women:

Nancy Akin, who argued with me, tried valiantly to disciple me, and gave me my first sewing machine.

Peggy Barker, who loaned me her electric typewriter.

Prudence Barker, who prayed for the needed miracles and saw them happen.

Leslie Cotton, who made many useful suggestions.

Nancy Pearcey, who introduced me to the home-school movement.

Christine Princivalli, who also made many useful suggestions.

And I'd like to thank these women for their encouragement: Lulli Akin, Jayne Korljan, Judy Lynne Smith, and Kim Williams.

My best friend and mildest critic is, of course, my husband Bill.

I must thank Franky Schaeffer for his enthusiasm and for actually agreeing to be my book agent; Lane Dennis for likewise agreeing to be my publisher; and Jan Dennis for his excellent work as editor.

The sweat and tears are mine, and perhaps some blood as well when this book is reviewed in certain quarters! And I thank you, my reader, for whom I wrote it in the first place.

Introduction

This book is an exposition of the Bible's "mystery passage," Titus 2:3-5.

> Likewise, teach the older women to be reverent in the way they live, not to be slanderers or addicted to much wine, but to teach what is good. Then they can train the younger women to love their husbands and children, to be self-controlled and pure, to be busy at home [literally, *home-working*], to be kind, and to be subject to their husbands, so that no one will malign the word of God.

The mystery is not what this passage *says*—its message is fairly obvious. The mystery involves why modern Christian writers on woman's role are so unwilling to face up to it. Titus 2:3-5 is the most important text in the Bible on married women's roles, capsulizing a young wife's marital, sexual, biological, economic, authority, and ministering roles. Yet women's books routinely ignore, mutilate, or even mock this passage. There appears to be a great desire to accommodate Christianity to our culture, and a corresponding willingness to dismiss the Bible's teaching as a remnant of outdated, male-dominated culture.

What happens when women throw out what the Bible says about women's sphere because it "merely reflects ancient patriarchal culture," and then launch forth into a lifestyle that reflects *our* culture? This book will answer that question.

Christians have accepted feminists' "moderate" demands for family planning and careers while rejecting the "radical" side of feminism—meaning lesbianism and abortion. What most do not see is that one demand leads to the other. *Feminism is a totally self-consistent system aimed at rejecting God's role for women.* Those who adopt any part of its lifestyle can't help picking up its philosophy. And those who pick up its philosophy are buying themselves a one-way ticket to social anarchy.

Am I overstating the case? Well, who would have believed in 1955 that in twenty short years over one-third of all mothers with children under the age of *three* would be leaving their infants in day-care?[1] But it happened! The reason it happened, in a land where apple pie and motherhood used to be sacred, is that Christians, along with everyone else, had already accepted the basic outlook on which feminism is based. Feminism is self-consistent; the Christianity of the fifties wasn't. Feminists had a plan for women; Christians didn't.

Although the Bible teaches distinctly what a wife's role should be, this teaching had been getting more and more muted in the churches until it was almost muffled entirely. Women did not know their calling, or why it was important. They became restless.

Motherhood in the fifties, for example, had been reduced to a five- or ten-year span, lasting only until the youngest of the two or three "planned" children was in kindergarten. With an empty house full of labor-saving appliances and a family which no longer seemed to need her, it was understandable that a woman felt trapped at home. She was not expected to *produce* anything at home; her very inactivity was a status symbol for her husband, proving he could afford to maintain her in idleness. All the action seemed to be out there in the men's world, while she felt bored and useless.

Feminism claimed to be the answer to the housewife's dilemma, and women were captivated by the freedom feminists promised. Sentimental arguments about the importance of motherhood fell flat against the obvious truth that the children already weren't home most of the day. Ham-fisted attempts to "keep those uppity women in their place" just flung fuel on the feminists' fire. Women were tired of being sex objects and housekeepers. They wanted more scope for their talents.

The sad truth is that the "traditional" role which feminists attacked in the fifties had already lost its scriptural fullness.[2] Christian women were staying home out of habit, not out of conviction. Women had been robbed of their role, even through they were "in their place." *And they were robbed by the church.*

The Christian churches in this country had actually paved the way for feminism to succeed, even as preachers orated about the sanctity of motherhood! Denominations endorsed family planning and "therapeutic abortion." Church meetings were scheduled for every night of the week, giving out a clear message that family life was unimportant. Ministry was considered more worthwhile than motherhood, as missionaries were expected to leave their children in boarding schools as a matter of course. Church life centered on the church building, not the home. Even in the church building, children were whisked out of sight into the nursery, children's church, and their own Sunday school program.

At every turn Christian women found that their biological, economic, and social roles were considered worthless. *Men's* ministry, *men's* money, *men's* building and programs—*these* were the areas that mattered.

Today we are reaping the fruits. Role obliteration is the coming thing in evangelical, and even fundamentalist, circles. If women can't be women, by golly they will be men! All because two or more generations have grown up and married without ever hearing that the Bible teaches a distinct role for women which is *different* from that of a man and *just as important*.

Homeworking is the biblical lifestyle for Christian wives. Homeworking is *not* just staying home either (that was the mistake of the fifties). We are not called by God to *stay* home, or to *sit* at home, but to *work* at home! Homeworking is the exact opposite of the modern careerist/institutional/Socialist movement. It is a way to take back control of education, health care, agriculture, social welfare, business, housing, morality, and evangelism from the faceless institutions to which we have surrendered them. More importantly, homeworking is the path of obedience to God. Homeworking is based on what the Scriptures say. Nowhere in this book will you find a "Scripture seems to say this, but that can't apply to our culture," or "The Bible says this, but . . ."

Homeworking, like feminism, is a total lifestyle. The difference is that homeworking produces stable homes, growing churches, and children who are Christian leaders.

Each section of this book is dedicated to one of the womanly roles listed in Titus 2:3-5: loving your husband, loving your children, homeworking, being kind and subject to your husband, and what happens if we do (or don't do) all this.

Every great fire starts with one small spark. It is my hope and prayer that this book will be the "spark" which leads Christian women to fall in love with their families again and to determine to be working wives—*in the home!*

Part One:

BACK TO WIFELINESS

" . . . train the younger women to love their husbands . . ."
(Titus 2:4)

1   The Great Con Game

Today's women are the victims of the second biggest con game in history. (The first was when the serpent persuaded Eve she needed to upgrade her lifestyle and "become like God.") The courts rip away our legal protection via "no-fault" divorce, nonexistent alimony, and joint custody. "Women's" magazines follow in the footsteps of *Playboy* and *Hustler,* degrading us to the level of unpaid prostitutes by glamourizing uncommitted sex. Employers are losing their commitment to providing our husbands with a living wage, reasoning that we, their wives, can always get a job to make up the slack.[1] Cigarette and alcohol manufacturers gleefully haul in big bucks from the exploding new women's market, while our cancer and alcoholism rates skyrocket. Community colleges everywhere are scrambling to cash in on the huge wave of "displaced homemakers," meaning women who have been ditched by their husbands and are now forced to earn bread and rent money. All in the name of Liberation.

What makes this oppression so strange is that it is self-inflicted. *Women* have pushed through the "liberated" divorce laws which allow husbands to collect alimony from wives and allow adulterers and perverts to retain custody. *Women* are the ones working feverishly to remove children from their parents' care and place them in state institutions (we will see how they are trying to do this later on). All over America, in your town and mine, right now women are working to abolish the traditional family, to legitimize infanticide, homosexuality, and adultery. They have already succeeded in making abortion legal; now they are struggling for the right to murder one's child once he or she is born—or better yet, to let the State decide which children shall or shall not live. This total rejection of women's unique biological role is also called Liberation. And finally, women are pressing for state control over our personal property and lifestyles as well. (We will look at this move toward totalitarianism in Chapter 13.)

Christian women have fallen in with the lifestyle of the so-called women's movement in large numbers, not seeing what is waiting around the corner. Jean Shaw noted this phenomenon in a 1980 article in the *Presbyterian Journal:*

> Christian women . . . may not enter employment in such large numbers, but their lifestyle in the past has not proved to be radically different from that of their non-Christian neighbors. . . . Even mothers of very small children won't be away from work for long.[2]

Since then, Mrs. Shaw's prediction has proved correct. Christian magazines have fallen over each other in their eagerness to endorse outside careers for wives, even mothers of infants. The general feeling in the church seems to be that women have no special God-given role, and that careers for wives are harmless, or even beneficial.

Is careerism harmless? Another way to ask this is to ask, "Is *feminism* harmless?" Feminists, after all, created the female career movement, not Bible-believing Christians. True, feminism is more than careers for women, but can careerism be separated from its feminist roots? Or are careers for wives the symptom of a feminist philosophy that is beginning to infect our churches?

What would you say if I could prove that modern Christian women are being duped into becoming devotees of a false religion which bills itself as the "primordial, always present, and future Antichrist"?[3] What if our "harmless" embracing of feminist career goals is intertwined with and leads to moral, social, and economic collapse for our country? What would you say if the price of so-called Liberation turned out to be enslavement to a totalitarian regime? How about theology? Did you know that inerrancy and a "modern" role for women are at odds, and that in fact every advocate of Liberation within the church has abandoned inerrancy?

Do you find this hard to believe? Let's look at some proof.

Humanism on the Half Shell

Those who have never been involved in the feminist movement, as I have, don't realize that feminism is a religion. *Feminism is only human-*

ism on the half shell. To humanists, man is the measure of all things. To feminists, the measure of all things is woman. *Woman, to feminists, is God.*

At the first national all-woman conference on women's spirituality, which was held in Boston on April 23, 1976, feminist idolatry came out into the open. (It had been revealed earlier than this on a regional scale. I remember my feminist high-school teacher introducing us to the concept of reviving witchcraft as the original "women's religion.")

> After listening attentively to two addresses . . . the audience became very active. . . . they chanted, "The Goddess Is Alive—Magic Is Afoot." The women evoked the Goddess with dancing, stamping, clapping and yelling. They stood on pews and danced barebreasted on the pulpit and amid the hymnbooks.
>
> In fact, the women were angry at all religions of the fathers and took this opportunity to mock and defy those religions in a church they had rented for the occasion. . . . Proclaiming that the "Goddess Is Alive" in a traditional church setting is proclaiming that . . . being female is divine. . . .[4]

Naomi Goldenberg, our reporter of this incident and a feminist herself, is quick to assure us that the "Goddess was never symbolized as an idol or a picture in this or any other ritual." That is because feminism dispenses with external idolatry and goes straight to self-worship.

> Each woman is encouraged to keep a small altar in her home to be used for meditation and for focusing her will. At the Boston conference, women were advised to use mirrors on their altars to represent the Goddess. That way, they would be continually reminded that *they were the Goddess* and that they had divine beauty, power and dignity.[5] (emphasis mine)

To those outside, feminism is usually seen as a nonreligous movement striving only for fairness for women. To those inside, it is a different story . . .

> The feminist movement in Western culture is engaged in the slow execution of Christ and Yahweh. Yet very few of the women and men now working for sexual equality within Christianity and Judaism realize the extent of their heresy.[6]

Both feminists and mainstream churchgoers agree that the church is adapting to "nonsexist culture." Does this mean a change in Christianity (and Judaism)? Naomi Goldenberg thinks it does: she has become a witch. Still, some disagree with her prediction that feminism will destroy all traditional religions.

Many scholars of religion disagree with the radical direction I have predicted. They say that Christianity and Judaism can survive the very basic changes that will have to be made when these religions adapt to nonsexist culture. These scholars insist that a religion is whatever its followers define it to be. Christianity and Judaism, therefore, are said to consist of whatever those who call themselves Christians and Jews practice as religion. Theoretically then, Christianity could exist without Christ and Judaism could exist without Yahweh's laws as long as Christians and Jews *thought* of these departures from tradition as being in basic harmony with their faiths.[7]

Christianity without Christ? Is that where adapting to nonsexist culture is leading us?

Castrated Christianity

Mary Daly, who calls herself a Christian feminist, says this:

To put it rather bluntly, I propose that Christianity itself should be castrated by cutting away the products of supermale arrogance: the myths of sin and salvation that are simply two diverse symptoms of the same disease. . . .

I am suggesting that the idea of salvation uniquely by a male savior perpetuates the problem of patriarchal oppression. . . . Jesus Was A Feminist, But So What? In an admirable and scholarly article Leonard Swidler marshals historical evidence to show convincingly that Jesus was a feminist. What I think I perceive happening in the rising woman consciousness is an affirmation that goes something like this: "Fine. Wonderful. But even if he wasn't, *I am.*"

What is happening now is that these primordial eunuchs [she means women] are rising up to castrate the system that castrates— the great "God-Father" of us all.[8]

What makes someone who calls herself a Christian say something like that? That answer, of course, is that she is no longer a Christian. This woman elsewhere lauds the feminist movement for its "dynamic that drives beyond Christolatry,"[9] as if worshiping Jesus Christ were idolatry. She is busy exchanging God the Father and Christ for an idol made in her own image, and only regrets that she and her friends did not do this sooner. "We have not been free to use our own power to name ourselves, the world, or God," she laments.[10] Her solution is feminist religion: "The unfolding of God, then, is an event in which women participate as we participate in our own revolution."[11]

Alice Hageman, another member of Mary Daly's Harvard Divinity School Women's Caucus, links careerism with what she sees as the necessary rejection of the Christian God.

> Does it [the Christian faith] offer women spiritual and intellectual resources so that they can unashamedly derive satisfaction from work done outside the home? . . . Perhaps most centrally, are we within the churches capable of eliminating the familial images which crowd Scripture and liturgy—beginning with God the Father, and His earthly counterpart, the priest-father?[12]

Ms. Hageman also joins this call for abolishment of God and endorsement of female careers, including ordination, with a wish to eliminate the "anti-body bias of Christianity. . . so as to enable women (and men as well) to experience and rejoice in the gift of their sensuality."[13] This linkage is important, because (as we shall see) woman's biological, economic, marital, sexual, and church roles are all interconnected, and feminism is an assault on them all.

Are these women who cry out for the castration of God just a handful of harmless weirdos? No. All over this country Women's Studies departments are springing up in universities, dedicated to propagating feminism as religion. Just this spring I received a bulletin from our local university that contained this course offering:

417 Women's Spirituality
Exploration of women's spirituality beyond traditional, patriarchal religions. The significance of the ancient Goddess traditions for women today, individual spirituality as a manifestation of personal power, and the transformation of spiritual power into political power. *Prerequisite:* WoSt 317 or consent of instructor.[14]

What is "WoSt 317," which is required before women can learn how to be spiritual? Here it is:

317 Woman and Religion

The roles of women in religion; the early Goddess traditions; attitudes toward gender in Judaic and Christian traditions; *feminist attempts to reform these traditions;* and women's spirituality beyond traditional, patriarchal religions.[15] (emphasis mine)

Feminists are indeed anxious to "reform" our "traditional, patriarchal" Christianity. Some have already begun to do so. I refer to the evangelicals who are writing and lecturing on women's role, whose articles get printed in Christian magazines and whose books are used for women's Bible studies. They call themselves the "biblical feminists."

The most crucial question the biblical feminists have raised is how to interpret the Bible. . . . They think that since the Bible was written in a patriarchal culture, the biblical writers are prejudiced by that culture against women's rights. . . . According to this approach, the Bible is fallible and it can contradict itself. In effect, this view exalts human reason, by which man then determines what is and what is not God's authoritative word. . . .

To summarize, the biblical feminists see irreconcilable contradictions in the Bible's teaching on women. These contradictions are resolved by acknowledging that the Bible reflects human limitations. . . .

Biblical feminists do not believe that God has given us his word, true and trustworthy, the unchanging standard for beliefs and practice. Instead we have a hodgepodge of information (some of it is God's pure word, and some is only man's advice, molded by his male-dominated culture), and God has left us on our own to figure out which parts to obey and believe. Human reason becomes the final authority, the judge of Scripture.[16]

Susan Foh, who wrote those words, is right. Her book *Women and the Word of God* thoroughly exposes the "biblical" feminists' departure from Bible belief, in a way that I have no space to duplicate here. (You can read her book, or even read *their* books, if you feel you must see firsthand how entire passages of God-breathed Scripture are obliterated by feminist "exegesis.") Yet the very writers Susan Foh exposed—Paul Jewett, Letha Scanzoni, Virginia Mollenkott—are still honored in evangelical circles. Anti-Christian feminism is *inside* the church.

Again people might ask, "What's the big uproar? Sure, feminists originated the women's movement, but Christians don't go along with their radical excesses. We are just taking feminists' good insights, like about working wives, and leaving the rest alone." It's not that simple. Feminism is a religion. Like all religions, it has a Great Assumption. Christianity's Great Assumption (which unlike other religions' is verifiable by historical evidence) is that the Bible is true. Feminism's Great Assumption is that woman is the measure of all things. Translated, the burning question becomes, "What will fulfill me as a woman? Anything that interferes with my sovereign 'fulfillment' is to be destroyed—and I mean *anything*."

Let's take a look at what our nice, tame, evangelical feminists are willing to destroy.

What Happens When Women Stray
First, they endorse abortion.

Yet, at the same time, is abortion entirely out of the question for a Christian couple faced with an unplanned pregnancy at a time when it could be detrimental to the whole family? . . . What about a Christian couple who learn through genetic counseling that tests show their baby will be a mongoloid, or the wife who contracts rubella early in her pregnancy and knows her child is likely to be malformed? Does Christian morality insist that these pregnancies be carried through, even though bringing the child into the world may cause extreme emotional distress and financial hardships for the family? We think not.[17]

To feminists, biblical or otherwise, woman's biological role of motherhood as designed by God is at best embarrassing and at worst worthless. Babies are an option for those who "do not want to deny themselves the experience of parenthood,"[18] and disposable when they interfere with our emotions or finances.

Complete role obliteration is what feminists, biblical or otherwise, are after. "And if there are no significant distinctions, this fiction can be maintained only by the use of abortion-on-demand as a means of coping with the most profound evidence that distinctions really do exist," as Dr. Francis Schaeffer points out in his book *The Great Evangelical Disaster*.[19]

Dr. Schaeffer also mentions the effect that obliteration of role distinctions must have on sexual relationships: "For if there are no significant distinctions between men and women, then certainly we cannot condemn homosexual relationships."[20] And, as a matter of fact, the biblical feminists do endorse homosexuality. One year after her book

Women, Men and the Bible came out, Virginia Mollenkott collaborated with Letha Scanzoni (the co-author of *All We're Meant to Be)* to produce the book *Is the Homosexual My Neighbor?* In it, they ask

> Who is my neighbor?
> Who is my friend?
> Could it be the Samaritan?
> Could it be the homosexual?[21]

They answer this question by first dismissing the traditional (read "biblical") Christian position that homosexuality is sin, and then the traditional psychoanalytic teaching that it is an illness. Their position?

> Since the acceptance of lifelong homosexual unions would solve a great many problems, provide helpful guidelines for both ethical living and ordination decisions, this alternative to traditional attitudes is worth exploring in greater depth.[22]

They also refer with approval to a panel of Christians in the mental health professions whose majority view was that

> God's perfect will is for the monogamous heterosexual family. However . . . Christians burdened with an involuntary homosexual orientation could choose a committed homosexual relationship as within God's "permissive" will rather than an unwanted celibacy.[23]

Contrast this with Letha Scanzoni's view on heterosexual singleness in *All We're Meant to Be:*

> An unsupportive husband can be a millstone, dragging a woman down and holding her back from all she could otherwise be. A woman should determine *before* marriage what kind of husband can work together with her rather than against her. If such a man can't be found, a lifetime of singleness would seem preferable to a marriage in which a woman's gifts would be stifled and in which the husband and wife could not share fully their total selves.[24]

So out of this emerges an ethic: homosexuals should be free to indulge in sin to avoid "unwanted celibacy," while heterosexuals would be better off as celibates than married to a nonfeminist husband. Feminism is worth sacrificing marriage for, but the Bible's teaching on homosexuality is not.

Mollenkott and Scanzoni find it hard to hold the line anywhere against homosexuality, just as Dr. Schaeffer would predict. "Perhaps it is wise to keep *pedophiliacs* or *pederasts* [child molesters] from teaching children. But from the standpoint of the children's safety, there is no more reason for barring an ordinary homosexual from working with children than there is for barring an ordinary heterosexual from the same job."[25] They cannot quite bring themselves to explicitly prohibit child molesters from teaching children—perhaps it would be wise to do so but again, perhaps not. *Moral* safety is not even an issue. Homosexuals in their view will make fine teachers of Christian children, as well as excellent role models.

What else do the "biblical" feminists want? Ordination for women, of course—which oddly enough (or not so oddly) is coupled in their minds with careers for wives. "If a woman has been called and gifted by God to be a pastor or a priest," writes Virginia Mollenkott, "it is a fearful thing for the organized church to block her from that ministry. And if a Christian woman has been called and gifted for some career outside the home, and her husband blocks her by refusing to assist with the care of their mutual home and their mutual children, isn't he frustrating the work of the Holy Spirit?"[26]

Ms. Mollenkott elsewhere makes it clear that if a husband refuses staunchly to become Mommy's little helper, the wife has a right to make the "difficult decision" to "abandon the relationship in search of a more affirming life-style."[27] So careerism justifies divorce of an uncooperative husband. Children, sex roles, biblical church government, and now marriage itself are all targets of the "harmless" evangelical feminist movement.

Stop and think calmly about this for a minute. We are being asked to embrace a lifestyle which *unbelievers* would have considered perverted only forty years ago. We are being asked to kill our babies, endorse homosexuality (and perhaps become lesbians), nag our husbands to do our job so we can do theirs—under threat of divorce—and all in the name of *Christ!*

But the words *Christ* and *God* are just a smokescreen. The evangelical feminists are really *much* more anxious to convert us to feminism than they are to convert feminists to Christ. (The Scanzonis' sociology text for college students, for example, makes no attempt to put in a good word for Christianity, but instead mocks and downgrades traditional Christians and their beliefs.) This is the way liberalism has invaded Christianity in the last 150 years—singing the Siren song of deeper insights and wielding the weapon of superior scornfulness at our outmoded peasant ways. As James Fitzpatrick points out in his illuminating book on liberals and their ways, *Jesus Christ Before He Became a Superstar,*

> The updaters don't ask us to turn against Christ. They *use* him to prepare us for the next step toward wisdom—the direction of which varies according to the pet ideology of the updater.[28]

Some people think that no nice Christian should talk about anyone the way I am talking about the feminist leaders within the church. But they who teach should be judged more strictly (although our policy for the last 150 years has been to call the wolves "brother" and "sister" and to refuse to expose them until they throw *us* out of the church). But *somebody* has to point out that the Empress, just like her husband the humanist Emperor, has no clothes. Feminists have picked up the threadbare heresies of humanism, and only a mistaken sense of chivalry keeps us from seeing that all they want is to strip off our robe of righteousness so they won't be embarrassed standing all alone in their theological nakedness.

Careers for wives is *not* a single issue. It is the symptom of a massive loss of Christian perspective involving, as Scanzoni and Hardesty inform us,

> the nature of sexuality, the meaning of marriage, questions about vocation, ordination, friendship, homosexuality, abortion . . . equal pay, employment discrimination, child care, educational opportunity, care for the aged. . . .[29]

The list Scanzoni and Hardesty present is an echo of what secular feminists see as the goals and results of their movement:

> Feminism since the early 1960s has begun to color interpersonal relations, the language we speak, family life, the educational system, child-rearing practices, politics, business, the mass media, religion, law, the judicial system, the cultural values system, and intellectual life.[30]

The movement toward outside careers is *not* a Christian invention. "The American materialistic feminist tradition favoring women's economic independence and socialized domestic work" gave it birth in the nineteenth century.[31] That movement itself grew out of "communitarian socialism, anarchism, free love, and feminism."[32] This is *not* a grouping which strikes one immediately as shining for Christ.

The Bible has a lot to say about woman's role, none of it resembling feminist dogma. And what the Bible says is *important*. It will help us understand why our society is deteriorating so rapidly; why the church seems impotent in the face of social revolution; how Christians lost control of America in the first place; and how we can go about *taking it back*.

2   Beyond the "Me" Marriage

These are the times that try women's souls. For the first time in American history, a marriage is more likely to break up than to last until death does it part. Single-parent families are forming at twenty times the rate of two-parent families, and you know who the vast majority of those lonely single parents are: women.

Here's what one serious article from a major national magazine has to say about where current trends are taking us:

> Over the next five decades, experts say, society will redefine its concept of the family. . . . Serial marriages, a growing trend even now, will be a normal and planned-for part of adulthood. Tomorrow's children will grow up with several sets of parents and an assortment of half and step siblings. . . .
>
> Already it is predicted that by 1990 up to 50 percent of all children will have experienced divorce and remarriage in their families.[1]

The people who wrote this article were not kidding. Their predictions are not all for the far distant future, either. 1990, the year by which 50 percent of all American children are supposed to have lived through a divorce and remarriage, is almost here.

The Infected Church

Is the skyrocketing divorce rate confined only to the non-Christian world? Don't we just wish it were! You know and I know that churchgoing families have run on hard times. Witness the spate of books about the family. We are groping for something, anything, that will help our churches ride out the tidal wave of brokenness sweeping over America.

Responses to the Christian family's pleas for help have taken two main forms. Some evangelicals, acting the part of the permissive parent, assure us that divorce is actually a sign of our flowering personhoods and that "it must be OK, dear, because all your friends are doing it." This is like calling skunk cabbages roses to make them smell better. Others take to the road to publicize their latest findings on Wonderful Marriage, Intimate Marriage, Exciting Marriage. These seminars appear to offer some help, so church folks attend in droves. Unhappily when the weekend is over, families are still breaking up and couples are more discontented than ever.

It doesn't have to be this way.

Some say that this sorry state is a sure sign of the end times. But end times or no end times, the church is *always* supposed to be the light of the world. God expects us to shine brightly, not flicker fitfully! The church is also supposed to be the salt of the world, which even in small amounts flavors the mass and protects it from decay. We *can* and *should* be influencing the world to get better; it shouldn't be influencing us to get worse.

If the Christian family is falling into disrepair, it is not because our God is not powerful enough to maintain us in the midst of a corrupt society. New Testament Christians faced a society that in some ways was even more decadent than ours, with cult prostitutes, infanticide, and gladiators battling to the death for the crowd's "entertainment." Yet history witnesses that the early Christians had outstandingly stable and holy home lives. If we can't say the same, perhaps it is because we have walked away from what the New Testament Christians had. Perhaps in our zeal to be relevant we have replaced Christian culture with twentieth-century humanist culture.

Divorce among Christians is not normal. It is God's plain signal to warn us that we have gone astray. Divorce in the church tells us that the church has left the path in its preaching on marriage.

A wrong view of marriage is like a man whose ankle is out of joint. Because his ankle is crooked, his knee sticks out sideways. Because his knee is twisted, his hip angles oddly. Because his hip is skewed, everything he does is clumsy. Similarly, the way we young wives handle our duty to "love their husbands" affects how we treat our children, how we behave in our homes, and what contribution we make to our church and our community. Husbands come before children; and homes, as the basic building-blocks, come before church and State. Husbands are just as responsible as wives for keeping their families together. All the same, the new theories of marriage affect the wife's role first. All of them share in common a radical new role for women.

Let's look now at three popular views of Christian marriage and see if we can see why the glue is leaking out of the joints of the Christian family. We shall then consider what God *really* designed marriage to be, and what we can do about it.

Searching for Companionship

The first popular view is that God created marriage for companionship. One writer explains,

> God's own answer to the question of what marriage is is found in Genesis 2:18: "It is not good for the man to be alone. I will make him a helper who approximates [or corresponds to] him." In other words, the reason for marriage is *to solve the problem of loneliness.*
>
> Marriage was established because Adam was alone, and that was not good. *Companionship,* therefore, is the essence of marriage.[2]

Later this writer states, "God provided Eve not only (or even primarily) as Adam's helper . . . but as his companion."[3]

This analysis may sound good, but it directly contradicts the Bible passage our writer is quoting. God did say, "It is not good for the man to be alone," but the *reason* he gave was that Adam needed a helper. God could have given Adam a *dog* if all Adam needed was a companion. God could have given Adam *another man* if companionship was all Adam needed.

Of course Adam was not drooping about, overcome with loneliness, yearning for a companion. How could he be lonely, face to face with God? Adam was *alone:* incomplete, not lonely. He needed a helper. He needed a woman.

Groping for Intimacy

The second popular view of Christian marriage can be labelled "Intimacy." Intimacy theology is one step beyond companionship theology. Here is what one believer in intimate marriage has to say:

> The traditional family pattern provided defined roles for males and females, rendering the marriage institution more secure, though more rigid. . . . That this traditional system can also be found

among modern blue-collar workers should indicate to us that it is important to *provide biblical justification* for the intimate and romantic relationship between husband and wife advocated by books and conferences on marriage.[4] (emphasis mine)

He is contrasting the traditional view of marriage, with its separate roles for men and women, with his new view of marriage as an "intimate and romantic relationship." He goes on,

> Can we justify . . . marriage as intimate companionship?
> Jacob's love for Rachel and Isaac's for Rebekah include both romance and intimacy. But the view of the prophets is most decisive. The fact that they chose marriage as the most appropriate analogy of God's love for Israel reveals more than anything else the Hebrews' lofty concept of the marriage relationship. . . . [It also reveals some faulty theology on this writer's part, because *God* chose to use marriage as an analogy, not the prophets.]
> The richness of the marriage relationship reaches its fullest expression in the New Testament. Paul, following the example of the Hebrew prophets, compares the union of Christ and the Church with the union of husband and wife.[5]

This, too, sounds good. That is why so many people are fooled by it. But it's one thing to talk glowingly of romance, and another to prove that *romance is the reason for marriage*. That is what intimacy theology is really saying, when you strip it to its bare essentials.

Let's take another look at romance as the "biblical justification" for marriage. Jacob and Isaac's lives with their wives were not all romance. In fact, Jacob stayed married to Leah, whom he disliked quite strongly, until she died. And what about the marriage of Yahweh and his people, or Christ and his church? Does this union consist mainly of romantic encounters, or do our spiritual experiences come as a result of our fruitful obedience to God? Did Jesus say, "If you love me, you will obey what I command" (John 14:15), or "If you love me, we will have neat times of spiritual fellowship"? Did Jesus say, "I chose you to go and bear fruit—fruit that will last" (John 15:16), or "I chose you so I could contemplate your wonderfulness"? Of course our fellowship with God is important. But in this life romantic emotions are no more the *essence* of the Christian life than they are the *essence* of marriage.

Romance is the blossom on the flower of marriage, not the root. It is beautiful, it is a gift of God, but marriage *can* survive without it.

What happens when couples begin to grope for intimacy? Here is our warning: "It is to be expected that as friendship becomes more important in marriage, *more marriages will end in divorce*. It is more difficult to be a friend than to be a master; it is more difficult to be a friend than to be just property"[6] (emphasis mine). Thus a spokesman for intimate marriage announces *it will cause divorce!* The only way he can justify the total failure of his teaching is by claiming that the alternative is slavery, which is not true.

And as a matter of fact, the attempt to turn a perfectly good marriage into an intimate marriage has led to many, many divorces. I think, for example, of an article published awhile back in a major evangelical magazine about divorce in the church. The author told of a couple she knew who had for years jogged along, sharing their interests in the kids, the house, his job, and so on. Then someone talked them into having a "second honeymoon." So they dutifully packed their bags and headed off to become "intimate." On the way to their resort, they began to talk about "us" rather than their common interests, as they had always done before. After only one day they returned, shocked to discover that when it came to talking about "us" they had nothing to say. The author says she said, "Uh, oh," when she heard this, and "sure enough, soon after they divorced."

What was wrong with this marriage? From a biblical point of view, *nothing*. But *intimate marriage isn't biblical*. Intimate marriage *demands* that marriage be self-centered. It insists that kicks and thrills are the reason for marriage's existence. It tries to squash everyone into one mold—that of hedonistic teenagers—and destroys all who can't fit.

Signing on the Dotted Line

The last popular view of marriage is the social contract. John and Letha Scanzoni, two "biblical feminists," present this model in their sociology text *Men, Women and Change*. Here is how it works:

> In an equal-partner marriage, both spouses are equally committed to their respective careers and each one's occupation is considered as important as that of the other. Furthermore, there is role interchangeability with respect to the breadwinner and domestic roles. Either spouse may fill either role; both may share in both roles. Another characteristic of an equal-partner marriage is the equal power shared by husband and wife in decision making. Lastly, the basic marital roles are simply husband and wife, and marriage is not considered automatically to require parenthood.[7]

In the contract theory of marriage, it is vital that each partner *gets* as much as he or she *gives*. So Jack promises to do the dishes on Wednesday in exchange for Jane taking out the trash. He has his checking account, and she has hers. If they still feel lonely, they may have a child in hopes that it will brighten up the place a bit, each hoping the other will take charge of diapers and midnight feedings (and during the day putting the baby in day-care). Everyone squawks loudly if his or her toe is stepped on, and has a sharp eye out for his or her rights.

The problem with all three of these views of marriage—companionship, intimacy, and contract—is that *they are all "me"-centered*. Companionship marriage focuses on my need to conquer loneliness. Intimate marriage hooks into my desire for romance. Contract marriage is tuned in to my career ambitions and financial goals. *If the need in question is not being met, or can be met better elsewhere, the whole reason for marriage disappears.*

Some people may say that these types of marriages are not "me"-centered but "us"-centered. I grant that companionship and intimate marriage bill themselves as "us"-centered, but if you reflect for a moment you will see that people very rarely get married because they want to keep *someone else* from getting lonely, or provide *someone else* with romantic experiences. Rather, people who think of marriage as being for companionship or for intimacy marry because they hope their *own* desires will be met.

I don't think the Bible teaches that marriage is for me, or even for us. But what *is* it for?

Back to the Garden

Once upon a time, Jesus tells us, there was an ideal marriage (see Matt. 19:4-6). And this is what it was like.

Adam stood free before God in all his glory. He was not lonely, because he had God to talk to. There is no record that Adam complained of any lack. But God had a plan for Adam, and something was needed to complete it. It was *God* who said, "It is not good for the man to be alone."

Now did God go on to say, "I will make Adam a playmate," or "I will make Adam a pal"? No. He said, "I will make a helper suitable for him" (Gen. 2:18).

God gave Eve to Adam to be his helper. Why? Because Adam had been assigned a project. God told them to "be fruitful and increase in number; fill the earth and subdue it." Without Eve, Adam could not possibly be fruitful and multiply. Nor could Adam, all by himself, fill the earth. Eve was needed for the couple to bear fruit. *The biblical reason for marriage is to produce fruit for God.* Marriage is to produce children and to make the earth fruitful for God. Christian marriage, in other words, is God-centered (producing what God wants) rather than me- or us-centered (meeting my or our desires). As with all of God's designs, our needs do get met, but by the route of faith. First we do what God commands; then to our surprise we find ourselves blessed. First we deny ourselves and take up our cross, and then we find the burden light and pleasant. Then we find ourselves. Then we find our hearts set free, and the love of God shed abroad in our hearts, and our marriages blossoming and blooming.

The Sister-Wife

Within a God-centered marriage, husband and wife want to behave as God directs. (Or, if only the wife is saved, she still wants to do her best to obey God in these difficult circumstances.) God requires young wives to "love their husbands" (Titus 2:4), and the "love" he asks from us is *phileo* love: brotherly love. It is based on our *relationship*, not our emotions.

Under God, brotherly love is the sustaining ingredient of marriage. Sisterly love is the same as brotherly love, and the opposite of the "having it all" mentality on which the modern careerist movement has been based. Instead of striving for "equality," the sister-wife honors her husband-brother above herself (Rom. 12:10). She is devoted to him (Rom. 12:10). Daily she encourages him (Heb. 3:13; 10:24, 25). She sympathizes with his troubles (1 Pet. 3:8) and refuses to slander him or grumble against him (Jas. 5:9). If he is a Christian, she will rebuke him when necessary and then speedily forgive him (Luke 17:3). She makes the effort to spend time with him (Heb. 10:25). Her goal is that they live together productively and in harmony (Rom. 12:16; Psa. 133:1). All these passages describe *phileo* love, and they all apply to Christian marriage.

Wifeliness, then, has two components: long-term *commitment* and daily *self-sacrifice*. But "me"-marriage reflects the feminist value of self-fulfillment. "I have to do what I want or I won't be any good for anyone else." "You can't love another without loving yourself." The Scanzonis point out this difference:

> Traditional sex-role norms prescribe that the wife's interest should be subordinate to those of her husband and any children they may have. . . . In contrast, egalitarian sex-role norms prescribe that a

woman should have autonomy and should find her fulfillment in her own achievement endeavors rather than through second-hand enjoyment of her husband's success. Under these egalitarian sex-role norms, a woman should be free to pursue her own interests without subordination to those of her husband and children.[8]

Autonomy is not what marriage is all about; partnership is. Autonomy means we determine our own goals on the basis of our own selfish interests. Partnership means God determines our goals and our roles, and both parties submit to God.

Why God Hates Divorce

Your husband is your partner. You are his partner. This is why God hates divorce. The prophet Malachi laid this message on the men of Israel:

> You flood the Lord's altar with tears. You weep and wail because he no longer pays attention to your offerings or accepts them with pleasure from your hands. You ask, "Why?" It is because the Lord is acting as the witness between you and the wife of your youth, because you have broken faith with her, though she is your partner, the wife of your marriage covenant.
>
> Has not the Lord made them one? In flesh and spirit they are his. And why one? Because he was seeking godly offspring. So guard yourself in your spirit, and do not break faith with the wife of your youth.
>
> "I hate divorce," says the Lord God of Israel. . . . (Mal. 2:13-16)

The reason the church is getting lax about divorce is that we no longer understand marriage. If a spouse has problems, such as drunkenness or fits of temper, the other one concludes it is not a "good" marriage and moves on. Those who take this perspective end up allowing divorce "for any and every reason," just as the Pharisees were doing in Jesus' day. Jesus answered the Pharisees that destruction of *any* God-ordained marriage is always wrong. "What God has joined together, let man not separate," said our Lord (Matt. 19:3-11).

The pertinent question then is, What has God joined together? Some marriages God refuses to sanction. In Old Testament times, for example, Jews were not allowed to marry unbelievers. God commanded the Israelites to put away their foreign wives, not because of "problems" but because the children would not be his. The foreign wives undoubtedly were good companions, exciting bedmates, and worked out their share of the marriage contract as well. Futhermore, their Jewish husbands enjoyed their marriages and thought they had good relationships going—*they* certainly didn't want to break up. But God said, "Send away all these women and their children." Why? Because the fruit of marriage—the "godly offspring"—was missing. (See Ezra 9 and 10, and compare with Deuteronomy 7:3, 4.)

In our day, God sanctifies the children of all legitimate Christian marriages, even if one partner is not Christian (1 Cor. 7:12-14). The fruit of your partnership with your legitimate husband is sacred. Only *adultery*, which breaks the partnership by pouring its resources into a spiritually fruitless extramarital union, as well as (in the case of an adulterous wife) jeopardizing the children's legitimacy, and *desertion*, which nullifies the partnership, are biblical grounds for divorce (Matt. 19:3-11; Mark 10:1-12; 1 Cor. 7:10-16).

Christians may never, never, never divorce Christians. The world only knows we are Christ's disciples by the love we have for each other (John 13:34, 35). John plainly says that if we can't love our brothers, whom we have seen, there is no way that we can love God, whom we haven't seen (1 John 4:20, 21). When Christians divorce, both parties still remaining in the church without serious discipline, the message the world gets is that we are grade-number-one, first-class, government-inspected hypocrites. And when it comes to mixed marriages of Christian and non-Christian, it's up to the Christian to show *more* love, *more* understanding, *more* forgiveness than the unsaved partner.

Christ called us to love our neighbors, not reject them.

The Fruit of Marriage
Since marriage should be God-centered, not me-centered, our main care must be to honor God's holy Name and to fulfill his holy purpose. A lax attitude toward divorce comes from putting the feelings of sinners before the feelings of God. God created marriage not first and foremost to meet our wishes, but to advance his Kingdom.

If marriage is only to satisfy my need for friendship, for sex, and to pacify the IRS, then the family really *is* irrelevant, just as feminists claim. A wife can be replaced by a dog, a temporary sex partner, or a tax shelter. This thinking has far-reaching consequences, of which increased divorce is only one. For all three models of marriage leave out one little ingredient that makes marriage different from all other human relationships: children.

What *is* the place of children in a companionship marriage? Are they needed at all? They are a downright *hindrance* to an intimate marriage, as the pesky little critters are always interrupting romantic moments. Social contracts provide for each *partner's* duties, but where do *children* fit in? As the Scanzonis have already told us, "equal-partner marriage is not considered automatically to require parenthood."[9]

Children are the essential fruit of marriage, not a mere accidental side-effect. Husband and wife unite in God's plan not for themselves alone, but for the sake of the fruit they will bear as well. Woman's role then begins to emerge as something distinct from man's. Neither man nor woman sees marriage as an end in itself, which can be discarded at pleasure, but as a medium for the great responsibility of subduing the earth, in which each party has a role assigned by God. With this understanding of marriage as a fruitful partnership, much of the discontent which drives couples to divorce withers away. If we realize God gave us goals which we must reach *together*, then we can put up with obstacles for the sake of the result.

Children are *not* unnecessary baggage dragging a marriage down, but an essential part of the family. This makes a big change in the way we look at sex, as the next chapter will show.

3   The Joy of Unkinky Sex

The whole world hasn't gone sex-mad. Just America, Sweden, America, Denmark, America . . .

Walk into a bookstore and you can't help getting hit in the eye by popular porn. First it was *The Joy of Sex* leering at us from bookstore windows. Now it's *The Joy of Lesbian Sex*. What "joys" will we be offered tomorrow? I don't really want to know.

All this grabbing and groping has not made couples any happier, mind you. The divorce rate, which had been fairly steady from 1950 through 1967, started climbing rapidly after books like Dr. David Reuben's *Everything You Always Wanted to Know About Sex (But Were Afraid To Ask)* were published. The divorce rate is now almost double what it was in 1966, and the actual number of divorces per year is up by 136 percent.[1] But in spite of the facts, Americans have been brainwashed into believing with a religious fervor that old-fashioned normal sex is boring and the death of marriage, while freaky sex will turn your husband on and make him love you.

The Infected Church, Again

Christians are not immune to this influence. We now have our own breed of evangelical sexperts whose advice reads like a watered-down version of the original pagan sex manuals. Listen to this, from a currently popular book on family ministry:

> Cultivation of sexual enjoyment can assume three forms. [Notice the assumption that sexual enjoyment is something we ought to work at, as an end in itself.] Couples can avoid boredom [the

natural result of the grim pursuit of fun for its own sake] by changing the surroundings. Periodic weekends away as well as different occasions or different places at home can enhance the experience. Variety in technique will also prevent the expression of sex from becoming matter-of-fact. In their manuals evangelicals Tim LaHaye and Ed Wheat have given popular expression to the rightness of agreed-upon variations in marital sex that are not harmful, such as mutual fondling and oral-genital expression. [We will see just how unbiblical these "agreed-upon variations" are.] Practicing other forms of intimacy during the physical act enriches the total context and meaning of sex itself. Reading love poems or prose aloud to each other and communicating in writing can be done as a prelude or accompaniment to sexual intercourse.[2]

So to enrich the "total context and meaning" of our Christian marriages, we should take pen and paper to bed with us and try to compose poems while making love! All to "avoid boredom"! Can you think of a better way to destroy a couple's sex life?

Picture Sally and Harry dutifully trotting off to the Christian psychiatrist's office. They attended one of those "intimacy" seminars awhile back, and now they find they have problems they didn't even dream of before. Harry couldn't make love and write poetry at the same time. The kids caught them messing around in the hall. And when Sally came to the door dressed in Saran Wrap, as she tearfully told the psychiatrist, "Harry just laughed at me!"

How ludicrous it seems for grown men and women, parents of children, to scuff through sex manuals in search of kinky new kicks. But the implications are actually very serious. *The new evangelical perspective on sex is an unwitting denial of God's basic plan for marriage and leads directly into role obliteration.* The couple hopping into bed with a sex manual in one hand and a pen and pad of paper in the other may not be aware of it, but in the very middle of their most united experience the root of their marriage is being attacked.

Back to the Garden, Again

The Genesis account of the creation of man and woman tells us two very significant things about human sexuality. First, God confines sex to marriage: "For this reason a man will leave his father and mother and be united to his wife, and they will become one flesh" (Gen. 2:24). Secondly, God commanded that sex be at least potentially fruitful (that is, not deliberately unfruitful): "God blessed them and said to them, 'Be fruitful and increase in number; fill the earth and subdue it' " (Gen. 1:28). This command follows immediately after the teaching that God created man in his own image as male and female. Human sexuality, as male and female, is meant to produce babies.

Because the whole creation has fallen since then, some couples, with the best will in the world, cannot beget and bear children. Older people also reach a point where childbearing is no longer physically possible. However, there is all the difference in the world between an old or sickly apple tree which can't bear fruit, and a healthy apple tree whose owner goes around every spring pinching off the buds to prevent blossoms from forming. We might feel sorry for the unproductive tree's owner, but someone who would deliberately pluck the buds off his own tree—that's really foolish!

But that's exactly our modern sexperts' attitude. They have divorced sex from fruitfulness. See, for example, how many pages their manuals devote to birth control and how few to fertility improvement. Their very obsession with technique shows that they are now presenting sex in popular pagan terms.

Sexual Gluttony

The world around us craves pleasure here and now. The world believes that "you only go around once in life" and therefore you ought to "grab for all the gusto you can." Experience, to them, is everything.

But don't we also hear noises like this within the church? Isn't the basic presupposition of much modern evangelical teaching on sex that the *experience* (meaning climax) is everything, and that just about anything that aids in achieving an exciting experience is valid?

I feel convinced that not only the world, but in some cases the church is suffering today from a bad case of sexual gluttony. Gluttony can be defined as *seeking an experience to such an extent that the basic purpose of one's actions is ignored or perverted.* Thus one who is a gluttonous eater may, like the Romans of old, self-induce vomiting, so he can cram down more food, when the *basic* purpose of eating is to nourish the body, and enjoyment of food is only a *secondary* purpose. As we say, a glutton is someone who "lives to eat instead of eating to live."

In the area of sex, our modern tendency is to put the sex act on a pedestal and to deemphasize or even reject the begetting of children. The Scanzonis, for example, make one of their arguments against having children that children interfere with the parents' sex life.[3] Even the "one-flesh" bond which sex creates must bow before the desire for thrills, as couples are led to feel dissatisfied with each other because their sex life isn't a totally wonderful experience.

The Bible teaches us that sex is only legitimate within marriage. It further teaches, as we have seen, that the natural purpose of marital sex is (1) physical oneness and (2) fruitfulness. Nowhere does the Bible say that the purpose of marital sex is climax, much much less climax at the *expense* of fruitfulness and oneness.

The feminist view of sex and our "modern" evangelical view of sex are one and the same thing. Both separate fun from fruit. Both make the wife (and husband) inessential. Both lead to perversion.

Perversion

The Bible defines perversion as "exchanging natural relations for unnatural ones" (Rom. 1:26). This passage is interesting because it shows *women leading the way into perversion:*

> Because of [their unwillingness to worship him] God gave [the rebellious human race] over to shameful lusts. Even their women exchanged natural relations for unnatural ones. In the same way the men also abandoned natural relations with women and were inflamed with lust for one another. Men committed indecent acts with other men, and received in themselves the due penalty for their perversion. (Rom. 1:26, 27)

Literally this passage says, "The females exchanged the natural function for that which is against nature, and in the same way also the males left behind the natural function of the females. . . ." The word "women" in the NIV which I translated "females" and the word "men" which I translated "males" are used in each of Jesus' references to the creation account—God "made them male and female" (Matt. 19:4; Mark 10:6). But the most noteworthy feature of this passage is that the word women, or females, comes from the root meaning "to nurse or give suck."

Theologians have often interpreted this passage to mean that when God gives up on a race or nation, first the women become lesbians and then the men follow their example and become homosexuals. This is certainly part of the truth, but I don't think it's the whole truth. Historically men are more likely to turn to homosexuality, and to turn to it in large numbers, *before* women become lesbians. Nor need the passage be talking about lesbianism at all. All it says is that the females exchange their natural function for that which is against nature. We then ask, "What *is* their natural function?" Since the word used for female is connected so strongly with the idea of nursing babies, whereas it has no connection at all with the idea of sexual activity, I believe that God is saying here that when women exchange their natural function of child-bearing and motherliness for that which is "against nature" (that is, trying to behave sexually like a man), the men tend to abandon the natural sexual use of the women and turn to homosexuality. When men stop seeing women as mothers, sex loses its sacredness. Sex becomes "recreational," and therefore the drive begins to find new kicks.

All honest-to-goodness Christians agree that homosexuality and bestiality, both of which the Bible forbids in the strongest terms, are perverted. Both involve going outside the normal male-female marriage relationship. Both result in barrenness.

But what about marital "agreed-upon variations" that also result in barrenness? What about forms of coupling that *prevent* conception—the same forms that homosexuals use? Can these "agreed-upon variations" be what the Bible means when it talks about women abandoning their natural function? Can this type of sexual behavior be what turns men away from their wives and toward other men?

I believe the answer is yes, and here is why. Becoming "one flesh" is only *one* of the purposes for which God ordained sex. This purpose could be achieved by *any* sexual joining of any two living beings, marital or homosexual or whatever. But the *other* purpose, the one which gets swept under the evangelical rug, is fruitfulness. For fruitfulness it is absolutely necessary that coupling be marital, heterosexual, and genital-to-genital—and *nothing else*.

Please keep in mind that I am tallking about *coupling*, not *touching*. Fondling is one thing, and the sex act is another. The Song of Songs describes a couple rejoicing in each other's bodies, snuggling, kissing, and fondling each other. But that is not the same thing as substituting one portion of a wife's anatomy for another, or one part of a husband's anatomy for the normal one, or resorting to man-made objects as genital substitutes. This all is the stuff on which X-rated movies thrive, not Christian marriages.

God gives us the example of a man who was willing to express himself sexually with his wife in a nonfruitful fashion. The man was Onan, the son of Judah. According to custom, Onan had married his dead brother's widow. He had sex with Tamar, but because he didn't want children he "spilled his seed on the ground to keep from producing offspring for his brother. What he did was wicked in the Lord's sight; so he put him to death also" (Gen. 38:9, 10).

Some have said that Onan was a special case, because God had chosen Tamar to be the ancestress of Jesus, our Messiah. But neither Onan nor Tamar knew this. Any of Judah's children or (as it so happened) Judah himself could have fathered the heir of the promise. Nor was Onan's sin just not wanting to beget children for his brother. Shelah, his younger brother, never married Tamar at all, being equally unwilling to do his duty by his dead brother. Yet nothing happened to Shelah. What Onan did was perverted because he debased sex. He used Tamar for his selfish pleasure, but refused to give her children.

Perversion means using ourselves—our bodies, spirits, or minds—in a way God did not design. One example would be people seeking for some new gourmet experience by ingesting food through tubes put down their noses, rather than through their mouths. When one is sick one must eat this way, but for a healthy person to choose to eat through the nose would be . . . well, perverse! In the same way, modern sex techniques that divorce sex from fruitfulness are perverted. It doesn't matter if they are "fun," or "exciting"; they constitute rebellion against God's design for sex.

All forms of sex that shy away from marital fruitfulness are perverted. Masturbation, homosexuality, lesbianism, bestiality, prostitution, adultery, and even deliberate marital barrenness—all are perverted. As far as turning oneself on via porn books and movies, surely it ought to be clear to everyone that being sexually turned on by the imaginary or real exploits of others is *exactly* what Jesus meant when he said that looking at someone who is not your wife and lusting after her in your heart is committing adultery (Matt. 5:28). People who talk about a Christian's "freedom" to read such books and see X-rated movies or to fantasize sexual encounters as an aid to lovemaking are really missing the point. If that turns you on, you are committing adultery. If someone says it doesn't turn her on, but continues to read the books and see the movies, she is lying. Anyone who *wants* to see a porn movie can't "handle" it. Anyone who would go out of her way to watch others commit adultery is obviously not one of the "pure" to whom "all things are pure." We are all free to spend our weekends digging around in outhouses; yet there is no mass exodus to the country each weekend to indulge this marvelous liberty! Anyone who uses "Christian freedom" as an excuse for indulging in pornography is just showing where his or her heart really is. In the words of the Bible, they are using freedom as a cover-up for evil.

It is important to realize that something may titillate simply because it smacks of evil. Fallen human nature *enjoys* perversion. Therefore, Christian women who dress up like prostitutes in various kinky ways to excite their husbands need to seriously consider what they are trying to do. Do you want to train your husband to respond sexually to kinky dress, or to *you*? *Anyone* can wear a Frederick of Hollywood black lace nightie, and if it's the subtle hint of wickedness in clothing or in technique that your husband is responding to, it's going to give him a taste for *more* titillating wickedness. Diverting your husband's attention from unity and fruitfulness into the sewer of hedonistic gratification is what Romans 1:24-28 is talking about. First God gives people over to sexual impurity; then he gives them over to shameful lusts; finally he gives them over to a "depraved mind, to do what ought not to be done." In the terminal stages, perversion is sought simply *because* it is unnatural and wrong. That's what makes it a kick. So first we have impurity; second we have greater impurity, as the first experiments get "old" and don't thrill like they used to; finally, anything goes as people desperately search for some new way of perverting sex so they can rouse their jaded passions one more time.

Off the Pedestal and Into the Gutter

Our society has been separating sex from the responsibilities and joys of having children for over thirty years. Do you like its *new* attitude toward sex? Wives, who used to be regarded primarily as mothers and therefore sacred, have been knocked off that pedestal. We are now seen as fancy vessels for men to relieve their sexual frustrations. Look at the ads in magazines, in the stores, on TV and billboards. Is this a noble picture of women, for our bodies to be used to sell everything from jeans to toothpaste? Think about the flood of pornographic materials, which oozes wider and more loathsome every year. Consider how children are getting coerced into sex, being abused by adults who have lost all understanding of sex as including reproduction and who therefore see no need to protect those who have not yet reached the age of puberty. Consider also how this attitude has undermined marriage. Many husbands no longer look at their wife as the mother of their children, but as their legal mistress. Is it surprising that they divorce their wives whenever someone better-looking comes along?

Christian women are not called to be flamboyant mistresses or desexed business partners. We are *women, females,* able to bear and nurse children. We don't need to dress like prostitutes or behave like actresses in an X-rated movie to enjoy our sexual nature. We want our husbands to respond to *us,* not props; we want to learn to respond to *them,* not fantasies.

When all is said and done, sex is not the most important thing in life. The Bible says that husbands are captivated by *love,* not sex (Prov. 5:15-19). Even an older woman, the "wife of your youth," can compete successfully with all the world on these terms.

When Satan tempted Jesus to pervert his divine power for the sake of sensual self-indulgence, Jesus said, "Man does not live by bread alone, but on every word that comes from the mouth of God" (Matt. 4:4). If I may apply our Lord's words to the sin of our society I would say, "Man does not live by *bed* alone." Kinky sex is not a glittering toy we can fondle without harming ourselves. It does not proceed from the mouth of God, but from the *Deep Throats* of the world. It abases women and casts contempt on our beautiful ability to bear and nurse children. It endangers children, as the line of puberty means nothing where kinky sex is concerned. It places men under temptation to pervert themselves with men, by turning them on to homosexual styles of coupling that do not require a female partner.

Marriage is more than just a man and a woman. Marriage is a family: a husband, a wife, and all the sweet little children God gives them. We love our husbands not as sex objects whose main mission in life is to turn us on, but as partners with us in the glorious task of bearing fruit for God, of filling the earth and subduing it. Feminists can't understand this kind of love; I certainly didn't when I was a feminist. For them, marriage must (if it is contracted at all) be an equal exchange, with each party doing exactly the same thing. Feminism makes even heterosexual marriage homosexual: the union of a man and a would-be man who wants to "control her own body"—that is, mutilate it, sterilize it, try desperately any way she can to keep it from betraying the fact that God made her female.

Hard on the heels of God's insistence that young women should be trained to love their husbands comes his command that we should be trained to love our children. Children are the Waterloo of feminism—especially babies. So in the next section we will go "Back to Babies" and see who is right—feminists or God.

Part Two:

BACK TO
BABIES

". . . train the younger women to . . . love . . . their children . . ." (Titus 2:4)

4   God's Least-Wanted Blessing

In the summer of '69 I was tramping off to summer school each day with the hope of earning enough credits to escape high school one year early. A young man in my class had a Volkswagen van, and he used to drive us all to a local ice-cream joint during our morning break. One day he casually mentioned to me that he was going to a rock festival the next week, and would I like to go with him? I declined, so he took someone else. That is how I narrowly missed the ultimate youth happening: Woodstock.

Think of it—100,000 young people, high on drugs, sex, and music. All those kids, free to do whatever they wanted, without any parental restraint and *with their parents' money.*

The Unwanted Generation

My summer school classmate did not buy that van himself. Neither did the majority of Woodstock-trippers earn their wheels and clothes with their own sweat. Mom and Dad were paying for their offspring's flirtation with decadence. Did the kids honor them for it? No; they resented it bitterly.

I remember the hate and disgust my generation felt for their parents. It was a generation that felt abandoned, rejected, unloved. And all the money and freedom their parents offered to appease them only made them angrier.

"Mom and Dad? Huh! Those old buzzards don't want me around interfering with their lifestyle," were the words I heard long-haired dropouts spit out again and again. And it was true. Without realizing it, Mom and Dad had adopted a new attitude toward their children. The Turned-on Sixties generation felt it, resented it, and fought back. *They were the last generation of kids to have the backbone to do so.* The kids of the Liberated Seventies and Gay Eighties feel totally helpless and therefore don't rebel en masse in those spectacular ways. It's not that kids today are more satisfied; they just have no hope at all. They are the unwanted generation, and they know it.

With the advent of family planning in the fifties, motherhood began to be questioned. In the sixties, the push was on for abortion "rights." In the seventies, abortion was legalized and motherhood became just another option on the menu of life. Today *motherhood has become a hobby.* Couples don't *want* babies—certainly not more than one, or maybe two, and those *after* they have paid for the new car and made some progress on the mortgage.[1] When the one or two have dutifully arrived, that is that.

Not only have non-Christian mothers and fathers lost their natural affection, but this spirit has crept into our churches as well. I remember how much it shocked me the first time I heard a Christian mother (of one!) complain about how much work her baby was and swear she'd never have another one. Now that kind of remark is commonplace. Women, even Christian women, seem to feel no shame about rejecting the whole idea of motherhood, and their own children (who are the "little nuisances" they malign) along with it.

An antichild attitude is nothing new under the sun. In 1835 John Kitto (author of the immensely popular *Kitto's Daily Bible Illustrations*) said,

> It may be safely predicated of any woman of Israel, if she had already many sons, that the gift of another would still be great joy to her. . . . But again, how is it—owing to what vice in our social system, or in ourselves, does it happen—that there are among us tens of thousands, to whom the promise of children would be a sorrow and a trouble, rather than a comfort and a joy?[2]

Kitto, a deaf man who had ten children in the days before welfare, charges his fellow-Englishmen with lack of faith.

> Alas for our faith! which will not trust God to pay us well for the board and lodging of all the little ones He has committed to our charge to bring up for Him.[3]

Kitto would not have imagined a woman who could *afford* to feed a child failing to embrace motherhood with joy. And throughout the ages the church has always felt like Kitto.

The Bible says young women should be trained to love their children (Titus 2:4). It seems this training would be especially helpful today.

How Not to Love a Kid

Of course, the very women who make snide remarks about childbearing and motherhood would be horrified if you told them their comments were unloving. The reason is that they never intended to be unloving. They consider themselves to be loving mothers, and they are—but not always by the Bible's standard. Love nowadays means many different things, not all agreeing with God's definition.

What is love? Well, what is love *not*? We can probably all agree that love means we should not neglect or reject our children. It is a bit more difficult to convince people that we should not *worship* our children. Those who have only one or two seem particularly prone to this condition. Christopher Robin of the Pooh Bear stories is an example of a worshiped child. Dr. Spock brought this concept up-to-date with his insistence two decades ago that children were basically good little creatures who knew best how they should be raised. More recent efforts along this line include the well-publicized Year of the Child and the emergence of a brood of "children's rights" advocates.

We will have to look again at the question of children's rights in Chapter 7, because this innocent-sounding term is the thrusting edge of an attack on *parental* rights. But for the moment let's just pass on quickly with the thought that as God, our Father, demands certain things from us (including gratitude) and chastises us for our misdeeds, so earthly parents are ordered by Scripture to remain in firm control of their children's lives, rather than waiting in worshipful submission on their every whim.

Acquirers and Nurturers

Loving our children also means not making them into our personal ego trip. Sue Remmus describes this "acquirer" mentality which looks at first blush like love until you see that all the attention, possessions, and other favors the parents dispense are all for the sake of their own glory.

"I want it all," gushes one mother of one—smartly dressed and made-up, currently-coiffed, cigarette waving between long, manicured fingernails. This working mother typifies the "acquirer" mentality so prevalent among the instant-gratification set.

"Acquirers" treat their children as possessions, good for decoration and useful for reflecting stylish taste. Children are pulled out, put on show for a few minutes, then sent back to their quarters. . . . Acquirers do not spend their lives together with their children, they go on "as before," in spite of the children. Children's feelings are not taken into account, their needs do not come first. Babies are artificially fed (or token breastfed for a week or two) and sent off to early schooling. . . . Children do not accompany parents anywhere, except on specifically child-oriented excursion. . . . All child-parent interaction is geared to the convenience of the parents. . . . Hugs are perfunctory, squeezes of affection used in lieu of kissing (which might smear the mother's lipstick). . . . The father was not present at the birth of the child, and is proud of the fact. Or if he *was* present, it was in addition to the routine fetal-monitor, anaesthesiologist, chief of obstetrics, a couple of medical students, and forceps. His wife certainly did not breastfeed on the delivery table. They both thought everyone was just great, and the wife kissed the doctor for giving her such a beautiful baby. The baby cried and everyone laughed with delight as they whisked him away. . . .

At home, the baby is deposited in his new room to be looked after by the baby nurse. . . . The baby is beautiful, even though he seems to cry an awful lot. He looks so cute all dolled up in his designer baby clothes. He is another splendid acquisition![4]

The fact is, our society has become so antichild that people are actually pressured into "excusing" their children as toys or hobbies. Women rave about the "marvelous experience" of childbirth more than they do about the child himself or herself. Motherhood must become chic in order to be justified. All those cute T-shirts for pregnant women with "Mommy" stenciled on them, all those cute coordinated quilts for baby's room, are not proof that our culture overflows with love for children. They prove, rather, that children have been resurrected as pets.

Children Are a Blessing

Sue Remmus contrasts acquirers with natural nurturers, who "take their children along everywhere they go. They like discussing things with their children. They *like* their children."[5]

Now we're getting closer to the biblical view of loving our children. The Bible says that *children are a blessing*, even without designer baby clothes. It's a pity that most modern churches don't sing the Psalms, because several of them state this quite clearly. Psalm 127, for example:

> Children are the Lord's good gift.
> Rich payment are men's sons.
> The sons of youth like arrows are
> In hands of mighty ones.
> Who hath his quiver filled with these
> O, happy shall he be.
> When foes they [the whole family] greet within the gate
> They shall from shame be free.[6]

Or how about Psalm 128:

> Blessed the man who fears Jehovah
> And who walks in all his ways.
> Thou shalt eat of thy hand's labor
> And be prospered all thy days.
> Like a vine with fruit abounding
> In thy house thy wife is found
> And like olive plants thy children
> Compassing thy table round.[7]

Natural nurturers *like their children*. They are glad they have them. Here is God's attitude in a nutshell. The love of children that young mothers are supposed to be trained in is *phileo* love, brotherly love, fondness, natural affection, liking, friendship.

Don't you enjoy holding a sweet, warm little baby and watching him contentedly nurse at your breast? Don't you treasure that first little smile as your baby drinks you in, the most important person in his world? Isn't it satisfying to make a yucchy little bottom all clean and sweet, and can't you laugh at your offspring's gooey face, innocently awash in carrots and rice cereal? Doesn't it make you feel special that God has trusted you to nurture and protect this tiny morsel of helpless humanity?

As the baby grows, a nurturing mother shares the excitement of those first wobbly steps. She thrills to those baby lips calling, "Mama." A downy head pillowed on her shoulder; little fingers trustingly curled round her thumb; happy giggles when she tickles her toddler—what queen can buy these pleasures?

As the child's mind develops, a mother discovers a new friend. More and more the young personality emerges, and each new revelation is a surprise! Can Johnny *really* write a poem, or Jane *really* design a dress? Their thoughtful questions about heaven and hell, sin and salvation, duty to God and neighbor make you feel so anxious and proud for your baby Christians. Seeing the young Christian begin to flex his or her wings brings a surge of gratitude to God for allowing you to bring forth such a special person into the world.

Loving our children means just *enjoying* them and not fretting about the time and energy it takes to serve them. Children are fun for those tuned in to God's values. (I still like that boy who suggested that his family should "turn off the TV and watch the baby.") Hug them. Kiss them. Play with them. Teach them. Get down on the floor with the baby, romp with the toddler, bake cookies with the preteen, listen to the teenager. The mother who likes her children will find that they are a blessing.

Should Blessings Go Begging?

Jesus said that whoever welcomes a little child in his name welcomes *him* (Matt. 18:1-5). We welcome children when we are willing to bear them in our bodies and nurture them thereafter. Anticipating that some people would always disparage God's blessing of children, Jesus said, "See that you do not look down on one of these little ones. For I tell you that their angels in heaven always see the face of my Father in heaven" (Matt. 18:10).

I'm almost afraid to ask this, because family planning has become as American as motherhood and apple pie *used* to be—but I have to. *If children are a blessing, why don't we want to have them?* Can you think of any *other* blessing that Christians moan about and complain about and do their best to refuse? Wouldn't it sound ludicrous to hear Christians saying, "I'm so sick of all this money you've given me, Lord. Please don't give me any more!" or "I've had enough of the Holy Spirit's power poured out on me to last for the rest of my life. No more for me, thanks!"

A blessing is something you *want* to have. Health, for example. Who after surviving three winter flu seasons without catching cold would complain about her bothersome string of good health, or take to standing in drafts and downpours to avoid being that healthy in the future?

If the Bible says children are a blessing (and it does) but we don't see it that way, the fault lies in us.

Roling in Ignorance

A negative attitude toward childbearing and a correspondingly positive attitude toward careers, leisure, money, or any of the other worldly idols we are being handed in its place has serious consequences. I already pointed out in the last chapter how divorcing sex from fruitfulness leads to perversion according to the most likely interpretation of Romans 1:26, 27. But more than that, it is *a denial of the image of God in women.* God "made them male *and female*," and sterilizing the female half of the partnership defaces the image of God.

You may think I am making too much of the Genesis account of creation. "Surely," someone may argue, "there is more to being male and female than sheer biology." I am not sure what else besides our biological difference God could have had in mind when he said that his image in man is male and female—especially since the word for "female" comes from the same Greek root as "to breastfeed." But let's consider that point, for argument's sake. Suppose that by "male and female" God had in mind the androgynous mix 'n' match unisex lifestyle of our day. What then?

Well, dear friends, that cannot possibly be, because *the Bible teaches that childbearing is a wife's basic role.* Look with me for a minute at 1 Timothy 2:15—"but women will be kept safe through childbirth, if they continue in faith, love and holiness with propriety." Commentators perennially have difficulty with this passage, and no wonder, since it actually says, "women will be saved through child*bearing.*" The NIV translated it "childbirth," perhaps because the translators couldn't believe the Bible would say women were saved through childbearing. Wouldn't that be works righteousness? How can we be saved through anything but the blood of Jesus Christ, the Lamb of God?

The mystery is solved when we look at the context. Paul has just finished giving Timothy instructions about how men should pray and how women who profess to worship God should dress. Next Paul said women should learn quietly and submissively, not be teachers in the church. The next logical question would be, "Well then, what *can* women do for God if they are not supposed to teach?" Paul says that by persevering in our God-given role—childbearing—with a godly attitude, we will be saved. "Childbearing" sums up all our special biological and domestic functions. This is the exact same grammatical construction as Paul's advice to Timothy that Timothy should persevere in his life and doctrine, "because if you do, you will save both yourself and your hearers" (1 Tim. 4:16). Timothy's particular path to heavenly glory was his preaching and example. Ours is homeworking, all revolving around our role of childbearing.

After reminding women that they too have an important role, Paul then feels free to go on and discuss the qualifications of elders and deacons, secure in the knowledge that he has not slighted women by simply excluding them from church office without telling them they have an equally vital job.

James Hurley comes close to saying this in his book *Man and Woman in Biblical Perspective*. He says, referring to 1 Timothy 2:15,

> It is possible to understand this verse as a continuation of the discussion of women's role. The passage has been discussing patterns of conduct for men and women in prayer, in adornment and in teaching and worship. . . . I would propose the possibility that [Paul] is thinking . . . that Eve and women in general will be saved or kept safe from wrongly seizing men's role by embracing a woman's role. This allows the text to be read as it stands and keeps it in line with the issue at hand. . . .
>
> On the interpretation which I am proposing, we may paraphrase Paul as saying that women in general (and most women in his day) will be kept safe from seizing men's roles by participating in marital life (symbolized by childbirth), which should be accompanied by other hall-marks of Christian character (faith, love and holiness with propriety).[8]

A. T. Robertson, the great Baptist Greek scholar, puts it more directly:

> It is not clear that Paul does not have mostly in mind that childbearing, not public teaching, is the peculiar function of women with a glory and dignity all its own. "She will be saved" (*sōthēsetai*) in this function, not by means of it.[9]

We don't have to be timid in approaching this passage. Childbearing *is* woman's "peculiar function." It symbolizes our role just as preaching symbolized Timothy's role. Preaching *was* Timothy's role, and persevering in his calling he would be saved. In just the same way, having babies and raising them is our role, and we show we belong to God by persevering in it.

Another passage speaks of childbearing as a wife's calling, not just as an optional extra when the fancy takes us. Paul is speaking again: "So I counsel younger widows to marry, *to have children,* to manage their homes and to give the enemy no opportunity for slander" (1 Tim. 5:14, emphasis mine). People are incredibly ready to dismiss this passage as "just talking to widows," without ever asking why widows should have a duty to bear children and other women should *not*. I have never seen an evangelical magazine article that while endorsing birth control and careers for all *other* married women, pointed out that *widows alone* have no right to follow the crowd into the job market, because the Bible says they, and they *alone,* have a sacred duty to stay home and bear babies. This position would be ludicrous! Paul is not telling widows that they are a special class of wives who have to operate by different rules. He is telling them to settle down, marry, and *behave as normal wives,* instead of abusing their unmarried state to become drones and gadabouts.

Having babies is a Christian wife's calling, whether first-time bride or remarried widow.

By the Picking on Us Mums, Something Wicked This Way Comes

In Shakespeare's play *Macbeth,* a group of witches could tell that Macbeth was coming, and that he was wicked, by the pricking in their thumbs. Macbeth was willing to sell his soul for worldly ambition—what we now call "fulfillment." In the process, he destroyed all that was good around him and finally lost his life as well.

If talk of "duty" and "calling" sounds harsh to your ears, perhaps this will help put it in perspective. The pendulum is now swinging from the ancient duty of women to bear children to a new duty: controlling reproduction through family planning. The people attacking motherhood have another role in mind they'd like to impose on you. Here is what one famous thinker looks for when women no longer conceive spontaneously:

> In the ideal city . . . there is no domestic role such as that of the traditional housewife. Since planned breeding and communal child rearing minimize the unpredictability of pregnancy and the time demanded of mothers, maternity is no longer anything approaching a full-time occupation. Thus, women can no longer be defined in their traditional roles. However, every person in the ideal city is defined by his or her function; the education and working life of each citizen are to be dedicated to the optimal performance of a single craft.[10]

The thinker whose ideas were just summarized was Plato, the ancient Greek philosopher. Plato was nothing if not a logical thinker; he knew where taking away childbearing from women would lead us:

> Plato's bold suggestion that perhaps there is no difference between the sexes, apart from their role in procreation, is possible only because . . . *the consequent abolition of private property and the family entail the abolition of wifehood and the absolute minimization of motherhood.* Once the door is open, the possibilities for women are boundless.[11] (emphasis mine)

Right. Once marriage is abolished (Plato saw "private wives" as the root of all evil) and motherhood is cut down to the bare minimum of nine months of a planned pregnancy (planned by our omnipotent rulers), the possibilities for women *are* boundless. We can then be enslaved to *any* occupation our rulers choose! (Not that with private property abolished we will have much to comfort us as we return "home" to the communal hall.)

Plato saw that traditional, old-fashioned nurturing mothers were the grand fly in the ointment of his utopian scheme. Society could not be efficiently reduced to a faceless mass for its rulers to manipulate as long as women insisted on staying home, keeping house for one man only, and having babies at unpredictable times.

> Despite Plato's professed intention of having the women of the second-best city [Plato's attempt to construct a Utopia that the men and women of his time would actually accept], share equally . . . citizenship their role as private wives curtails their participation in public life for three reasons. The first is that they are subject to pregnancy and lactation, which is not controlled and predictable as it was in *The Republic,* where the guardians were to mate only at the behest of the rulers. In *The Laws,* since women are permanent wives, they are far less able to limit or time their pregnancies and cannot be held continuously liable for public and, especially, military duties. Second, the reinstitution of the private household makes each wife into the mistress responsible for its welfare, and it is clear that in *The Laws* a mother is to participate far more in early child care than did the female guardian [Plato's "Ideal Woman"] who was not even to know which child was hers.[12]

Poor second-class wives, unable to participate in military duties, and forced to know which children are theirs instead of being "free" to "mate only at the behest of the rulers"! Do you wonder why the Greeks of Plato's time didn't rush to adopt his ideal society? Then why are we in America rushing toward the planned family/communal child care/female soldier setup that Plato's own countymen knew enough to reject?

Rejecting babies is rejecting ourselves. Unless, that is, the prospect of being a faceless cog in a society of faceless cogs appeals to you.

Loving our children, then, means first of all *wanting to have babies.* This is simple and easy to say, but it's become harder to *do* nowadays, because of the massive propaganda efforts of feminists and their fellow-travelers, the Zero Population Growth (ZPG) people. Let's examine the arguments they have raised against the Bible's teaching that children are a blessing, and see why God's blessings can never go out of style.

5 Who's Afraid of the Big Bad Baby?

The real reason that couples are so attracted to family planning has nothing to do with the Bible. It has to do with fear. We're afraid that we can't afford a large family. We're afraid that we wouldn't be able to control so many children. Some of us fear that without family planning we would have to give up cherished parts of our present lifestyle.

Some of these fears are legitimate, and some are not. Feminists have played on our normal fears like a virtuoso on a harp, and have added a few grace notes of their own. Their motive is obvious—large families and an "adult" lifestyle don't mix. Having babies and raising them takes precious time away from their sadly shallow goals in life, which are, in the words of two evangelical feminists, "pursuing individualistic interests and making their own name for themselves."[1] Some Christian leaders have also blown smoke into the discussion, wheezing about our responsibility to plan our own future as if it were scriptural to "plan away" God's blessings. And the Zero Population Growth people (ZPGers) are busy throwing cold water on every married couple they can find in hopes of defusing the "population bomb."

It is strange that a helpless little baby, weakly gurgling in her crib, can arouse such near-panic among adult people. "Oh, babies *look* helpless, but they're just putting on an act," the people who want to control our sex lives tell us. Actually, they say, babies are the scourge of the age. Babies "wreck" families and can "cost" a woman "her mental and physical health" or "even her life."[2] This, from a conservative Baptist minister who really ought to know better. Evangelical feminists chime in with figures about the financial costs of having children, the "lost opportunity" costs, the strains on marriage, and even the frightening fact that having a baby means "an investment of enormous amounts of time and energy which the parents might otherwise have put into individualistic pursuits."[3]

It doesn't look like the poor little kid has a chance, does it? Babies have been weighed in the balances and found wanting. But let's take a closer look at the scale and see if there isn't a big fat thumb leaning on the wrong side.

Fear of Beggary

Every so often some magazine publishes an article in which experts announce that they have carefully calculated the cost of having a baby, and that it will cost us $200,000 or some such outrageous sum to bring up one little person. The unspoken moral is, "Don't do it! You can't afford to have a baby!"

The Scanzonis quote a study done by Thomas J. Espenshade in their sociology text, a study based on census data from the sixties.

> He found that a lower-income family with one child will spend 40 percent of its income in childrearing over the eighteen-year period. An upper-income family, in contrast, spends only 26 percent of its income in rearing one child to age eighteen. Costs rise as the child grows older [note the assumption that children are forever consumers and never do any productive work], and of course costs rise as more children are added to the family. However, the cost of the first child is approximately twice as much as the cost of a second child in a two-child family. In actual dollars (based on 1960-61 prices), Espenshade estimates that over an eighteen-year period, families spend the following amounts in rearing one child: lower-income families, $38,787; middle-income families, $42,565; upper-income families, $49,145.[4]

This sounds very scholarly and impressive. We are presented with figures calculated right down to the dollar amount—"It will cost you at least $38,787 in 1960 dollars to raise one child, Mrs. Smith! Are you sure you can afford this investment?" But be wary: *these calculations, and all calculations like them, cannot be scientific or accurate.*

First, nobody can produce figures to the dollar amount—that is, *accurate* figures—when dealing with these sorts of calculations. When an expert gives you figures to the dollar, he's guaranteeing their accuracy plus or minus *one dollar.* That's what makes dollar-amount figures so impressive. But the huge range of variables in calculating child-rearing costs over eighteen years for all sorts of different people, climates, lifestyles, etc. means that honest figures ought to be plus or minus *tens of thousands,* not one dollar!

Second, how can it cost lower-income families 40 percent of their income for the first child and 20 percent for the second (and presumably each subsequent) child? That would mean that *no* lower-income family could afford more than three children (four children would cost 100 percent of their income!). Yet population alarmists are continually pointing at Third-World countries where the poorest of the poor are, contrary to their advice, raising kids by the dozen. If they say it costs more to live in America than it does in Bangladesh, I agree. Our present repressive Socialist laws *do* force us into costlier lifestyles than some of us would voluntarily choose. But all the same, does anyone honestly believe that no lower-income family in America which survives on its own funds contains more than three children?

I grew up in a lower-income family myself, the oldest of seven children, during the very sixties that the Scanzonis were pricing. My father had a nice-sounding title—college professor—but an embarrassingly small salary (as is traditional for college professors). Any young fellow fresh out of engineering school made more than my dad with his seven children and years of experience. In spite of this, he gave several of us years of extremely expensive figure skating lessons (including membership in the prestigious Boston Figure Skating Club), clothed us, fed us, and took us camping. Not one of us had to be flung to the wolves to lighten the family budget.

We are the richest people in history, yet the most fearful about the costs of child-rearing. Perhaps it's because we don't realize how superfatted our lifestyles are, and how little our children really need in order to grow up happy, healthy, and godly. Those people who would love to regulate life so that we would all have to choose between an enforced upper-class lifestyle and going on welfare don't understand children at all. Does a boy really *need* a room of his own, summer camp, Montessori preschool, designer jeans, a ten-foot-high stack of records to play on his personal stereo, and all the other goodies the anointed now deem essential for everyone else's children? In one word, no. Kids survive on peanut-butter sandwiches as well as they do on steak (some might say better). Wearing hand-me down clothes is not the ultimate social scandal. Food, clothes, shelter, and love are enough to make *any* Christian content (see 1 Tim. 6:8), even a kid.

Fear of Bondage

This is a very seductive song, which (I hate to admit it) I used to strum incessantly when I was a feminist, driving my poor long-suffering mother wild. It goes like this: "As children grow older, privacy increasingly becomes a problem." (Thrum, thrum.) "Spontaneous moments of romance at unusual times become difficult." (Thrum.) "Even if husbands and wives agree on child-rearing practices, the actual carrying out of all the day-to-day responsibilities involved may seem costly in terms of freedom."[5] By now you are supposed to be staring about with glassy eyes, wondering where all your freedom went and wishing you had never had a baby in the first place.

The Apostle Peter has something to say about this Song of Bondage. When I first read his words, I was filled with awe. Peter spoke directly about my selfish feminist outlook, warning me of those in the church who would try to lead me back to those blighted pastures I had just escaped.

> These men are springs without water and mists driven by a storm. Blackest darkness is reserved for them. For they mouth empty, boastful words, and, by appealing to the lustful desires of sinful human nature, they entice people who are just escaping from those who live in error. *They promise them freedom, while they themselves are slaves of depravity*—for a man is a slave to whatever has mastered him. (2 Pet. 2:17-19, emphasis mine)

Let's review for a minute what kind of "freedom" the Scanzonis and the other evangelical feminists want us to reject childbearing in favor of. They endorse *abortion, homosexuality,* and *divorce.* The Scanzonis even speak approvingly of "co-marital sex" (that is, consenting *adultery),* although they do tread a little cautiously on this thin ice. Referring to their hypothetical couple Tim and Trudy, they caution that "there is no way at this point to know for certain . . . whether incorporating co-marital sex into their lives would improve or damage their particular relationship."[6]

What "freedom" do babies cost us? Do they interfere with our freedom to love and serve God? No; they interfere with our freedom to indulge "the lustful desires of sinful human nature," as Peter puts it, ranging from common childish selfishness to full-fledged adult depravity.

The Scanzonis show us how the quest for autonomous female freedom leads to fear of babies with another of their hypothetical case studies.

As Julie became interested in commitment to a career, her conception of her role moved from *traditional* (being a wife and mother is a woman's most important calling, and a woman must subordinate her interests to those of her family) to *egalitarian* or *modern* (a woman should strive to use all her talents and abilities to achieve in the economic-opportunity sphere, just as a man is expected to do). No longer was Julie so willing to give up her work in order to bear and rear children. She began wondering if she even wanted any children.[7]

Careerism makes an unplanned baby a "disaster," a usurper attacking the mother's precious freedom:

> Women who hold more traditional sex-role norms may think of an unplanned pregnancy as a "surprise" perhaps, but they are not likely to think of such an event as a "disaster" as might be the case with women holding egalitarian sex-role norms and individualistic aspirations. Women who strongly believe in pursuing their own interests (such as career achievement) cannot afford to be indifferent to the costs of children. Any children to be born to them must be carefully planned both as to numbers and timing. . . .
>
> But what if an unplanned pregnancy occurs among nonsterilized couples holding egalitarian sex-role norms and pursuing individualistic interests? Are such couples more apt to think of abortion as a backup measure than are more traditionally minded couples? . . .
>
> Among married couples who feel that children would be costly and in conflict with individualistic interests, abortion may seem a viable option in the case of an "accidental" conception.[8]

Is Letha Scanzoni just trying to dispassionately assess the costs of child-rearing for the secular college students who will be reading her sociology text, or is she trying to talk them into *not wanting children at all*? Is she just informing these students that some selfish couples will choose abortion rather than give up some of their "individualistic interests" in order to share themselves with their very own baby, or is she trying to *make abortion seem a respectable option*? Remember, she is the same person who said, "Does Christian morality insist that these pregnancies be carried through, even though bringing the child into the world may cause extreme emotional distress and financial hardships for the family? We think not."[9]

If careers for wives make babies a "disaster," then *careers have become the disaster.* Babies "tie us down" only if our hearts are yearning to be elsewhere. Not that the grass is really all that much greener in the office building, anyway. Is the old nine-to-five grind, or rat race as it is commonly called, really more wonderful than dandling your very own baby on your knee or teaching her to play "peek-a-boo" while she squeals with delight?

Yes, babies are the scourge of the age—for those wrapped up in selfish "individualistic interests," who have forgotten entirely that *their* mothers sacrificed to have *them,* who have no intention of taking up their crosses daily and following Jesus, and who thereby proclaim they are not worthy to be his disciples (Matt. 10:38).

Medical Fears

Most of us have probably heard some statement like, "It's much more dangerous to have a baby after age thirty-five," or "Birth defects increase by 50 percent in babies born to mothers over age thirty." In rejecting an article my husband Bill wrote about birth control, the editor of a well-respected Presbyterian journal replied, "After all, there are *medical* reasons why a woman should call a halt to childbearing eventually." Supposedly all sorts of horrible diseases and disasters will occur if a woman has the temerity to keep getting pregnant.

As the oldest of seven children, all of whom are perfectly healthy and some of whom are athletic champions, I was a bit skeptical of such claims. My mother was no twenty-five year-old when she brought my youngest sister Barbara into the world (although she *looked* younger than the mothers of my contemporaries; my grandmother says pregnancy keeps your skin young). In our neighborhood, which had quite a few large Catholic families, I couldn't remember one unhealthy child or mother. Could it be that Catholics "are not like the Egyptian women" (see Ex. 1:19)? Or is someone playing monkey games with medical statistics to frighten us away from having babies?

I am willing to grant that a woman who has her *first* child past age forty is likely to have problems, as is one who has been using birth control for years and slips up at that late date. You would *expect* a female body that had been lying barren for so many years, in which all the healthiest young eggs had already been lost, to have trouble adjusting to pregnancy. And then there are the cumulative effects of years of chemical dosage. Coming off the Pill, a woman's hormones may not yet have gotten the message that they are supposed to function normally now.

The medical studies which scare us with percentage points—so many birth defects, so many maternal deaths—invariably fail to take these factors into account.

Why don't we hear about the medical dangers of *not* having children? I asked my obstetrician what my chances were of getting cancer from having babies, and he told me there was no need to worry. The women he sees with cancer of the uterus are women who never had babies. Apparently God meant for women to have babies, and when we don't do so on a regular basis, it can cause problems. But you don't have to rely on my obstetrician's word alone.

> R. V. Short in a discussion meeting at the Royal Society in 1976 . . . pointed out that women living now represent the first generations to ovulate thirteen times a year for most of the adult life. The difficulties that many women have with menstruation may indicate that we are doing too much of it; the fact that they can be alleviated with progesterone, the hormone that sustains pregnancy, seems to bear out Short's hypothesis. There are signs that the menstrual cycle is a stress upon the organism, and particularly upon certain parts of it, such as the breast, which may go through massive changes associated with the cycle for more than ten, and often nearer twenty years. . . . Short suggests that some of the diseases associated with our low birth rate—for example, breast cancer— might be caused by some such mechanism.[10]

Short also mentioned that cancer of the ovaries and of the uterine lining "seem to be increased in nulliparous women [women who have never given birth], presumably as a result of the increased ovarian activity associated with nulliparity."[11]

But beyond the biological perils of simple barrenness—which result from preventing our female bodies from performing their natural function—many common contraceptive methods have perils of their own. Some formulations of the Pill are suspected of being abortifacient—that is, of causing the fertilized egg to fail to implant rather than preventing fertility in the first place. And when once a Pill-user conceives, the baby may have unexpected problems.

> Birth defects in the children of oral contraceptive users seem to result only if contraceptive steroids are still circulating in the body at the time of conception, although there is some evidence that

children of women who have *ever* used oral contraceptives may be less bright than others. Gross visible defects such as limb reduction and triploidy [a chromosomal abnormality resulting in sexual deformities] do occur.[12]

Since the Pill is the most commonly used contraceptive, someone should be telling us that it is not medically innocuous. Besides the common side effects of depression, vitamin deficiencies, bloating, sluggishness, brown facial marks, and so on, there are less well-known dangers to Pill-taking. Women subject to hypertension or blood clotting could die from taking the Pill.[13] Furthermore, "15 percent of women on the Pill become diabetic or peridiabetic, and a Pill user should be tested for glucose tolerance once a year."[14] Back when I was taking the Pill, my doctor never told me *that!* But that is not the end of the story:

Fungal infections can plague women, causing discomfort, pain, and disgust, costing time and money as they search for effective treatments, inflict the treatments on their unfortunate partners as well as themselves, and eventually manage to clear up the discharge and the smell only to find it returning at the first sign of unusual sexual activity or tiredness, or without apparent rhyme or reason. . . . The risk of local infection is much higher [for Pill users].[15]

Furthermore, since the natural defense mechanisms in the vagina are thrown out of whack by the Pill, "the Pill may be an accomplice in the rising incidence of cervical cancer in many areas."[16]

And just to cap it all off, it turns out that thanks to the Pill even totally monogamous couples can now get venereal disease.

Candida albicans existed as a member of the flora of a healthy vagina, but the changes in the sugar balance of the vagina consequent on Pill taking turned it into a destructive pathogen causing painful inflammations in both men and women and completely changing the nature of sexually transmitted diseases, for *candida can become a pathogen in totally monogamous people.* Recently candidiasis has been isolated as the cause of episodes of acute pelvic inflammation. Researchers have found a positive correlation between the use of sex steroids and chlamydial infection as well.[17] (emphasis mine)

The IUD is another device women frequently use in the mistaken belief that it is a harmless means of preventing conception. One thing they may not know is that the IUD is not a contraceptive; it actually causes abortion of the already-conceived baby.[18] Moreover, this form of "birth control" turns out to be at least as risky as trusting one's body to God.

The dissected womb of a woman who has had an IUD in place for several years shows the pattern of the device clearly worn into the layers of tissue . . . some areas overgrow, others are eroded, others dead and dying.

On the one hand, women are told that the device is a boon to millions of women who have never had any problems with it, and on the other, every intern knows that the first question to ask a woman reporting to emergency with severe abdominal pain is whether or not she has an IUD. . . .

A woman who accepts an IUD may expect to have her blood loss doubled as a consequence. . . . Even among the well-nourished women of Sweden, iron deficiencies were found in a group of women who lost more than 80 ml of blood at each menstruation. . . .

Perforation and infection are both most likely in the initial stages; something like a third of all women receiving IUDs will be without them two years later, and have no pleasant memories of the experience. . . .

The device does not become safer or more effective the longer it is left in. The unluckiest women of all are those whose initial tolerance of the device encourages them to rely upon it and eventually take it for granted. . . . One unfortunate woman in Atlanta, who had had repeated episodes of pelvic inflammatory disease but was determined to keep her IUD, on which she had evidently come to rely, died of pelvic actinomycosis. This is the first recorded case in which the IUD and only the IUD was the cause of death. Actinomycosis is the body's reaction to the presence of a foreign body.

The continuing risks associated with the IUD have been well summarized by Vessey and Doll: "Of these the most important are uterine perforation and pelvic inflammatory disease. In addition unplanned pregnancies occurring in women using an intrauterine device are much more likely to be ectopic or to end in spontaneous abortion than usual and there is some evidence that such abortions are particularly likely to be septic, occasionally with fatal results for the mother." The increased risk of pelvic inflammatory disease is now so generally recognized as attaching to the IUD that the FDA now insists that each device carry a warning to the consumer on the packet.[19]

As far as pregnancy with an IUD *in situ,* it can have "hideous results ranging all the way from birth with an IUD embedded in the fontanel, to septic abortion and death."[20]

Other contraceptive methods, while less hazardous than the Pill and the IUD, are medically counterproductive in that they make the sex act to some degree ludicrous or unpleasant. Germaine Greer shares with us this tribute to the diaphragm and its power to render intercourse ridiculous:

> The diaphragm is a rubber dinghy for spermicide. The fit is crude, being merely the largest circumference which can be got to stay taut inside the vagina after it has been inserted by pressing it between finger and thumb and making sure that it is pushed up well behind the pubic bone. . . . Once this large, springy object is thickly piled with spermicide, it is remarkably difficult to keep the circular spring compressed between finger and thumb. The loaded diaphragm is quite likely to shoot out of the inserter's tentative grasp and fly through the air, splattering glop in all directions. The spermicide is usually cold and dense, with a slithery consistency; it is meant to coat the cervix, but succeeds in coating everything else as well with chilly sludge. If intercourse continues so long that this sludge is dissipated, it is a sign that a fresh injection is required, so that a night of love becomes a kind of spermicidal bath. . . .
>
> The least thing stains its pallid rubber and the merest breath of damp makes it perish, so the obscene gadget is forever hanging about, draped over the bathroom faucet, to the immense interest of tradesmen and casual visitors.[21]

Ms. Greer has kind words for the condom as an effective birth control method,[22] though she does note that "in America the Food and Drug Administration has virtually destroyed the condom's potential attraction as a method of fertility control by insisting on a minimum thickness which is the highest anywhere in the world."[23] She does not mention its cost, which can become quite substantial for an active couple, or the depressing and unromantic interruption of marital activities which occurs while the husband is searching for and sheathing himself in rubber, so that instead of a warm human being his wife finds herself getting intimate with a small model of the Goodyear Blimp. Since the condom does have wide associations with "promiscuity, bought sex, and disease," mainly because most American husbands are too sensible to rigidly enforce its rubber discipline on themselves, the Christian husband might find himself embarrassed to go into his friendly neighborhood drugstore and order a gross or so (a reasonable year's supply).

There are, of course, other methods of birth control besides Pills, IUDs, condoms, and diaphragms. Kinky sex is by its very nature antifertile. Germain Greer in her book *Sex and Destiny* tries to build a case for the practice of *coitus interruptus,* and even suggests anal sex as a possibly superior method in some cases to our Western contraceptive hardware.[24] I believe she is making a medical mistake in seriously considering the latter; the frightening speed with which AIDS spreads has brought public attention to the fact that homosexuals' dirty styles of intercourse, which are duplicated by fashionable heterosexual kinky sex, make the body prey to a variety of infectious diseases, and can even break down its immune defenses entirely. As to the former, the biblical example of Onan does not encourage us to follow in his footsteps.

My main point is not that some contraceptive methods are much more unpleasant or hazardous than others, or that some may well be more hazardous or unpleasant in the long run than normal childbirth. The point to remember is that *no contraceptive method is entirely risk-free.* Even celibates get cancer, and the less dangerous birth control methods are also less effective. Perhaps God will give you the same number of children whether or not you coat yourself with sludge or sheath your husband in rubber. In that case, why go through the discomfort of contraception needlessly?

When you consider the risks of cancer, birth defects, septic abortion, uterine perforation, fungal infections, and on top of it all perhaps an unplanned pregnancy anyway, which women face who use contraception, one really wonders why doctors talk as if only mothers had medical problems.

But even if bearing children were as dangerous now as it was in the Middle Ages (when women were willing to do it), that does not prove Christian women should avoid pregnancy. God says through the Apostle Paul,

> Therefore, I urge you, brothers, in view of God's mercy, to offer
> your bodies as living sacrifices, holy and pleasing to God—which is
> your spiritual worship. Do not conform any longer to the pattern of

this world, but be transformed by the renewing of your mind. Then you will be able to test and approve what God's will is—his good, pleasing and perfect will. (Romans 12:1, 2)

My body is *not* my own, to do with as I please; it belongs to God. If he says, "women shall be saved through childbearing" (1 Tim. 2:15, literal translation), and "Sons are a heritage from the Lord, children a reward from him. . . . Blessed is the man whose quiver is full of them" (Psa. 127:3, 5), and "Your sons will be like olive shoots around your table. Thus is the man blessed who fears the Lord" (Psa. 128:3, 4), why should you and I not "honor God with your body" by having babies (1 Cor. 6:20)? Feminists say that unrestrained childbearing is slavery. God says, "Don't you know that when you offer yourselves to someone to obey him as slaves, you are slaves to the one whom you obey—whether you are slaves to sin, which leads to death, or to obedience, which leads to righteousness? . . . Just as you used to offer the parts of your body in slavery to impurity and to ever-increasing wickedness, so now offer them in slavery to righteousness leading to holiness" (Rom. 6:16, 19). *You and I don't have a choice between slavery and uncontrolled freedom.* We have a choice between *slavery to self-indulgent sin* or *slavery to God.*

We Christians know this is true in other areas. Routinely we send missionaries off to work in unsavory climates, knowing full well that they will probably come down with amoebic dysentery, be overheated (or frozen), receive inadequate medical care in second-rate hospitals, and on the average live ten years less than other people. But we don't tell people not to be missionaries. Instead, *we commend missionaries for their courage.*

Missionaries go to foreign countries to beget new Christians; mothers get pregnant to beget new Christians. Even if maternal missionary work has some hazards (and what missionary work doesn't?), the noble way is to face them with courage. Likewise, we really ought to honor women with medical problems—diabetes, asthma, quadraplegia, arthritis, heart problems—who are willing to serve God with their bodies as mothers. These are the unsung heroines of the modern church.

Devotees of evil will sacrifice all they have—money, health, reputation—to maintain their lifestyle. If the actual threat of venereal disease or AIDS does not deter the wicked from their pursuits, why should the mostly phantom threat of "medical problems" deter us from ours? God will stand by his daughters who are willing to serve him.

Fear of Overpopulation

After medical fears, the next fear in line is fear of overpopulation. The population bomb has been dropped on homeworking wives, making those with large families bear the responsibility for the world's problems. As two evangelical feminists explain,

> At one time, a husband and wife were considered selfish if they chose not to have children; now it is not unusual to hear praise for such couples. Those now labeled "selfish" are couples who insist on having a large number of children, thereby aggravating societal problems because of population growth pressures. Bringing children into the world has come to be seen as a luxury rather than a duty or necessity. . . .
> There are fears that too many people will enter life upon a planet with limited resources and where the quality of human life could be severely affected by overcrowding.[25]

Overpopulation is the great excuse for feminist barrenness. More than that, it is a slogan used to persecute those who hold out against a feminist lifestyle. The word *overpopulation* turns a couple who are sacrificing their time, money, and energy out of love for their children into "selfish" people who are "aggravating societal problems."

Let's just ask ourselves one question: *Where is all this noise about overpopulation coming from?* Is it coming from the Bible? No; the Bible is remarkably silent about the dangers of overpopulation. In fact, it makes no provision for limiting family size at all. But you *will* find commands to *have* children.

Both before and after the Flood God commanded couples to "be fruitful and increase in number; fill the earth" (Gen. 1:28; 9:1). God calls this population increase a "blessing."

In Exodus 23:26 God promised the Israelites that if they did just what he said, none of them would miscarry or be barren. This too is called a "blessing."

God promised the Israelites in Deuteronomy 28:11 that if they obeyed him he would grant them great increase of children, livestock, and crops. (Keep in mind that the entire country of Israel is a very small area about the size of Rhode Island. God was promising them a population explosion in a limited area with limited resources.) On the other hand, in Hosea 4:10 God warned the Israelites who were rebelling against him that though they indulged constantly in illicit sex their numbers would not increase. Since children are a blessing, and since God was angry at those rebellious Israelites, their increased sexual activity alone would not lead automatically to a population increase.

In our own New Testament age, God tells wives to "have children, to manage their homes and to give the enemy no opportunity for slander" (1 Tim 5:14). (Though this passage is initially addressed to widows, after the directive that they should marry, the rest of God's instructions apply equally to all young wives.)

So through all ages of the church—Adam, Noah, the patriarchs, Israel, and now the New Testament age—believers in the Messiah were happily having as many children as God gave them, and rejoiced in their fruitfulness when God blessed them with children.

But now, unbeknownst to the writers of the Bible, we have entered another age—the population explosion age. Sociologists have discovered that the earth is now full enough. In fact, it is *too* full. Supposedly Christians were meant to obey God's commands to be fruitful and multiply only up to a point. When the earth's population reached the Magic Number (whatever it was), then suddenly a Christian's duty switched from having children to *not* having children. Nobody knows exactly when this moment occurred, but the facts stare us in the face. The earth is definitely overcrowded.

Or is it?

Population bombers believe in the discredited theories of Thomas Robert Malthus, an English parson of two centuries ago, who taught that people always lived on the edge of starvation, and that increasing the food supply only produced too many people, who then starved for lack of food. This theory provides the main justification for the birth control and abortion ethic. As one such ethicist writes,

> The state will forever be poor, if its population surpasses the means by which it can subsist. . . . It is unjust to cut short the days of a well-shaped person; it is not unjust, I say, to prevent the arrival in the world of a being who will certainly be useless to it. . . . Who then has a greater right to dispose of the fruit than she who carries it in her womb?[26]

Kenneth Mitzner, founder of Mobilization for the Unnamed, discovered this quote. But "does anyone really believe," he asks, "that France was overpopulated in 1795? Does anyone really believe that the Marquis de Sade [after whom "sadism" is named] made these statements because of a humanitarian concern for the welfare of society?"[27]

The main problem with Malthus's theories, apart from their selfish and proabortion uses, is that *they never have worked.*[28] According to Malthusian dogma, the U.S.A. should have been destroyed by famine long ago. Yet centuries of healthy population growth have brought us a *better* standard of living, not disaster. When the same theory is applied to other countries and other centuries, it fails every time. History contradicts it. As the Bible says, "A large population is a king's glory, but without subjects a prince is ruined" (Prov. 14:28).

Not only does history disprove overpopulation dogma; so does science. Several learned works have thoroughly debunked the premises of "overpopulation crisis." Among these, the most notable examples are *Grow or Die!* by James Weber (Arlington House, 1977), *The Ultimate Resource* by Julian L. Simon (Princeton University Press, 1981), and the most massive and learned tome of all, *The Resourceful Earth: A Response to 'Global 2000'* (Basil Blackwell, Inc., 1984), which is a collection of writings on population and resources by twenty-eight scholars, edited by Julian L. Simon and Herman Kahn.

However, you do not need to wade through massive volumes to discover the scientific facts about population. The above works were designed to beat falsehoods to death with reams of facts, not merely to expose them. The proof that overpopulation is not a crisis, or even a problem, can be summed up in a magazine article. In fact, I am going to quote from just such an article: "The Population Bomb Threat: A Look at the Facts" published in the June 1977 issue of *Intellect*. The author is Jacqueline R. Kasun, professor of economics at Humboldt State University in California.

> There is a notable shortage of facts regarding the size and rate of growth of world population. The best population information exists for the developed and industrialized countries. . . . As Ansley J. Coale, director of the Office of Population Research at Princeton University, states: "Of the 31 countries that are usually listed as highly developed, 21 now have birthrates below replacement.". . .
>
> Compared with many other countries, both population density and rate of growth are relatively low in the U.S. There are about 22 persons per square kilometer in the U.S., compared with between 100 and more than 300 for various countries in Western Europe. . . . The rate of natural increase in the U.S.—0.6% in 1974—is below the average for developed countries. [Since then it has dropped below replacement level.]
>
> Thus, there is no population explosion in the U.S. or in the other developed countries. . . .

On this question of the world's food-raising potential, a number of major studies have reached a common conclusion, which does not support the view that mass starvation is imminent. This conclusion is that there is a *very large, unused potential for world food production.*

For example, in 1974, the University of California published the results of a major survey of world food resources showing that *the world presently uses less than half of its available arable land.* . . .

Colin Clark, former director of the Agricultural Economic Institute at Oxford University and noted author of many books on population-resource questions, classified world land types by their food-raising capabilities and found that, if all farmers were to use the best methods now in use, enough food could be raised to provide an American-type diet for 35,000,000,000 people, almost 10 times as many as now exist! Since the American diet is a very rich one, Clark found that it would be possible to feed three times as many again—or 30 times as many people as now exist—at a Japanese standard of food intake. Nor would these high levels of food output require cropping of every inch of available land space. Clark's model assumed that nearly half of the earth's land area would remain conservation areas. . . .

Nor does any shortage of fertilizers, irrigation water, or energy threaten world food production, in the view of Clark and the University of California researchers. . . .

Over the past decades, there have been recurrent predictions of the imminent exhaustion of all energy and basic metals, but the facts have not borne out these prophecies—and indeed they should not. It is a familiar chemical principle that nothing is ever "used up"—materials are merely changed into other forms. . . . Two major economic studies of the availability of basic metals and fuels found no evidence of increasing scarcity over the period 1870-1972. . . .

Insofar as metals are concerned, they exist in tremendous quantities at lower concentrations. Geologists know that going from a concentration of six percent to one of five percent multiplies the available quantities by factors of 10 to 1,000, depending on which metal is concerned.

In the case of fuels, the U.S. is currently in the position of having exhausted its own sources of low-cost petroleum. [Again, this was written before several major new deposits were discovered.] This is not correctly described as a "crisis," however, since higher-cost petroleum supplies are still available in this country and extremely large deposits of coal remain, to say nothing of the possibilities for substitutes such as solar energy. . . .

Barry Commoner, professor of plant physiology at Washington University in St. Louis and director of the Center for the Biology of Natural Systems, explains that the environmental damage found in modern industrial societies is primarily the result of highly polluting technologies which have been recently adopted, rather than a consequence of population growth. He points out that, between 1947 and 1970, population in the U.S. increased 40%, but pollutants due to the use of synthetic pesticides increased 267%; nitrogen oxides in motor fuel increased 630%; inorganic fertilizer nitrogen increased 648%; and detergent phosphorus increased 1,845%.

What these figures mean is that the only hope for cleaning up the environment lies in a direct attack on the polluting technologies responsible for the damage. The fact that the anti-population-growth movement is so heavily subsidized by the leaders of some very polluting industries suggests that the population panic may be intended to deflect sincere environmentalists from attacking the real roots of pollution. . . .

Despite the congestion near the urbanized sea-coasts, most of the planet is still largely empty. As Felice points, out, "We could put the entire world population in the state of Texas and each man, woman and child could be allotted 2,000 square feet [the average home ranges between 1,400 and 1,800 square feet] and the whole rest of the world would be empty."

The reason we feel so crowded in our entire modern milieu is that we use space inefficiently, especially in our transportation systems. . . . Thus, during the decade of the 1960's in the U.S., while the human population increased by a modest 13%, we acquired 34,000,000 additional cars, creating as much additional congestion as if we had added more than 1,000,000,000 people, or more than 50%, to the human population! . . .

The simple expedient of moving about in buses, trains, and trolleys, or on foot, instead of in personal automobiles would reduce congestion, as well as urban air pollution, by 90%.

In closing, it should be noted that children are not merely claimants on social resources. Children do not diminish, but add to, the welfare of those who have them, just as truly as material possessions do, and they create far fewer environmental pressures than do the ubiquitous vehicles of the so-called "advanced" societies.

Admittedly, we live on a finite Earth and, if world population growth were to continue for many centuries at the two percent rate estimated for the present, problems could be expected. History shows, however, that, when countries begin to modernize, an initial stage of rapid population growth is followed by a spontaneous reduction in fertility. This happened in Europe and North America and can now be observed in most less-developed countries.

Therefore . . . the so-called "population crisis" is more truly a myth and an alibi than a fact. . . .[29]

Overpopulation does not exist. *Unbelief does.* The only reason a large number of people become a curse to themselves and others is that they do not believe in the Lord Jesus Christ.

Scripture draws a fundamental distinction between the children of the righteous (of whom there are never enough) and the children of the wicked (of whom there are always too many). The children of the righteous are blessed (Psa. 37:26). The man who fears the Lord and delights in his commands will have children who are "mighty in the land" (Psa. 112:2). "Blessed are his children after him" (Prov. 20:7). On the other hand, curses are on the children of the wicked (Psa. 109:10-13; 37:28).

Today many of those who have turned away from God are refusing to have children. Scripturally, this could very well be God's curse on their movement. But just because *they* are not willing or able to raise up a new generation to carry on *their* work is no reason why we shouldn't raise up a new generation to carry on ours.

Fear of Rabbithood

Population alarmists have convinced most of us that without birth control people breed like rabbits. If it were not for scientific family planning, so they say, out would pop a baby each year. Couples, overwhelmed at the thought of twenty or thirty children, head off to buy IUD's or vaginal thermometers.

But God doesn't dispense his blessings that automatically. In Bible times, when nobody used birth control (except Onan), Sarah had only one child. Rachel had two. Rebekah had two. Zebedee's wife had only two sons (if she'd had more, you can bet she would have been lobbying for a special spot in Christ's kingdom for them too!) Noah only had three children—even though he lived 950 years! Take time to examine the

Bible genealogies, and you will find that really *big* families are the exception, not the rule. Population expert James Weber informs us that the average birth rate in developed countries is two to three children per family, and in developing countries only five to six instead of the dozen or so that population bombers constantly depict.[30] Throughout history the rate of population increase has been infinitesimally small, and at times it even *drops*. This is as we should expect, since God controls who gets what blessing. It takes more than a desire to reproduce for a nation or a family to get God's blessing.

Nor does the Lord just drop twenty children on a Christian couple. And if he did give you twenty children, not only would the process take a good long time, during which the older ones would grow up and leave, but the Lord would supply all you need to raise them as well. As my Hungarian grandmother says, "The Lord doesn't give you a little lamb without giving you a pasture for him." And my mother says, "You get stronger with every child." Both sayings are true.

Fear of Persecution

We don't need to fear that we will breed like rabbits. But should we fear those who fear us breeding like rabbits? ZPG zealots are trying to get the political power to persecute parents of large families. In the meantime they are using every means at their disposal to get out the message: Large Families Are Disgraceful!

In our mostly black neighborhood, somehow the people seem to have escaped being infected with the antichild attitude of our age. When I go out walking with our three small children, everyone says, "How sweet!" But there are many suburban neighborhoods, or ritzy city sections, where a mother would feel *ashamed* to be seen in public with more than two children.

You can encounter an antichild attitude even in the maternity ward! After a woman has delivered her third or fourth child it is common practice in many hospitals for the nursing staff to encourage her to have her tubes tied before she leaves the hospital with her new baby.

My friend Lesesne, who is now the mother of five, told me about her experience in a hospital staffed by ZPG types. When she had her first baby everybody smiled and made her feel good about being a mother. When she had her second, the nurses said, "How nice. Now you have your boy and your girl." When she had her third, eyebrows went up— "Oh, you want a *large* family." Lesesne heard children crying on the floor overhead, and nurses screaming at them, "Shut up, you little brats!"

When she found out that all the doctors in the women's ward performed abortions, the whole picture added up—*these guys don't like children!* She switched to a prolife hospital and doctor twenty miles away from then on.

(By the way, it is not only an extremely effective prolife statement, but good common sense to refuse to use a doctor who performs abortions or a hospital that allows them. To expect an abortionist to perform heroic lifesaving procedures for your baby while he routinely deals out death to hundreds of others is to require professional schizophrenia.)

If my friend Lesesne, living in a somewhat isolated rural community, could run into persecution for having "too many" babies, so could anyone. Population bombers are adamant that motherhood is sinful. James Weber quotes one major ZPGer as calmly suggesting,

> It can be argued that over-reproduction—that is the bearing of more than four children—is a worse crime than most and should be outlawed. One thinks of the possibility of raising the minimum age of marriage, of imposing stiff penalties for illegitimate pregnancy, of compulsory sterilization after a fifth birth.[31]

It's amazing how casually believers in overpopulation can chat about taking away our basic freedoms. The reason, as distinguished psychologist Fredric Wertham says, is that

> The superfluous people, and especially their parents, are regarded as really guilty. . . . The consequence is punishment. You may have the right to exist, but you lose the right to procreate. If someone in authority tells us that we have no right to procreate, it is only one step further for him to tell us we have no right to live.[32]

Fear of God

I won't say that in a day like ours when evil is called good and good evil we won't be persecuted for embracing motherhood wholeheartedly. But as Jesus said, "Rejoice in that day and leap for joy, because great is your reward in heaven. For that is how their fathers treated the prophets" (Luke 6:22, 23).

However, we don't have to go about cringing in fear of the population bombers, even if we are timid types. Not yet anyway. They talk a lot, but so far none of their brave new ideas has made it into law. Now is the time to make the most of our opportunity to bear children for

Christ, while we are still unhampered by legal restrictions. As for the future, I'd like us to follow the example of Philip Henry, the father of the great Bible commentator Matthew Henry. When the English government lifted restrictions on Nonconformist preaching, Philip Henry's friends begged him not to preach openly. They warned that the govenment could then tag him as one of the men to crack down on when they brought back the old penalities, which everyone expected they would. "Many thoughts of heart he had concerning this use he made of the liberty," wrote his son, "not knowing what would be in the end hereof; but after serious consideration, and many prayers, he saw his way very plain before him, and addressed himself with all diligence to the improvement of this gate of opportunity. Some had dismal apprehensions of the issue of it: and that there would be an after-reckoning. But, saith he, let us mind our duty, and let God alone to order events, which is his work, not ours."[33] The government did briefly suspend preaching liberty again, as his friends had feared. But the upshot of it all was that although Mr. Henry suffered some personal abuse and loss of property, the Nonconformist ministers had made such good use of their liberty to preach when they had it that England never again put a believing Christian to the flames.

We don't have to fear beggary, bondage, death, disease, rabbithood, or even persecution. As I said before, some of these fears are legitimate to a certain extent, and some are not. But all of them, if I may say so, are beneath us as Christian women. As the prophet Isaiah said,

> The Lord spoke to me with his strong hand upon me, warning
> me not to follow the way of this people. He said:
> "Do not call conspiracy
>   everything that these people call conspiracy;
> do not fear what they fear,
>   and do not dread it.
> The Lord Almighty is the one you are to regard as holy,
>   he is the one you are to fear,
>   he is the one you are to dread,
> and he will be a sanctuary;
>   but for both houses of Israel he will be
> a stone that causes men to stumble
> and a rock that makes them fall. . . .
> Many of them will stumble;
>   they will fall and be broken,
>   they will be snared and captured." (Isa. 8:11-15)

Why should we stumble at God's teaching? Let us say like Isaiah, "Here am I, and the children the Lord has given me" (Isa. 8:18). The Lord is the only one worth fearing. The Lord is the only one worth dreading. Not snide neighbors. Not antibaby activists. And definitely not babies.

6 Family Banning and Planned Barrenhood

To love our children means we don't reject them. Yet, if I am not mistaken, a very significant undercurrent in the careerist movement, which comes from its mother the feminist movement, is the rejection of children. Women declare, "We don't want to be tied down to a house and children!" More than once women have told me straight out, "The reason I work is that I'd go crazy staying home all day with the kids."

It's no coincidence that those within the church who push hardest for careers for women also say the most negative things about children. The Scanzonis, for example, devote ten pages of their sociology text on the family to listing the costs of having children and eulogizing a childless lifestyle.[1] Their attitude toward children may be gleaned from this quote:

> But is it true . . . that couples have babies merely because of societal pressure (since societies cannot continue without replacement of their members)? Or is having babies simple a matter of nature's trickery—a kind of cosmic con game in which persons are carried away in the ecstasy of sexual pleasure only to be rudely awakened by a squirming, squealing, demanding infant who emerges to mock the lovers with an attitude of "Aha! You thought you were just having fun, but look what you got instead—me!" Or might it be that people have children because they want them or value them? No doubt all three explanations contain elements of truth.[2]

But rejection of children does not stop with name-calling. "Squirming, squealing, demanding" infants who "emerge to mock the lovers" are the enemy who can wreck a mother's career. Far from loving our children, feminists try to make us hate them as the chief obstacle to our total liberation, and we must deal with them ruthlessly. They must be fought and repulsed before they can invade our lives. Thus: abortion.

The Blood of the Children

Abortion is the ultimate rejection of a baby. In abortion, the baby is cut to pieces, pulled apart by suction, poisoned, or burned to death, or even removed alive to be put to whatever painful and lingering death seems best to the kind doctor who wants to help the baby's mother pursue her "individualistic interests" in the "economic-opportunity sphere." During all of this, *the baby feels pain.*

But what happens *during* the abortion is only half the story. Abortionists now reap a rich profit from selling the bodies of those poor mutilated babies to be made into—guess what? *Cosmetics!* As Dr. Olga Fairfax says,

> Since there are 1.5 million abortions every year, there is an abundant source of fetuses for commercial use.
>
> There's a triple profit to be had. The first is from the abortion (estimated at a half billion dollars a year by *Fortune* magazine). The second profit comes from the sale of aborted babies' bodies. The third profit is from unsuspecting customers buying cosmetics.
>
> Babies' bodies are sold by the bag, $25 a batch or up to $5,500 a pound. The sale of late-term elective abortions at D. C. General Hospital brought $68,000 between 1966 and 1976. The money was used to buy a TV set and cookies and soft drinks for visiting professors.[3]

Before abortionists realized they could make big bucks out of babies' bodies, unborn babies were treated like trash. One abortion center in Richmond

> filled a long bin on the rear of its property with the remains. . . . Its trash compactor neatly massed 100 babies' bodies which were then tied up in plastic bags and thrown on top of the bin.
>
> "The hungry dogs came along and dragged the bags away. There were frequent fights and the contents of the bags would be strewn up and down the streets until the dogs separated the gauze, sponges and pads and devoured the placenta, bones and flesh of the babies," said a mother.[4]

It is not particularly pleasant to hear of city dogs being trained to enjoy the taste of human flesh. Even worse, however, is the taste for human torture being developed by respectable medical men.

Dr. Robert Schwartz, chief of pediatrics at the Cleveland Metropolitan Hospital, said that, "After a baby is delivered, while it is still linked to its mother by the umbilical cord, I take a blood sample, sever the cord and then as quickly as possible [what, Dr. Schwartz? Weigh the baby? Give her to her mother so she can nurse? No, while the baby is still alive] *remove the organs and tissues.*" [emphasis mine]

Tissue cultures are obtained by dropping still-living babies into meat grinders and homogenizing them, according to the prestigious New England Journal of Medicine. . . .

A $6,000,000 grant from the National Institute of Health [supported by your and my tax dollars] enabled one baby (among many others in the experiment done in Finland) to be sliced open without an anaesthetic so that a liver could be obtained. The researcher in charge said that the baby was complete and "was even secreting urine." He disclaimed the need for anaesthetic, saying an aborted baby is just garbage.[5]

There's more . . .

In March of 1973, Connecticut's Attorney General presented an affidavit to the U.S. Supreme Court regarding a Yale-New Haven experiment in which a baby boy was dissected without anesthesia before he died. The next month the *Washington-Post* reported that Dr. Gerald Gaull, chief of pediatrics at New York State Institute for Basic Research in Mental Retardation, "injects radioactive chemicals into umbilical cords of fetuses. . . . While the heart is still beating he removes their brains, lungs, liver and kidneys for study. . . . Also in 1973, a medical journal reported experiments carried out on live-born fetuses [he means living babies] who were decapitated [he means their heads were cut off] in order that their heads could be perfused to study carbohydrate metabolism.[6]

Don't let high-sounding language fool you. The very year that abortion became legal, doctors carried out experiments that involved cutting off babies' heads and keeping them *alive* for months, and torturing babies by removing their organs or cutting them into pieces, while they were *alive* and *able to feel pain.*

And the atrocities go on. Will the unborn be regarded as handy little organ sources? Will our preborn brothers and sisters become a source of spare parts?

Listen to the newscasters—they are already pleading nationwide for organs. . . .[7]

These are not academic questions. A twenty-eight-year-old engineer who "found life on a dialysis machine intolerably restricting" and couldn't get a kidney transplant from a family member since he had been adopted and didn't know who his natural parents were thought of a "novel solution" to his problem. "The man's wife would get pregnant and, after five or six months, have an abortion. The kidneys from their own pre-born child would then be transplanted to the husband."[8] His idea is especially noteworthy since not only is he, the father, plotting to murder his own son or daughter, but because we have come to the point where such ideas are *respectable* in our media circles.

Babies Are People Too

The abortion people have thrown up a dense fog over their nefarious doings by constantly refusing to use the proper English word for the person they are killing—"baby." Instead they prefer "embryo" or "fetus" (actually *fetus* is Latin for *child*). However, the Bible makes it clear that a baby is a human being made in the image of God from the moment of conception. David says he was "sinful from the time my mother conceived me" (Psa. 51:5), not "protoplasmic tissue was conceived, which upon emergence from my mother turned out to be me." Jeremiah was Jeremiah within his mother's womb, where God had already chosen him to prophesy against a country much like ours (Jer. 1:5). The Bible rhapsodizes over how wonderfully God fashioned you and me within our mothers' bodies (Psa. 139:13). And in Proverbs 23:22, the ultimate pro-life passage, God says, "Listen to your father, who gave you life . . ." God does not say "Your *mother* who gave you life," but "your *father*." Babies are not the sole property of their mothers, over whom she has godlike and total authority. From the moment of *conception,* which is the only time a father has anything to do with producing a baby, a baby has been given life by God. The 1973 *Roe v. Wade* decision which legalized abortion in the U.S.A. was not only a sin against all American children yet to be born, by making them the absolute slaves of their mothers, but was also a sin against all American fathers, by depriving them of their God-given right to protect and nurture their own children.

So we know that the Bible says a baby is a person from the moment of conception. Now we come to our big mistake. Prolifers have been acting on the assumption that the reason women get abortions is because they don't realize the person they are killing is a person. Well, those who believed that were wrong:

> The unborn child is a human life, but taking that life is justified if the social reasons are "high enough."
>
> This attitude was expressed by many of the woman law students who sponsored a debate on abortion at Emory Law School in Atlanta on November 18 [1983].
>
> The students' sentiments shocked Richard W. Summers, executive director of the Rutherford Institute of Georgia, who was invited to participate in the debate. He had expected many of the women to avow that there is *not* life in the womb.[9]

What reasons are "high enough" for a mother to kill her baby?

> Protecting pregnant teenagers from the psychological distress of bearing a child, helping poor women who aren't able to care adequately for a child, and preventing children from coming into the world "unwanted."[10]

So the true reason for abortion has finally come out. Women are willing to kill their babies because *they don't want them,* and *they don't care if the "fetus" is a living baby or not.* They have goals of their own, which they euphemize as "high social reasons," such as going through law school childless. According to the feminist philosophy, woman is the measure of all things. As a goddess, she has the right to kill and make alive (though unfortunately not the power to do the latter), and no responsibility to anyone but herself. She may or may not fully understand the magnitude of the crime of destroying her own baby's life, but her action was not based on respect for anyone else in the first place.

The underlying sin beneath the abortion holocaust, is, then, *selfishness.* And the first people to admit it would be women who, since their abortions, have become Christians. They know they didn't get their abortions because of high philosophical reasons, but to serve their own selfish desires. They didn't want to inquire, "Is there really a baby growing within me?" In some cases they *knew* it was a baby, and in some others they had actively avoided discovering this fact. But even in the cases where a new Christian didn't know before she was saved that her "fetus" was a baby, she knows her abortion was not the result of innocent love, but of selfishness. She was thinking, "What will be best for *me?*" She was responsible for her sin.

Thank God—even the horrible sin of abortion can be forgiven, and a woman who repents of it and believes in Christ is your and my sister as much as anyone else. However, there is one deep question that needs to be asked and answered: Why do so many women *want* abortions? Where did the abortion holocaust come from?

Ray Joseph, editor of the *Christian Statesman,* puts this most feelingly:

> I was accompanying my close brother, the pro-life speaker for that Sunday evening meeting in downtown Pittsburgh. . . .
>
> We were meeting with a small group of Sunday night faithfuls, people who found themselves in the strangely uncomfortable position of cultural holdouts, or even throwbacks, the faithful few who felt bewildered as they witnessed the opening of the bloodgates, the result of an abortion practice which had now been declared legal by the highest court of the land. . . .
>
> The close brother said, "The culture has shifted its presuppositions." Indeed it has. And . . . WHY?
>
> The church used to be culturally dominant. But today it has become nearly culturally impotent. What has happened? What kind of mentality, what form of teaching, beginning where and taught by whom, is responsible for this massive shift from dominance to impotence? Where did it go wrong?[11]

We will now attempt to answer these questions.

Who Killed the Stork?

I believe the reason that Christians have not been successful so far at stopping abortion in this land is because we have not yet understood and confessed *our part in bringing it about.* Typically the Christian understanding of abortion has been, "The central issue in abortion is the question of human life. But the great assumption of the proabortion movement is that the fetus is not a human being."[12] However, as we have just seen, the lid is off the abortion racket; everyone knows that "fetuses" are human. In fact, they are pushing for more and more experiments on and organ transplants from these poor little human beings. Yet women still have abortions. Neither have abortionists repented of their half-billion-dollar-a-year business just because daily exposure to the "products of conception" proves conclusively that those are hands and feet and heads and toes that they are handling.

Now that Bible-believing Christians have woken up to the enormity of abortion, have we stopped it? Has it become illegal? Even though it remains legal, does that mean that *inevitably* more and more women must want abortions? No to all these questions. So there must be something wrong with our response to abortion.

Typically Bible-believing Christians have reacted to abortion in the way outlined by Rev. Dean Smith in an article entitled "Abortion: Doing Justice and Preaching Peace" in the March-April 1984 issue of the *Christian Statesman*.

How shall we as Christians respond to this [abortion]? First, do justice.

He asks us to recognize our responsibility to protect the weak and innocent. He calls us to challenge the lying abortionist terminology, to take political action, to press for men's responsibility for their children.

Second, preach grace . . . call people to repentance from sin.

O.K. so far.

Preaching grace and lovingkindness means offering compassionate alternatives to women with crisis pregnancies.

Can we offer an unwed mother an atmosphere in which she would be made to feel welcome? . . . How many women from Christian churches have had abortions rather than face the church as an unwed mother?

The unwed mother may need a place to stay. So we must be personally and corporately prepared to offer hospitality, financial aid, and other assistance. . . .

A mother may need to work. So the church may need to provide a day care center. . . .

What does God want you to do in response to this message? First, He wants you to be involved. He wants you to pray for the cause of life. And He wants you to support with both your prayers and your finances Christian Action Council, People Concerned for the Unborn Child, Lifeline, and other pro-life ministries.

Write your congressman and other representatives. . . .[13]

The typical Christian response, as expressed in this article, is that our sins have been (1) lack of political involvement and (2) lack of acceptance for unwed mothers. This is not correct. We are not all called to be lobbyists or politicians any more than we are all called to be preachers. Nor do we *owe* it to every unwed mother to provide her with money, a home, a day-care center, and a job (to say nothing of pushing her into this feminist careerist lifestyle). Mercy? Yes, for *repentant* sinners. Compassion? Yes, for those who *ask for help*. We do need to repent of our sins before God; but political naiveté and a strong stand against fornication are not sins. Nor have they *caused* abortion.

The church's sin which has caused us to become unsavory salt incapable of uplifting the society around us is *selfishness, lack of love, refusing to consider children an unmitigated blessing*. In a word, *family planning*.

Creating the Unwanted Generation
Murder arises in the heart, as Christ reminds us (Matt. 15:19). Abortion is first of all a *heart attitude*. "Me first." "My career first." "My reputation first." "My convenience first." "My financial plans first." And these *exact same choices* are what family planning, which the churches have endorsed for three decades, is all about.

Women abort their babies for two reasons: *selfishness,* and a *low view of the value of children*. The latter is the crucial factor, since no amount of selfishness would make a woman rob herself of what she believed to be a blessing. But into whose hands did God entrust the message that children are a blessing? The church. And who for the past thirty or forty years has been denying this very message by endorsing family planning? The church.

When the church came out in favor of family planning, it produced certain effects. Outside careers became truly possible for women with the blessing of the church. Only when a woman deliberately chose to stop having children and was able to carry through on her plans would she be able to launch into a career without fear of "interruptions." This was the first wave. The second wave was a sudden demand for abortion, to insure that her new career plans *were* failsafe. Along with this came a decreased dependence on her husband, leading to marital stress as she felt more free to do her own thing without bothering to consult him. You know the rest of the story. Epidemic divorce, abortion-on-demand, child abuse, the popularity of homosexuality (with women trying to become men, who wouldn't be confused?), infanticide, and so on. All because children are no longer considered a blessing.

This is not to say that the church is totally responsible for legalized abortion and the social ills that inevitably follow in its wake (though a good many liberal church people *were* involved in groups like Clergy and Laity Concerned that actively worked for the repeal of abortion laws). People like Margaret Sanger and her organization Planned Parenthood, the Women's Liberation Movement and its apologists, and the militant and extremely well-organized secular proabortion groups like NARAL (National Association for the Repeal of Abortion Laws, later National Abortion Rights Action League), NOW, and the ACLU brought about the change in U. S. abortion laws. But because the church did not confront these groups at the most basic level by insisting that children are an *unqualified* blessing, we unwittingly contributed to the overwhelming antichild attitude that eventually resulted in *Roe v. Wade*. And as long as this antichild mentality remains firmly rooted in society as well as in the church, it will be extremely difficult to stop abortion. Thus Christians have a responsibility to stop talking and acting like children are a hindrance, an interference with the "real" things of life—upward mobility, careers for wives, recreational sex, etc. As long as Christians maintain the same hedonistic lifestyles as the world, thereby showing that what really matters to us is our own comfort, our supposed concern for the unborn will appear either irrational or hypocritical. Only by living consistently can we make the kind of prophetic, authentic statement the world will hear.

The two methods Christians use to plan their families—(1) spacing and (2) limiting family size—both have one thing in common: *they make a cutoff point on how many blessings a family is willing to accept.* Can anyone find one single Bible verse that says Christians should refuse God's blessings? Children are an *unqualified* blessing, according to the Bible. But the only way the world is ever going to know this is to see Christian couples who are willing to have and enjoy large families.

Let's take these methods one by one. *Limiting* as a family planning method separates sex from reproduction. It produces the same mental attitude as a "child-free" couple has, since once the desired number has been reached there is the same call for sterilization and the same unwillingness to conceive. Limiting encourages an antimotherhood attitude, since a woman who already has had children and does not want any more is apt to be looked up to as an expert by those without children. They think she is basing her decision on experience, and it makes them afraid to become mothers themselves. And all this talk about, "That's all we want—just two (or four, or one)" is incredibly discouraging for the already-born sons and daughters, who have to listen to their own parents explain how children (meaning *them*) are too much trouble to want any more.

Spacing has the same effects as limiting, by a slightly different route. Spacing is the attempt to usurp God's sovereignty by self-crafting one's family. Who can tell but that one special combination of genes will produce the greatest revival preacher the world has ever known, or the greatest musician, or the most wonderful mother? By discarding, month after month, our opportunities for reproduction, we are not only limiting our family size but limiting God's opportunities to *choose the best children for us.* God can, of course, override our attempts at birth control. But he much prefers to cooperate with us, and does not usually choose to beat us over the head with unwanted blessings.

Psalm 127, the Psalm which tells us that children are a heritage and a reward from the Lord, also warns us that "unless the Lord builds the house, its builders labor in vain." Scripturally, your "house" is your family. The past two generations have been trying to build their families themselves, consulting their own goals and convenience—and you see the results.

Family planning is the mother of abortion. A generation had to be indoctrinated in the ideal of planning children around personal convenience before abortion could become popular. We Christians raise an outcry against abortion today, and rightly so. But *the reason we have to fight those battles today is because we lost them thirty years ago.* Once couples began to look upon children as creatures of their own making, who they could plan into their lives as they chose or not, all reverence for human life was lost. Children as God's gifts whom we humbly receive are one thing; children as articles of our own manufacturing are another. You can do anything you like with what you yourself have made.

Children today are their parents' toys or hobbies. They exist for their parents' desires alone. So they are banned from all adult functions (including Sunday morning worship), deposited in day-care from infancy, and even abused sexually. The incest rate has increased so dramatically that one expert recently expressed his opinion that in one out of every six families a father is raping his daughters or a brother is raping his sister.[14]

God help the children of family planning: the poor, abused, unwanted generation.

The Wanted Family

There *is* an alternative to scheming and plotting how many babies to have and when to have them. It can be summed up in three little words: trust and obey. If God is willing to plan my family for me (and we Christians all do believe that God loves us and has a wonderful plan for our lives), then why should I muddle up his plan with my ideas? Only God knows the future. Only he knows how much money we will have next year, or when I will reach menopause, or when his Kingdom will desperately need the unique talents of my yet-to-be-conceived son or daughter. Why not leave the driving to him?

Naturally couples wonder what will happen if they flush their Pills down the toilet and toss out their vaginal thermometers. Let's go behind the scenes and look at a couple who did—namely, Bill and me.

When I first discovered the Bible's teaching on children as a blessing rather than a curse, I had a career of sorts and a headful of fuzzy notions about fertility. I was sure that I would immediately get pregnant once I got off the Pill.

I was wrong.

For three long years nothing happened at all. *Nothing!* This is by no means unusual. Fertility specialists have an abundance of clients who triumphantly decided to conceive . . . and then discovered they couldn't. We tried this, that, and the other thing. Nothing worked. Finally we thought of actually admitting God was in control of the situation and *praying* for a baby. You might laugh, but the idea that babies just automatically pop out when couples are "unprotected" by birth control was so ingrained in both of us that we had never thought of it as a matter for prayer! Six weeks later I found I was pregnant.

At this point our circumstances were far from ideal. We were on our way to linguistics school in blistering-hot Oklahoma with $200 to our name. But you see, our situation at the time of conception had nothing to do with our circumstances at the time of delivery. In fact, according to the Bible *nobody's* present circumstances are an infallible guide to their situation next year, or even tomorrow (Jas. 4:13-16). God timed that baby to divert us from a missionary career that we now see was not the place for us. He also proved himself faithful in providing for the needs of two homeless and penniless parents-to-be. We had no money; but God provided us with a place to stay and a job for Bill. We had no medical insurance; but Bill's medical plan was changed at the last minute to cover my preexisting pregnancy. (This last was a minor miracle, and not our doing, since Bill's employer was New York State and the bigwigs in charge of insurance didn't know we existed!)

Since then, God has graciously given us two more children. I have never become pregnant until we prayed for a baby. Our children were born a year and a half and two and a quarter years apart respectively. This is actually less than the normal spacing experienced by families that don't use birth control. Between the nine months of pregnancy and the year or two that God designed women to breastfeed their infants, most women will have a reasonably long time after conceiving one baby before they can expect success in conceiving another. As I pointed out in the last chapter, in countries where women have no fear of conceiving, the lifetime average for children per family is only five or six. My experience with the Catholics in my childhood neighborhood bears this out. The Sullivans, with twelve children, had by far the largest family. (They were proud of it too, I might add!) Most families had four to seven children. Nobody had twenty or thirty.

If you let God plan your family, nobody can say exactly what his plan will be—except that the blessing of an extremely large family is rare, like all special blessings. You could normally expect to have children at least two or three years apart, as long as neither you or your husband develop any severe health problems or have bad accidents involving the reproductive system, in which case you will have few, if any, more children. As the older children mature, they will be able to help with the younger ones and take a lot of the housework off your hands. Soon the older ones will marry; so you can't expect to have dozens of children in the house at one time even if you have a large family. While other women are having hot flashes and growing moustaches and experiencing all the other delightful effects of early menopause, you will sail serenely along with your youthful complexion (although maybe not a youthful waistline!). While other women are smitten by empty nest syndrome and midlife crisis and all those other modern ailments affecting women whose span of motherhood only lasts to age forty, you will still have little ones who need you. When you finally start slowing down, the last will be grown, and you will be a real expert on mothering, able to lend your invaluable help with your grandchildren and the children of the younger women in the church.

I do know of one case—just one—where a couple had five children in six years. For various reasons the wife was unable to breastfeed, and the children just came right along. However, in this case if they had not had children that close together they would never had had them at all. The wife developed cancer of the uterus after the birth of her sixth baby and had to have it removed. She had come close to dying of starvation as a young girl in Poland, and her poor nutritional background as a child and adolescent was probably the cause of losing her womb at such an early age.

It is foolish to assume that because I am fertile today I will be tomorrow. We can't count on the blessing of fertility lasting forever, any more than we can count on always being able to run the 100-yard dash in fourteen seconds. I believe that once we start looking more realistically at our fertility, seeing it as a fragile and special blessing which many people will never have and which everyone eventually loses, we will have a higher respect for babies. If we really could create children any time we wanted, it would be a different story. But to arrogantly decide we can produce a baby any time we want, when it is beyond our unaided power to conceive, is flying in the face of the facts.

If I don't want a baby today, but do tomorrow, I may find when tomorrow comes that I have already missed my only chance.

Evangelism Through Reproduction

We Christians can sometimes be inconsistent. We'd fight and scream if someone tried to stamp out our evangelistic efforts (the FCC is still getting postcards in response to the bogus rumor that Christian programming on radio and TV was going to be outlawed). Why doesn't it bother us that, thanks to family planning, the number of Christians in the next generation is being thinned out from *within*?

Let's say that Christians are 20 percent of the U.S. population. If each Christian family had six children, and the humanists, feminists, and others kept on having an average of one (which is realistic, considering how they feel about fruitful heterosexual marriage), then in twenty years there would be sixty of us for every forty of them. In forty years *90 percent of America would be Christian!* That is *without* outside evangelism. All we'd have to do would be to have children and raise them for Christ. Even if Christians were only 2 percent of the population (which I think is more accurate), then in two generations, at the reproduction rates I already mentioned, we would be over 40 percent of the population.

Norman Podhoretz, editor of *Commentary* magazine, observed in 1971:

> The Devil, if he exists, does not command us to be fruitful and multiply. If he exists, he exists for the purpose of tempting or seducing as many of God's creatures as he can into a refusal to choose the breeding of life. . . .
>
> As he seduces into suicide not with the praise of death but with the dream of an escape from death, so he seduces into sterility not with denunciations of the generative act but with the promise of sexual riches and sexual delights. . . .
>
> Would he not, if he existed, be pleased with the size and condition of his American flock? Could even he with all his cunning ever have dreamed that so many would come to preach sterility and even to sterilize their very own selves?[15]

The devil *does* exist, and he has fooled us into giving up our God-given role as *the greatest evangelists in the world* for the sake of measly carnal careers. The church's enemies know what they are doing when they push careers for women. They know they are trying to make us unfruitful. As University of California biologist Garrett Hardin, a leader in the Zero Population Growth movement, says,

> How can we reduce reproduction? Persuasion must be tried first. Tomorrow's mothers must be educated to seek careers other than multiple motherhood. Community nurseries are needed to free women for careers outside the home.[16]

Among Planned Parenthood's "examples of other proposed measures to reduce U.S. fertility" are

> increased homosexuality; chronic economic depression; *requiring women to work* and providing few child-care facilities; compulsory abortion of out-of-wedlock pregnancies; compulsory sterilization of all who have two children—except for a few who would be allowed to have three; confining childbearing to only a limited number of adults; and stock-certificate type permits for children.[17] (emphasis mine)

It's no accident that the very organization that calls itself Planned Parenthood has been the great driving force behind abortion's popularity in this country. Planned parenthood leads to abortion, homosexuality, careerism, "chronic economic depression," and all that smacks of antihuman ugliness.

I have my own sins to confess. I was a feminist and spouted this rhetoric. But you and I together can take great hope from this promise of God:

> "If my people, who are called by my name, will humble themselves and pray and seek my face and turn from their wicked ways, then will I hear from heaven and will forgive their sin and will heal their land." (2 Chron. 7:14)

This promise was given first to the people of Israel, but it is ageless. God's people sometimes do go astray. But he promises he will heal their land—even this sick, sinful, bloody America—if only we, his people, repent.

Christians have made the mistake of taking on our enemies without making sure first that God was on our side. We have acted as if we have done nothing wrong and have nothing to confess; as if America's slide from a God-fearing people to an openly God-defying people was an accident we had no control over and nothing to do with. But if the culture is corrupt, the fault lies in the salt. Had the salt remained salty, it would have preserved the meat.

What kind of example have we been? What kind of examples *will* we be? Will we teach our daughters about woman's role, about the dignity of bearing children, about God's sovereignty over our bodies? Or will we assert the "right to control my body," that cornerstone of self-worshiping feminism? Will we humble ourselves, admitting that we have sinned? Will we pray and seek God's face? Will we turn from our wicked ways and embrace our role as willing, even joyous, mothers of children?

Woman's role is more than having babies. But motherhood is a watershed. It divides the sweetly flowing waters of biblical womanhood from the bloody flood of abortion and feminism. Yes, we should picket abortion clinics and donate to prolife lobbies and write our congressmen and most especially preach *against* fornication and *for* faithful marriage. But here is what we should do *first*. If Christian women and their husbands all across this land—in cities, in suburbs, in the country; in apartments, houses, and mobile homes; young and old, rich and poor—all bowed their heads to beg God's forgiveness for hardening their hearts against the children he had planned to give them, and pledged that they would start having and nurturing as many as God gave them, I really believe God would heal our land and send revival. When the hearts of the fathers are turned to the children, the land no longer has to be struck with a curse (Mal. 4:6).

In the next section we will look at raising children: how to nurture our children once we have them, and why God gave this job to parents, not institutions.

Part Three:

BACK TO MOTHERING

"... train the younger women to ... love ... their children ..." (Titus 2:4)

7   Who Owns Our Kids?

A child is born. Pain is dimmed by anxiety as the baby emerges—is he or she all right? You listen for the cry, and relax as the baby gives vent to a wail, repeating the age-old response at being pushed into this strange new world. The doctor tells you, "It's a girl!" "A baby daughter!" you think, and bless God for this little miracle—no, this *major* miracle, that a tiny human has been brought forth out of your body. Quickly you count fingers and toes—all there, again thanks be to God, though even if they weren't you'd count it an honor to love and mother this new little person who is already being soothed on your breast. "My baby!" you think in pride and bursting delight.

The doctor or midwife is smiling, your husband is smiling, you are smiling. But there's still someone unhappy about your moment of joy. Like the evil fairy in the story "Sleeping Beauty," they have not been invited to the party and they resent it. As Malificent cursed the baby princess, so are they casting an evil eye on your baby daughter.

Call these people the "Coercive Utopians."[1] They know what's best for everyone's children, including yours. They even know how many children you should have had in the first place. Feminists ZPGers, Socialists, Big Brother—whoever they are, their agenda is the same. They want total control over everyone and everybody, including our children.

Garrett Hardin, a member of the ZPG wing, speaks for them:

> The right to breed implies *ownership* of children. This concept is no longer tenable. Society pays an ever larger share of the cost of raising and educating children. The idea of ownership is surely affected by the thrust of the saying that "He who pays the piper calls the tune."[2]

In a country where you need a license to do just about anything, from putting a new porch on the house to driving a car to going fishing, motherhood is, as Alvin Toffler, author of *Future Shock*, puts it, "the last realm of the amateur." Totalitarians can't stand amateurs; they believe strongly that only experts, meaning themselves, should have the power to do something as important as shape a human life. Impressed by the fistfuls of credentials these experts have been waving in their faces for the past 150 years, the American family has quietly surrendered more and more of its power to institutions. Now our very surrender is turned back on us to whip us into total submission. If "society" bears so much of the cost of raising our children, surely "society" should do it all. So says Mr. Hardin.

Encouraged by the American family's willingness to part with its offspring, government is gearing up to be Big Mother. This has taken two forms: (1) a deliberate attempt to vest all parental authority in the State, and (2) a simultaneous attempt to physically remove children from their parents' custody under the guise of "education." Let's take a look at how it's done.

Children's Rights and Government as Mother

We are hearing an awful lot about child abuse nowadays. The media, who couldn't care less as a general rule about the life or feelings of an unborn child, wax lyrical about the rights of that child once he manages to be born and proves he is not handicapped in any socially unacceptable way. Daily magazines, newspapers, and TV regale us with horror stories of battered children, and passionate pleas are made to protect all children from this kind of abuse.

To the unwary this all sounds quite innocent. Who could be *for* child abuse? But the "children's rights" movement has only one goal in mind: government as Mother.

When you sift the rhetoric through, you find that the argument goes something like this:

(1) Some parents abuse their children.

(2) We don't think that's right.

(3) *So,* government must take control over families to make sure parents don't abuse their children.

(4) *And,* parents who abuse their children will have their children taken away.

(5) *And, government will define the word "abuse."*

From point (3) on, this entire train of argument is unscriptural.

Strange as it may seem to us modern Americans, the Bible does not give anyone the right to remove a child from his or her parents' custody, abuse or no abuse. In Old Testament times, if a parent killed or raped a child, he was not given a slap on the wrist, he was executed (Lev. 18:6, 17, 24). This would, of course, strongly deter parents from serious abuse. If a child ran away, it is possible that the fugitive slave law would have applied, whereby an Israelite was forbidden to return a runaway non-Israelite slave to his abusive foreign master (Deut. 23:15). Beyond this, if a parent permanently damaged a child the law said, "eye for eye, tooth for tooth" (Lev. 24:20).

In contrast with the Bible's humane way of controlling parental license while keeping the child *within* the family, the modern children's rights movement is designed to get the child *out* of the family. Even if a parent has committed horrendous sexual or other sins, he or she is not punished. Rather, he or she is an object for "rehabilitation." This only makes sense when we see that justice and the child's best interests are not what the children's rights people are after. *They want to control our children,* pure and simple, and the sentimental appeal of "preventing child abuse" is merely a wedge they are using to crack the American family apart.

What happens when they get their way? In Sweden, a Socialist democracy, children's rights have been implemented. Parents can no longer spank their children, although the Bible commands us to do so (Prov. 13:24; 23:13, 14). Indeed, it is considered "abuse" for a mother to *scold* her son or daughter! Children are drilled in school on their rights, and encouraged to turn in their parents if they offend. Perhaps it is not a coincidence that Swedish youngsters have one of the highest suicide rates in the entire world.

For us as Christian parents, children's rights means *we have our children only as long as the government lets us.* Any attempt to control a child at all, from spanking to sending him to Christian school to sending him to his room, is grounds for the state screaming "Abuse!" and stepping in to take him away. In places where the children's rights people are active, parents have been convicted for ridiculous things like forbidding their children to attend movies. Right now cases against parents who teach their children at home are routinely brought under the banner of "educational neglect," even if the parents in question have Ph.D.s and their children do better on standardized tests than public school children. Children are "neglected" if the parents are trying to teach them *instead of letting the State do it.*

Abuse, in short, is raising your children in any way those in power dislike—such as raising them as Christians.

Why Johnny Is in Public School

But the government *already* has control over the vast majority of American children. Public education was the American family's first move toward socialism. Samuel Blumenfeld, author of *Is Public Education Necessary?*, tells us,

> Knowing that our country began its remarkable history without public education—except for some local common schools in New England—and that the federal Constitution did not even mention education, I was curious as to why Americans had given up educational freedom for educational statism so early in their history, adopting the notion that the government should assume the responsibility of educating our children.
>
> Out of this labor came some fascinating discoveries: that American intellectual history is inseparable from its religious history; that public education was never needed, and that literacy in America was higher *before* compulsory public education than it is today; that socialists, who were very active in the public school movement, began operating covertly in secret cells in America as early as 1829, before the word socialism was even invented. . . .
>
> Besides being buildings, cash flow [$81 billion dollars in 1977], a powerful establishment of professionals, and a legal structure that maintains and regulates it all at taxpayer expense, public education is also a process whereby the American youngster is molded into an American adult. . . . Today, most of the young adults who emerge from the process read poorly, write miserably, have stunted vocabularies, cannot do arithmetic well, know little geography and less history, and know virtually nothing about the economic system in which they live. At school they fall under strong peer pressure, are introduced to drugs and sexual promiscuity, while their teachers preach the moral relativism of secular humanism as a substitute for the outmoded moral codes of religion.
>
> The truth is that the system that prevailed prior to the introduction of compulsory public education was not only quite adequate . . . but served the public need far better than anything we have today.[3]

Mr. Blumenfeld, whose book is incredibly well-documented, traces the compulsory public education movement to the following sources:

(1) The Harvard-Unitarian elite, who having discarded the biblical

belief of man's basic sinfulness now believed that man was only evil because society was evil. Change society, change man. Get all the children young enough and change society.

(2) Socialists, under the influence of Robert Owen, the founder of the New Harmony Socialist experiment (which totally failed by the way). Socialists also believed in getting children away from their parents while they were young and teaching them Socialist doctrines before they learned to become "wicked, selfish capitalists."

(3) The decline of Calvinism in America. As people, under the restraints of the government and church life which Calvinists had established, behaved better and better, it became easier to forget that all men have evil hearts. So if not all children grew up to be perfect, it must be the fault of their parents, because all children *could* be perfect, if we only taught them right.

(4) The Unitarian- and Socialist-founded educators' associations were the last force behind public education.

The public education movement, then, did *not* arise out of a crying need for quality education or for education for the poor (we already had both of these), but because an elite wanted govenment to control children's moral and spiritual beliefs. In the beginning would-be public educators appealed to Christian ministers, promising great opportunities to indoctrinate even non-Protestant students in the gospel. That was why public education needed to be compulsory—so we could *force* children to be good, whether their parents wished it or not.

Well, chickens will come home to roost, and bad ideas cannot succeed in spite of good intentions. In a recent hearing concerning the future of private schools and home schools in Wisconsin, the Wisconsin Education Association Council representative "made it clear that his group could not allow home schools to exist that teach ideologies that conflict with the majority opinion of the state."[4] I need hardly mention that the "majority opinion of the state" is no longer by any stretch of the imagination Christian, and that parents are turning to private schools and home schools precisely to *escape* the compulsory "moral" training they know their children will receive in the public schools. Moreover, in Wisconsin legislation is on the docket to give the State Superintendent of Schools "rule making authority" and to give the local superintendent "the right to determine whether any private school in his district was in fact a private school for compulsory attendance purposes and he could do this on his own as often as he wished."[5] This proposed bill also denies private school status to schools "held on premises that are primarily a private residence," or where the teacher "is related to more than 50 percent of the student body"—a clear attempt to outlaw all home schools and many struggling new private schools in Wisconsin. Freedom of religion, anyone?[26]

At the same time, school officials all over the country are pressing for earlier compulsory school age, longer school days, and longer school years. "Legislation is pending in Indiana to lower the school entrance age from seven to five with mandatory kindergarten. Similar legislation is on the docket in South Carolina, Wisconsin, Nebraska, Missouri, Illinois, Kansas, Nevada, and other states."[7] Already Kentucky and Maryland have made kindergarten compulsory.

Does anyone really think that the same schools that can't teach children to read and write will suddenly start producing geniuses if only they can force children to remain on school premises more hours at an earlier age? Public schools have proved they are incompetent. Now their very incompetence is the grounds for demanding *more* power, *more* money, *more* control over our children!

Make no mistake about it—education is not the issue here at all. The issue is (1) more money and jobs for teachers and administrators, (2) influence over children's minds (that is why the NEA doesn't want home schools which teach competitive ideologies), and (3) free day-care for working wives. Isn't it an *odd* coincidence that immediately after careers became respectable for mothers of preschoolers, the NEA started pushing for nice long school days and nice long school years? Full-time baby-sitting at last! And the earlier age at which they want our children—that would never have worked in the bygone days when mothers enjoyed having their children home, but it's great for all those paying day-care costs right now. Thus the Feminist Revolution can finance itself out of the wallet of the American taxpayer.

Please notice that all this proposed legislation is about *compulsory* education. The states are not being asked merely to provide new facilities for parents who want to send their children to school earlier or longer, but to *force* all parents to do this, whether they want to or not.

Why this drive to restrict parents' freedom?

It all comes back to those coercive utopians again: those people who want to get us wives out of the house and into the work force, who want to force us (or at least our daughters) to be barren.

"In any deliberate effort to control the birth rate," [Kingsley] Davis contends, the government also has "two powerful instruments—its command over economic planning and its authority (real or potential) over education. The first determines (as far as policy can) the economic conditions and circumstances affecting the lives of all citizens; the second provides the knowledge and attitudes necessary to implement the plans. . . . The schools define family roles and develop vocational and recreational interests; they could, if it were desired, redefine the sex roles, develop interests that transcend the home, and transmit realistic (as opposed to moralistic) knowledge concerning marriage, sexual behavior, and population problems."[8]

The public schools, you see, are the coercive utopians' catechism classes. Since coercive utopians refuse to reproduce themselves the normal way, public education becomes their avenue for passing on their beliefs to the next generation—through other people's children. Public school is their private school. Whether the cause be developing "world citizens" as opposed to patriotic Americans, "sexually active" as opposed to moral teenagers, Socialists instead of believers in free enterprise, or feminists instead of Mommies, there are textbooks designed to teach it and a curriculum designed to enforce it.

I sent away recently for an outline of the typical course of study followed by public schools from kindergarten through grade 12. Grade 10 social studies featured "The search for peace" and "Role of women in today's society." Grade 11 included, along with significant historical events such as the Civil War, the "struggle for women's rights" and again, "the role of women in today's society." And once again, in twelfth grade, social studies featured the "role of women in today's society."[9] This outline was based on thorough curriculum research, including guides of curriculum from all fifty states.

Michael Levin, a professor of philosophy at City College of New York, writes in an article in *Commentary* magazine that "one of the most extensive thought-control campaigns in American education history has gone completely ignored. I am referring to the transformation, in the name of 'sex fairness,' of textbooks and curricula at all educational levels, with the aim of convincing children that boys and girls are the same."

The major textbook publishers—such as McGraw-Hill, Macmillan, Harper & Row, Lippincott, Rand McNally, Silver Burdett, Scott-Foresman, Laidlaw Brothers, and South-Western—have lists of guidelines requiring their writers to promote a feminist world view, according to Levin. . . .

The federal government is currently supplying hundreds of thousands of dollars through something called the Women's Educational Equity Act Program, whose purpose is to rewrite textbooks in a way that will reflect the feminist and minority view of the world to the exclusion of all other views.[10]

Parents for the past 150 years have been expecting public school to do the job of shaping their children's values. Now the bitter fruit of this error is appearing, as the public schools are demanding the right to indoctrinate children in values that may be directly *contrary* to the parents'.

Sex education courses are designed to brainwash children into accepting homosexuality and fornication as "valid forms of sexual expression." Values clarification classes systematically destroy the biblical concepts of an absolute right and an absolute wrong. One-world government programs in Social Studies are meant to destroy patriotism, while the study of "women's role in today's society" is a front for indoctrination in feminism. Economics courses teach socialism; English teachers assign pornography as required reading; even my high-school gym class featured instruction in occult Yoga techniques.

None of this can remotely be called "training up a child in the way he should go." What might be harder to see is that, biblically speaking, it isn't a school's job to teach even *good* values.

The Forgotten Responsibility

God gave parents, and parents *only,* the job of shaping their children's values. After Moses delivered the Ten Commandments to the people of Israel, he said,

> Hear, O Israel: The Lord our God, the Lord is one. Love the Lord your God with all your heart and with all your soul and with all your strength. These commandments that I give you today are to be upon your hearts. *Impress them on your children. Talk about them when you sit at home and when you walk along the road, when you lie down and when you get up.* (Deut. 6:4-7, emphasis mine)

God repeats this command for emphasis in Deuteronomy 11:19— "Teach them to your children, talking about them when you sit at home and when you walk along the road, when you lie down and when you get up."

Our responsibility to teach our children their moral and spiritual values cannot be delegated. Both Deuteronomy 6:7 and Deuteronomy

11:19 make it clear that this training must occur *at home,* throughout the course of the family's day together. No school teacher, no Sunday school teacher is there to teach your child when he lies down for sleep and when he gets up in the morning and when he sits at home in between. Nor are they usually available for lessons as he walks along the road. *If we want to raise godly children, we have to take this responsibility back.*

The only reason the USA is drifting toward educational totalitarianism is that up to this point parents have been willing to give up responsibility for their children. If parents start refusing to let their children be taken away, the NEA can do nothing. There are more of us than there are of them, and we can vote too. On the other hand, the early childhood education movement is tailor-made for those who are looking for a way to dump their kids without social censure. If we follow that route, the next step would be total institutionalization of children from birth on, so parents would be free to pursue their adult lifestyles without interruptions in the evening or on weekends. Alvin Toffler discusses this possibility seriously in his book *Future Shock.*

Christian Institutions Are Not the Whole Answer

Some Christian parents have turned to the Christian school movement after witnessing the demise of public education's academic standards and morality. This is fine, as long as Christian schools are in the business of imparting skills and facts. But too often, it seems to me, the Christian school becomes the source of moral and spiritual training in exactly the same way the public school used to be. Jay Adams writes in reference to the Christian school,

> The classroom context is ideally suited to . . . establishing and changing life patterns. First, it is a total environment milieu such as that described in Deuteronomy 6:7, 11:19. Secondly, there is a daily, sustained influence of precisely the kind it takes to establish or alter patterns. Thirdly, the penalty and reward system inherent in teaching, if used under the authority of God, provides ample motivation for most students. Lastly, the school reaches the student during the most productive hours of the day . . . and can demand and obtain from him his utmost output. . . . The potential impact of the Christian school teacher is immense.[11]

This makes those of us nervous who believe that the *parent* is the one to establish and change the child's life patterns. If the teacher tries to change my son or daughter, he is taking my authority, perhaps to change the very values I am trying to instill. Adams unwittingly invites teachers to subvert parents by using the metaphor of war.

> If the teacher does not help his students develop new patterns and change wrong ones and thereby influence the activity of the child both within and without the school milieu, the wrong patterns he brings from without will exert a harmful influence within the classroom. There is no escape; the teacher's stance must be: *attack or be attacked.*[12]

The teacher is not told to turn to the parents for help, but to "attack" what he sees as "wrong patterns" the child "brings from without" the school. However, what the child learns outside of school is the parents' direct responsibility, and might be the fruit of the parents' deliberate efforts. Teachers, then, may find themselves attacking the parents.

Teachers base their qualification to teach on academic credentials. Their qualification is academic *only,* and is as strong or as weak as their skills in those areas. Teachers are not ordained elders or theologians, nor should we expect them to be. I believe, with C. S. Lewis, that teachers who take it upon themselves to lead our children spiritually are "unjust to the parent . . . who buys it and who has got the work of amateur philosophers where he expected the work of professional grammarians."[13] It is also unjust to the teachers who *do* want to teach to expect them to play Mommy to thirty kids at a time.

Yet Christian schools regularly advertise that they "build character" and "train your child to behave like a Christian." Even math class must include a sermonette or it isn't "Christian." In 1980, Christian Schools International produced a list of what it considered the top ten goals for its students:

1. Personal integrity
2. Providence
3. Self-respect
4. Social respect
5. Stewardship
6. Oral communication
7. Social justice
8. Written communication
9. Social responsibility
10. Persistence

"Career awareness" placed twenty-seventh, and the learning of a foreign language dead last.[14] I am not happy with this list. Even as a list for *parents'* goals it falls short. Self-respect is not more important than respect for others, and why social justice should be sandwiched between oral communication and written communication is a mystery. But in plain fact *most of these goals do not belong to the school at all.* We send our children to school (at least, we should send our children to school) to learn things like reading, writing, and arithmetic, and even foreign languages, that we don't feel competent to teach them ourselves or that we don't have the time to teach. Personal integrity, stewardship, and persistence they should learn at home.

The Difference Between Discipling and Teaching
Now I know that "educating the whole child" is very much in vogue right now. Some say that discipling and teaching are the same thing, and that the child's teacher should take the parent's role in discipling. The public school people said it first; now it's catching on in Christian circles.

But discipling is *not* the same as teaching. Otherwise your husband would have to check out the lecturer's religious background before he attended a seminar on data processing. If teaching *always* includes spiritual discipling, he could be getting "discipled" by a Jehovah's Witness or a Mormon if the lecturer happened to be one! If teaching and spiritual discipling are identical, Christians shouldn't go to grad school, or read books written by non-Christians, or ask their non-Christian neighbors to show them how to connect the plugs on their home computer.

Discipling is not the same as teaching. *Spiritual discipling only occurs when (1) both parties agree to form a discipler/disciple relationship in the area of spiritual things, and (2) the discipler attempts to transfer his values to the disciple.* Your child *can* be taught math without being spiritually discipled. The problem comes when a math teacher takes it upon himself to make moral or spiritual changes in his students.

The other side of the coin is that we do our children's teachers no favor by expecting them to do our job for us. If you find it hard at times to direct your son or daughter in godly paths when you are dealing with him or her one on one, imagine what it must be like with thirty children all needing your attention day after day! There isn't *time* to teach thirty children academic skills and disciple them as well—which is one reason why public education is failing: it has tried to do both.

Home Schooling
There is more that could be said against institutional education, Christian or otherwise. For one thing, *peer pressure.* By far the greatest discipling influence over children in institutional settings is the influence

of their peers. If not even the Christian teacher has a warrant from God for discipling my son, how much less my son's ignorant and untrained friends? What good is it if we spend thousands of dollars for our children to attend a top-notch Christian school if they spend breaks huddled over *Playboy* magazine in the lavatory? Yet this very peer dependence is praised as positive "socialization."

Next there is the question of *money*. The great reason for Christian wives being forced out of the home is "to pay for the children's Christian school." My sisters, this should not be. Christian schools were founded in order to build up the family, not to force Mom onto birth control and into a job. If they have become that expensive, it's time to look for an alternative.

And as it so happens, *the home school movement is here and is snowballing*. Some families just can't afford Christian school. Many others have been persuaded by Dr. Raymond Moore's books *Better Late Than Early, School Can Wait,* and *Home-Grown Kids* that children do not belong in *any* institutional setting until they are physically mature and capable of reasoning effectively. This, to me, makes sense. I'm not going to send my children into a situation of facing possible temptation without my help until I'm sure that they are capable of behaving as mature Christians. When my son is as strong spiritually as Daniel, *then* let him go to Babylon. And not a minute sooner.

Home schooling breaks the institutional monopoly. As long as parents can only choose between free public school and expensive private school, lower and middle-income families have no choice at all. This kind of monopoly is not healthy for the country. Furthermore, an institution is *so* easy to burden with regulations—as Christian school administrators know. What with stratified peer groups, certified teachers, and public-school-style curriculum outlines, there sometimes is not that much structural difference between public and private schools.

Real competition keeps everyone honest. Already the competition from private school is forcing the public schools to show a little more interest in the reading, writing, and arithmetic they so disdained when they were the only game in town. Home school offers even greater possibilities for raising the level of American education.[15]

For parents and children, the benefits of home school are obvious: the academic possibilities of the best private school education at minimal cost, and without worries about the children's moral or physical safety. Home school curriculum runs about $100-$400 a year, and a mother can develop her own program for almost nothing with the help of second-hand bookstores and the public library. There is also the great savings in *time.* My friend L. says, "I am saving three hours a day in transportation time, not to mention having a *sane* family routine that is not being artificially interrupted to take a trip to school. And I have *control* over my life and lifestyle that other women don't because of their crazy schedules!"

But more than all this, home schooling allows parents to control their children's spiritual development. Without the option of home school, parents are locked into whatever the institutions in town are providing, which may be very bad and even at its best is not the same as their personal discipling. William McGuffey, the author of the famous *McGuffey Readers* which sold by the millions a century ago, had this to say about children's spiritual development:

> But, much as we [teachers] love, and ought to love those committed to our care, they are but our pupils, not our children. . . . None but the *natural* parent, can feel that natural affection, which is adequate to the duties of *properly educating* an immortal mind. . . .
>
> The teacher, I repeat, should know better than any other man, how to produce a given result in mental training; but the parent, who is the natural guardian, or in want of parents, the authorised adviser, alone has the right to say what that result, which is attempted, shall be. . . .
>
> Teachers must not only take children as they are; but must permit them to remain as they were, in the respects just noted. For where is the parent, that will patiently permit any teacher to obliterate those impressions; or change those characteristics; or to interfere with the formation of those habits, in his children, which he has been so solicitous to secure? . . .
>
> We must, as far as practicable, so arrange matters at *home,* that our children may come into the hand of the school-master docile, ingenuous, affectionate, intelligent, honorable, magnanimous, rational, conscientious, and pious children. These are the fundamental elements of a right character; and *not one* of them can be dispensed with, in the very commencement of a school education. . . . Which one would any parent be willing, were it possible, should spring up in the mind of the child, under the fostering care of any hand but his own? Where is the mother that would not resent the imputation, that her child had grown old enough to attend school without her having cherished or implanted in its opening mind, one and every one, of the principles above enumerated? . . .

Some of the above traits are *habits*—and all require to be cherished at first by a *parent's hand*. And if they are not, it will be less than miraculous should they survive the rude culture and chilling atmosphere of public instruction, in its best forms. They can be cherished at home. They are successfully cherished in many families. But we might challenge the world, to produce even a few instances, where they have been successfully cultivated, in any other field.[16]

So speaks a voice from the days when mothers and fathers still felt responsible for their children's moral and spiritual training, and when the children were much better behaved and far superior academically to our children today.

The issue has been raised as to whether Christians should ever put their children into a public school. Viewpoints are available on both sides. For myself, the issue goes deeper than whether child A should be put in school X or not. As I read the Scriptures, *public education is not a legitimate function of government* at all. God gave us rulers to punish the wicked and to encourage those who want to do good (Rom. 13:3, 4). It is not the bureacrat's and politician's job to "do good" with other people's money. "Doing good" is the duty of citizens.[17] Furthermore, both Deuteronomy 11:19 and 6:7 make it clear that *parents* are responsible for a child's education, not the State. From this point of view, the present breakdown of American public education is not surprising but inevitable. The State was never meant to do this job; we should not expect it to succeed.

Beyond the abstract argument as to whether public education is a proper function of government, the very real fact remains that *our* present public education system is religiously anti-Christian. Nor can the presence of Christian teachers in the classroom make up for the fact that they are required to teach a curriculum which is as doctrinaire in what it includes as in what it excludes (i.e., we get sex education but no lectures on the Ten Commandments, the role of women in today's society but nothing on motherhood and homeworking). This curriculum is further enforced by the requirement that "approved" textbooks must be used. These textbooks are very interesting as examples of rather poor preaching. If schoolchildren were ever allowed to taste real Christian preaching, they might detect the difference. However, the textbooks are spared this trial, since their contents are supposedly not sermons at all, but neutral "facts." It makes exactly as much sense to send a Christian child to a school that uses typical public school textbooks and curricula as it would to send him to Moon Goddess Grade School or Temple of Islam High. In fact, it makes less sense, because we could expect the latter to be at least open about their religious bias, whereas the public school disguises its religious propaganda as "scientific neutrality."

To sum up, I don't believe that any child below the age of independent, courageous moral convictions belongs in an institutional school setting. Some will arrive at this age earlier than others; none will arrive at it at four or five. Secondly, I believe that the future Christian leaders in our country are going to emerge from everywhere *but* the public school system. Modern public education is designed to destroy Christians, not produce them. I see no reason why we should send our children to public school and then worry about how to counteract its influence when we can simply sidestep it entirely. Thirdly, I have enough faith in the power of the Holy Spirit to allow you to disagree with me, for the present at least! Most of my home schooling friends laughed at the idea when they first heard of it. The same could be said for many parents now involved in the Christian school movement. All I ask is that you *investigate the facts.*[18] I think you'll then agree that a mother does indeed have good reasons for staying home.

The battle now raging will decide who owns our children. Christian schools and home schools are challenging the compulsory attendance laws and the very concept of government control of education. The NEA, the utopians, and the children's rights people are fighting back with every bit of power they possess. They were counting on silently stealing our children while we slept, but some brave souls on the watchtowers have warned us of their schemes. Will we surrender our children to them, docilely dumping them in day-care euphemized as "early education" and trotting off submissively to a job? Or will we hold the home fort? Our children can't be raised at home until they are spiritually mature if there is *nobody home to raise them.*

Who owns our kids? *God* owns our kids. And he has given us parents the responsibility of making sure they turn out to be his kids. In the next chapters we will see how to do this, and what it means to be a *mother at home.*

8 Beyond "No-fault" Child-rearing

My husband Bill and I squirmed uneasily in our seats at the back of the auditorium. It wasn't that we were nervous about keeping control of our three preschool children, who were sitting with us; they were being very good. What the speaker was saying was making us nervous.

Addressing an audience of Christian school parents, he spoke about how to appease their kids' insatiable desire to conform in matters of dress and morals. He gave hints on how to handle a sixteen-year-old boy who keeps getting drunk or a fifteen-year-old girl who insists on staying out past her 11 P.M. curfew. When he warned us that we'd better throw away our porn books and sex manuals because the kids certainly would find them, there was much shuffling of feet and looking at the floor. I was more jittery than anyone, not because we have any porn in our house, but because some of the other parents apparently *did*.

Outside in the hall, as we assembled jackets and zip-up suits, I noticed red Valentines on the wall of this Christian school with the names of the children on the different basketball teams. Each boy or girl had a nickname—"Skin Tight," "I Love Boys," and "Mattress," for example. I was blushing redder than the Valentines in embarrassment for the Christian values those nicknames so ingenuously denied.

Timid as I am in front of groups, I wish I could have spoken after the man we heard that evening. Every problem he mentioned as inevitable in the teen years—drugs, sex, rebellion, premature marriage, self-centeredness—is either *caused* or *aggravated* by the "normal" worldly upbringing which that Christian school and some of those parents seemed eager to copy. What you expect from a child dictates what you put into that child. The tragedy is that in our day when motherhood is so severely attacked, women are being brainwashed into not giving themselves to their children because *they don't think it will make any difference.*

One of the great arguments used to discourage Christians from wanting large families is that "there is no guarantee your children will grow up to be Christians, so why wear yourself out?" This becomes a self-fulfilling prophecy as parents, almost unconsciously, hold back from pouring themselves into what they see as a losing proposition. We have come to accept as normal the defection of our children from Christian values. Teenagers who prefer nihilistic and perverted hard rock records to classical music or hymns are not considered weird but *normal.* Ditto regarding slavish conformity to fashions (even immodest ones) in dress, speech, and behavior. Who today expects her sons to prefer reading the classics to watching *Three's Company,* or her daughters to be more interested in deeds of mercy than in car-dating?

Yet a sizable proportion of great church leaders have always come from Christian homes. I think of Jonathan Edwards, the leader in our country's greatest revival. I also think of Edwards's sons and grandsons, who were also Christian leaders, as were Edwards's father and grandfather. I think of John and Charles Wesley, whose mother was exemplary for piety. Was it just an accident that Matthew Henry, the great Bible commentator, was the son of Philip Henry, a man whose godliness inspired his bride-to-be to say, "True, I don't know where Mr. Henry came from, but I know where he is going and I want to go there with him"? And when our Lord and Savior came to earth, God did not choose "just any" parents to bring him up, but two who were shining examples of godly obedience.

"No-fault" child-rearing has been dinned in our ears until we actually believe that parents have no control over how their children turn out. But this is neither the witness of the Bible nor of history. All our modern talk of "phases," "natural teenage rebellion," and the like simply points to the fact that our modern, progressive methods *don't work.*

Those who insist that we should totally adapt to modern culture because "things are so different now" and "old ways don't work" ought to explain the difference between the way children behave today and the way they did, say, back in 1890—when boys dipped girls' pigtails in ink for fun, instead of raping them in the school basement, when drugs were no problem and school children didn't even know how to spell "marijuana." The same people who brought us juvenile delinquency and the teenage VD epidemic are now blaming their failures on us. Parents are not "expert enough" to raise children in this "difficult society." We ought to step submissively aside and let government do it.

But being a good mother is not impossible. You only need three things. First, *confidence.* I aim to supply some of this by looking at what the Bible says about raising children. Second, *feedback.* Without a way to measure progress, or lack of it, we are helpless. I believe God gives us this feedback through our children's behavior. When we take responsibility for their behavior, then we are in a position to change it. Third, *the blessing of God.* "Apart from me you can do nothing," Jesus said (John 15:5). However, the Bible shows God is more than willing to bless his people's children, *just as soon as his people are willing to raise them his way.*

So we will look at these three things—confidence, feedback, and God's blessing—to see why no-fault child-rearing *does not work,* and how parents who return to taking personal responsibility for their children will be able to raise a generation of great Christian leaders.

Fear of Rotten Kids

All God's promises concerning children are to "the righteous" only—that is, to those who *do what is right* in this area, not to any and all saved people, no matter how rebellious they may be. *Not every saved person is a righteous parent.* A father or mother may be elect, but be disobedient to God's way of raising children. The Bible warns us that Christian parents are perfectly capable of disobeying God's directions for raising their children. That is why God keeps telling his people (who are the ones he expects to read his Book) that "a child left to itself disgraces his mother," and "he who spares the rod hates his son" (Prov. 29:15; 13:24).

God says, "Train a child in the way he should go, and when he is old he will not turn from it" (Prov. 22:6). If you still fear that your children will not grow up Christian in spite of your best efforts, you have been infected with the germs of "no-fault."

We all know families whose children did not turn out well. We fall back on "no-fault" because we are afraid to hurt anyone's feelings by suggesting that the parents might have failed. And what about all those Bible families whose children rejected God? What about Isaac's son Esau . . . David's sons Amnon and Absalom . . . Jehoshophat's son Jehoram? If our children belong to God, how could this happen?

To answer this, let's look first at the biblical examples of unsaved children. Consider for a moment how Isaac, David, and Jehoshophat stack up as parents. Isaac played favorites and tried to overrule God's prophecy for the sake of a good meal. David committed adultery and murder, which is *not* a good example, and refused to discipline his sons for their wicked behavior. Jehoshophat was so easygoing he married his son to Jezebel's daughter! Don't you think you could beat those track records?

Isaac, David, and Jehoshophat were righteous in other matters but *un*righteous fathers. We can learn from their mistakes. God put their examples in the Bible so *we could do better,* not to discourage us (1 Cor. 10:6, 11).

As for Christian couples you might know whose children have turned out badly, let me ask you this. If the parents are not to blame, *who is?* Society? God? Does God say children are a blessing and then give us children who are fuel for hell? Does he really refuse to give the tools necessary to fulfill his own promise that a child trained in the way he should go will not depart from it?

If it's really true that a Christian mother or father can do everything right and have it turn out all wrong, then there's no hope for rebellious children at all. But if the parents are doing something wrong, they can repent and beg God to forgive them. They can do better.

It's not all bad to discover you are part of the problem. It just means you can be part of the *solution!* There is room for *hope!*

God's Fantastic Promise
Proverbs 22:6 says, "Train a child in the way he should go, and when he is old he will not turn from it." That sounds simple and straightforward: do your job and it will turn out O.K. But some people in the no-fault movement are trying to discourage Christian mothers from claiming this promise. They attack Proverbs 22:6 in two ways:

(1) They say that "when he is old he will not turn from it" only means that after years of sin the child will return to the Lord. According to this theory, the promise says nothing about your child's *middle* years. He'll be saved when you're in the grave, but meanwhile he can make you a nervous wreck.

This theory is wrong. Proverbs 22:6 never mentions departing from the Lord. It talks about *not* departing from the Lord. It does not say, "Train up a child in the way he should go, and though he may depart from the Lord he will eventually return to God when he is old." The true thrust of the promise is that even when your son is "old"—that is, mature and independent of you—he will *continue* to do what is right!

Mothers and fathers naturally worry about what will happen when their children are free to make their own choices. "Will they be good when we're not there to *make* them be good?" parents wonder. God wants to relieve our anxieties. Yes, they will be good even when they are mature . . . as long as we trained them properly.

(2) The second attack on God's promise in Proverbs 22:6 is more crafty. Some people have gone so far as to claim that Proverbs 22:6 isn't a promise at all! They say it means that if a child is trained up in the way he naturally wants to go, you won't be able to rescue him from his evil ways. They make it read, "Leave a child to his natural way and he will not depart from sin."

I am sorry to take your time refuting such an incredible misreading of this passage. I would not have believed anyone could teach this seriously had I not read it in a book written by a major evangelical author, heard it from two preachers, and run into a woman who had been taught this in her women's Bible study.

Take a concordance or lexicon and check this teaching out yourself. No way can it be right. First of all, the Bible says, "*Train* a child." It doesn't say, "Leave him to himself." The Hebrew word for "train" comes from a root meaning to narrow something down. Training means you're *narrowing down* your child's sinful tendencies, not leaving him to develop *more!* Furthermore, nobody needs to *train* a child to disobey. They come by it naturally. Those little mitts will be in the cookie jar before he can even lisp, "Thou shalt not steal." It makes no sense to talk about "training" children to do what they'd do naturally without any training at all! Finally, this view contradicts sound doctrine. Drawn to its logical conclusion, it would mean that every child from an overpermissive home is doomed to eternal damnation with no hope of salvation, because he "will not depart from" the foolish ways he learned. But that just plain isn't so! People from permissive backgrounds get saved every day. Just about my whole generation falls into the category of those who theoretically will not depart from sin; yet the Jesus Revolution occurred among exactly these people.

Why are no-faulters so anxious to dismantle Proverbs 22:6? Because they dislike its flip side. They just don't want to admit that a child's continuing bad behavior could be due at all to his parents' lack of discipline.

Parents are not the *cause* of their children's sins. Scripture makes that clear. Every baby is born with a sinful nature and sins without needing his parents to force him into it (Rom. 3:9-20). Nonetheless, God has commanded parents to train their children and to drive their natural folly out of them (Prov. 22:15). If a child's folly *remains,* it's because his parents are not doing their job. If they *are* doing their job, their children will not grow up to be fools. God has promised.

More Promises

No-fault child-rearing can't stand up against Proverbs 22:6. But I'd like to give you a few more scriptural reasons for rejecting no-fault.

First, think for a minute about the many, many Bible verses which tell parents how to raise their children. The Book of Proverbs alone contains forty-one verses on how to train your sons. Wouldn't it be strange for God to put such stress on telling us how to raise children the right way—*his* way—if it made no difference as to how they turned out?

Second, every elder is required to have children who "obey him with proper respect" (1 Tim. 3:4). His children are also supposed to "believe" and not be "open to the charge of being wild and disobedient" (Titus 1:6). The reason is, "If anyone does not know how to manage his own family, how can he take care of God's church?" So (1) God expects a man to be able to manage his family; and (2) when children are managed properly, they will believe and obey with respect. Managing children properly is something that *can* be learned and that *must* be learned before a man can try to manage the church.

Finally, although it is hard to be a good mother because "folly is bound up in the heart of a child," yet "the rod of discipline will drive it far from him" (Prov. 22:15). This verse shows us cause and effect. Godly childrearing (the cause) produces a godly child (effect). In Proverbs, wisdom is the opposite of folly. And in Proverbs, to be wise is to be *saved.*

Of course God is sovereign, and without his blessing nobody gets saved. But God is not capricious; he always chooses to bless the means he has appointed. He does not give us commands about how to raise our children and then fail to bless our diligent efforts with his power.

> Blessed is the man who fears the Lord,
>   who finds great delight in his commands.
> His children will be mighty in the land;
>   each generation of the upright will be blessed. (Psalm 112:1, 2)

God intends Christian parents to raise Christian children who are not just skin-of-the-teeth Christians but *leaders*—"mighty in the land."

If you take both God's promises and your responsibility seriously, you have every reason to expect success.

9 Raising Kids Without Confusion

One of the biggest reasons that mothers today are so anxious to get a job is simply in order to get away from the children. If I had a dime for every mother with a child in day-care who went to work "to get out of the house," I could buy Wyoming. This, as Hercule Poirot used to say, gives one furiously to think. Why are grown women incapable of bearing the society of their own children for more than a few hours a day?

The reason, of course, is that *the children are no fun to be around.* Misbehaving, bothersome children would wear anyone down. The prospect of facing all that hooting and hullaballooing alone for eighteen years is frightening. Thus, the drive for day-care, babysitters, Mom's days out, co-op child care, and so on.

I could say several things about this situation. I could point out, for instance, that if God gives us a job we have no right to shirk our duty even if we find it unpleasant. I could talk about taking up our crosses and denying ourselves. But actually I don't think motherhood *is* such a cross . . . if we approach it properly.

Fatalism and False Goals

Mothers today have been brainwashed into expecting failure. We have progressively lowered our sights to the point where, if our offspring make it through college without actually killing themselves or anyone else, we count it a victory. Both our *goals* and our *methods* have been eroded by the relentless drip-drip-drip of the pagan philosophies brought into the church in recent years.

As Christian mothers, our goal should be nothing less than to produce wise children who are self-motivated to do good and shun evil.

We are not striving for children who are merely educated and skilled, but children whose *loving behavior* proceeds from a *godly heart*. As the Apostle Paul puts it, "The goal of this command is love, which comes from a pure heart and a good conscience and a sincere faith" (1 Tim. 1:5).

This goal may seem self-evident; yet Christian parents today are under great pressure to substitute inferior goals for the true goal of godliness. Grades. Sports. Beauty. Popularity. These are all hawked about as "helping your child reach his potential."

Parents today are made to feel really guilty if they aren't putting every spare minute and every cent into turning out little Mozarts, Michelangelos, and Mickey Mantles. And as for the god of Popularity, it has actually gotten to the point where some Christian parents are *afraid* to make their children look or act any differently from non-Christians! Suzy *must* be a cheerleader, even if their skirts are cut to there and their shirts are a mere lick and a promise, or she'll be a social outcast. Junior *must* be on the football team, even if they play games on Sunday. They *must* date, *must* drink, *must* go to rock concerts—not because their parents believe these activities are more godly than doing something other than dating, drinking, or drooling over rock stars, but simply so they will be "normal."

The results of these false goals are not very pretty. Many a popular girl has made shipwreck of her reputation and her faith. Many an athletic superstar has fallen into drunkenness, drugs, and even worse habits from the example of his friends on the team.

God's goal for our sons and daughters, on the other hand, doesn't drive anyone to degeneracy. He wants them to *be like Jesus*.

Experts and Their Methods

Possibly nothing has caused so much harm to the family in this last century as the proliferation of experts. As Thomas Sowell, a black economist who sees most things clearly, says,

> Have you noticed how many disasters follow in the wake of "experts?" The period since World War II has been the great era of experts on raising children. Dr. Spock was only the tip of the iceberg. You couldn't turn on the radio or television, or open a newspaper or magazine, without encountering an army of experts on how to raise your kid.
>
> The first things these experts emphasized was that laymen were all wrong in their approach. What was needed was the sophis-

ticated, modern way to handle children, not simplistic or traditional methods. What followed was an unprecedented rise in juvenile delinquency, crime, teenage suicide, and pregnancy. The only thing going down was performance in school.[1]

Rare today is the mother who dares face her baby without a battery of books by Dr. Oracle, Dr. Infallible, and all their colleagues. And, of course, she couldn't *be* a mother without magazines. Magazines on "parenting" have led the way in convincing mothers and fathers that they know nothing about raising children and should passively accept the dictates of others. Such magazines grant themselves a godlike status, laying down the law as rigidly as if they were speaking to Moses out of the glory on Mount Sinai. An ad *Parents* magazine sent me in the mail, for example, offered to teach me:

- How can I build my child's self-esteem?
- How can I avoid spoiling my child? . . .
- What should I do for a "picky" eater?
- What should I do about thumbsucking . . . bedwetting . . . temper tantrums?
- Should I pick up my baby every time he cries?

The ad offered me "authoritative" answers to "questions like these," including "Am I an overprotective mother? . . . Is it right or wrong to spank?" Again the ad assured me that *Parents* was "an authoritative magazine" because it "brings you articles by some of America's most respected child psychologists, obstetricians, pediatricians, and other child-care experts." These experts consider themselves competent, on their own authority, to issue rules on such subjects as "Should You Have Another Baby—The Right and Wrong Reasons." The magazine thoroughly endorses careerism for mothers: "Going Back to Work—Seven Steps to Success . . . How to Choose a Preschool . . . Birth Control: What's New, Safe, and Foolproof?"

Do you think it's odd that a magazine called *Parents* advertises itself as giving "authoritative" advice on birth control? *Parents* has fallen into that trap because *worship of experts is part of the humanist/feminist religion.* Without God, man must become god and make his own rules. Such rules cannot include actually sacrificing oneself for one's children, for then one has no time to play god.

Our whole society is falling down and worshiping before the shrine of experts, particularly those of the supposed sciences of psychology and sociology. The result is that man's doctrine ("Dr. Infallible said so!") is actually preferred *above* God's.

Now don't get me wrong. I have nothing against psychology and sociology. But please, people, let's recognize that they are *not* sciences. Psychology is an art, and like any other art it is colored by the perceptions of the artist.

I could mention how often psychologists have been proved wrong, how often they contradict each other, how biased their data often is. (How many Christians do you suppose participated in all those "sexual response" tests? Would *you* let someone hook electrodes to your body and record your responses while you fornicated with twenty strangers? No? Well then, why should we pay any attention to the reactions of the degenerates who did?) Any "science" which depends for its results on the perfect neutrality of the psychologist-observer *and* the perfect honesty of his subjects is bound to be inexact. But let's just take a little look at whether, like other sciences, psychology produces the results its practitioners predict.

> The first indication that psychology might be ineffective came in 1952 when Hans Eysenck of the Institute of Psychiatry, University of London, discovered that neurotic people who do not receive therapy are as likely to recover as those who do. Psychotherapy, he found, was not any more effective than the simple passage of time. Additional studies by other researchers showed similar results. Then Dr. Eugene Levitt of the Indiana School of Medicine found that disturbed children who were not treated recovered at the same rate as disturbed children who were. A further indication of the problem was revealed in the results of the extensive Cambridge-Somerville Youth Study. The researchers found that uncounseled juvenile delinquents had a lower rate of further trouble than counseled ones. Other studies have shown that untrained lay people do as well as psychiatrists or clinical psychologists in treating patients. And the Rosenham studies indicated that mental hospital staff could not even tell normal people from genuinely disturbed ones. . . . When psychologists rush in to help, they are not particularly successful.[2]

William Kirk Kilpatrick, the author of the above quote and a Doctor of Educational Psychology, makes a further point:

Psychology and the other social sciences might be doing actual harm to our society. . . . On a larger scale, psychological values have run roughshod over traditional ones. And there are reasons to think there is something destructive about the new values. . . .

A rather blatant example . . . comes from Sweden, perhaps the most therapeutically oriented country in the world, where a law has been passed forbidding parents to spank their children. Further, it is a criminal offense to threaten, ostracize, ridicule, or otherwise "psychologically abuse" children. Presumably this means that parents can no longer raise their voices at their children or send them to their rooms. But there is no evidence that the Swedes are any less melancholy for this enlightenment. By all reports the young people are more bored and restless than ever.[3]

Psychology is only useful as a report of *one man's or woman's observations of human behavior.* In this form, it has always been with us and has often helped. In past times, an old man would sit at the city gates watching the people go by and chatting with the other old men. He would in this way accumulate experiences which he might sort out into statements like, "Eskimos don't seem to buy very much ice." He might even codify his observations into rules, such as, "Never try to sell ice to an Eskimo." His rules were not considered scientific oracles; he made no claim for them other than "I am an old man and this is what I have seen" (see Psalm 37:25).[4]

Psychologists, sociologists, and the like can tell us what they *see,* but they have no authority to tell us what to *do.* Hence our confusion. All the observations in the world can't tell us why a man, woman, or child ought to *do* something. If your daughter takes to vomiting on the rug every Friday morning, psychologists can give you hints for stopping this behavior. But *speaking as psychologists alone,* they cannot prove that the means they suggest are morally correct, or even that you ought to try to stop the vomiting in the first place. For moral judgments and moral actions we need the Bible.

Now, I can picture a flood of postcards coming my way asking, "What about Christian psychiatrists and psychologists?" I answer, "What *about* them?" Any Christian can give his opinion on what the Bible says. Any psychologist can share his observations with us. The danger arises when we make the mistake of thinking there is something sacred and anointed about a fellow-Christian's teaching just because he has a Ph.D. If I am not mistaken, this adulation of Doctors is just what Jesus had in mind when he warned us not to call our Christian brothers "Rabbi" (Matt. 23:8).

Dr. Mom, Ph.D.

God says the younger women should get their training from older women, not Ph.D.'s (Titus 2:4). Could it be that we *mothers* are the real experts on mothering?

What do experts have to offer, after all? Book learning (from books written by other experts) and their experience with children whose parents are desperate enough to pay for help. Beside this, they can observe children in institutional settings—such as day-care or the public schools. They can't observe a boy or girl on his or her home turf, at least not without interfering with the child's spontaneity, and certainly not without spending much more time than they want to for each case study. Most experts have never seen a child who doesn't watch TV. Some have never interviewed a child from a truly Christian home. They are, in short, the victims of biased data.

The Bible, on the other hand, does not make book learning or counseling experience the qualification for teaching other people how to raise their children. For church leadership the qualification is that *you have successfully raised children yourself.* Elders and older women both must meet this qualification before they are appointed to official church positions (1 Tim. 3:4, 5; 5:10; Titus 1:6). This makes immense good sense. Instead of "what you *hear* is what you get"—i.e., the only way you can judge an expert's teaching is whether it *sounds* good or not—the Bible says, "what you *see* is what you get." Does an older woman have godly children? Well then, we can listen to her with a good degree of confidence. The returns are in. Whatever she did, at least it didn't hurt. Since she is just a wife and mother like us, we won't be overawed into taking her teachings as gospel without testing them against the Bible. She is not only a *teacher,* but a *model.* You and I can hope to fill her position someday and teach the younger women ourselves. This cannot happen with experts. Finally, her years of experience in exactly the same situations we face have given her a rich fund of hints, ideas, and devices for putting scriptural rules into practice. She's been through it all, and she speaks from personal experience.

But who knows how the children of an expert behave? We see him on TV or we read his books, but we have never *met* him. If he is one of those people who makes a substantial part of his living touring the U.S.A., he may not even be raising his children at all. If they are turning out O.K., his *wife* is the one who should get the credit!

Furthermore, in order to become an accredited expert a man or woman has had to spend years at the feet of atheists. He or she has had to digest Freud, Jung, Fromm, and all their descendants. It is hard to be steeped for years in anti-Christian literature and not have some of it rub off on you. Many who follow this path do in fact succumb to the leaven of the Sadducees. Witness the destructive "Intimate Marriage" focus of so many Christian psychologists, or their emphasis on "communication skills" á là Transaction Analysis and P.E.T., or their permissive child-rearing techniques á là Spock.

Does this mean all Christian psychologists are wicked or inept? Of course not. Some may well have the qualifications of an elder, and *on that basis* they can teach in their local churches. *On that basis* they can write their books and give their radio talks. But a distant expert is still a poor substitute for a local mother. And his Ph.D. is not what qualifies him to teach us how to raise our children; his children are his qualification.

All We're Meant to Need

Our modern confusion about raising children (displayed in shelf after shelf of how-to books) is a result of depending on experts. The solution is partly to encourage older women to share their expertise. But what if you don't know any reliable older women? If the generation of our mothers and grandmothers had all been obedient to the Bible, we wouldn't be in such a mess in the first place. But we *are* in a mess, testifying to their failure. It is therefore not safe to ask just any older churchgoing woman to be your spiritual mentor. And a good, solid Christian grandmother is hard to find.

God intended motherhood to be a relay race. Each generation would pass the baton on to the next. But the baton has been fumbled. So it's our job—yours and mine—to pick it up. We have to do more than follow in our mothers' footsteps; we have to go directly back to the Bible ourselves, taking nothing for granted, and *rediscover the lost art of mothering*.

Is this difficult? Sometimes. It is harder to swim against the tide than to go with the flow. But it's not complicated. Instead of the trendy but endlessly confusing fashions in child-rearing, we only have to follow *one* teacher: God.

And God—bless his Name—keeps things simple. His Word is like light that shines brighter and brighter, not like thick fog through which only the initiated can grope.

Scripture breaks raising children down into two categories: *what you do* and *how you do it*. We are supposed to impress God's commands on our children ourselves. We are supposed to acquaint them with Bible history, and see that they acquire the necessary skills to be productive in life. That's the *what*. We are supposed to be strict with every sin, gentle with every genuine weakness, and to encourage every bit of good behavior. We are also supposed to live a good example before them. That's the *how*. Mothers are especially called to be gentle; fathers are especially reminded to be encouraging. But as long as mercy is mixed with justice, to a child it will spell love. And love will win his heart.

All the glitzy theories being peddled about fall short of God's perfect plan. They merely subtract from it. One expert tries to yank away the time a mother spends throughout the day impressing God's commands on her children and replace it with a dab of "quality time" in the evening. Another tells us to spank, but forgets to mention encouragement. Still another tells us to encourage but views spanking as a last resort, only to be used after a whole slew of other man-made disciplinary devices have been tried.

It's modern to want an instant method for producing wonderful children, which is why experts abound. But it's scriptural to hang in there and work at doing what God says. Raising kids right is hard work; there's no getting around it. But it doesn't have to be confusing. To raise kid right, we just have to raise them . . . right?

Raising Christian children is really not so difficult. *Unless* we hand them over needlessly to surrogates and experts who, unlike mothers, can't be expected to love them and who, unlike mothers, have no divine promises of success. We'll look at just how irreplaceable mothers (and fathers) are in the next chapter.

10 Home as a Greenhouse for Young Plants

NEWSFLASH! Today, in Notsogood Samaritan Hospital, a most unusual birth was recorded. Ms. Keepie Bizzy gave birth to a child who was *18 years old!* Discussing this unprecedented event with reporters, Ms. Bizzy said, "I think it will become the trend of the future. What woman wouldn't prefer a baby who was already toilet-trained and who could hold down a job instead of keeping you away from one?" According to eyewitnesses, young John Bizzy emerged from his mother fully clothed in a business suit; and after smiling at the camera he picked up a waiting briefcase (thoughtfully provided by the proud father) and headed out to work.

Is there one mother in the world who would believe that little story? I doubt it. Any of us who have had children know that a human baby is the most helpless infant of any species. It seems like a miracle that such a tiny, frail creature, all covered with blood and with a mouth clogged with mucus, can even survive. At birth, a baby can't lift up her head. She can't crawl to your breast to nurse, like the young of all other species. What awesome thoughts go through your mind, looking into that crumpled little red (or brown, or yellow) face, knowing that if you don't change her and feed her and love her, she will die.

Smother Mother, or the Fable of the Harmful Hothouse
But today's humanist society, in its constant struggle against reality, tries not to see that babies really are helpless and dependent little people. Just as the Scanzonis talk about a baby who "emerges to mock the

114

lovers" saying "Aha! You thought you were just having fun but look what you got instead—me!"[1] so all the Ms. Bizzies of this world devoutly desire to believe that children are born as adults. A mother's natural protective instinct is now called "smother love." The idea is that children have to face the world sometime, so they might as well be shoved out into it now. In fact, they *ought* to be shoved out into it now. This will help them "mature" faster. Supposedly children can handle the world as well as adults and do not need their parents' protection.

All the talk of "smother love" and the charming "independence" of day-care and latchkey children boils down to this: parents *should not* control their children's environment. It is their *duty* to hand their children over to others, whether parent-surrogates, peers, or the children themselves, who will then determine the children's environment. This is supposedly superior to good old-fashioned nurturing provided by Mommy and Daddy themselves.

Is it really better for children to face the world without their parents? Does the "hothouse" atmosphere of home actually *harm* children? Dr. Paul A. Kienel, the executive director of Association of Christian Schools International, forcefully deflates the "harmful hothouse" argument as it applies to Christian schools. His words apply equally well to home as a "hothouse":

> Christian schools are often referred to as *greenhouses* or *hothouses* that create a sheltered environment for children. The assumption is that a greenhouse is good for young and tender plants, but somehow the semi-protected environment of a Christian school is not good for children.
>
> The greenhouse plant-growing analogy carries some interesting parallels. Everyone knows, for example, the purpose of a greenhouse is to give young plants a head start. The ideal environment of the greenhouse protects the plants from destructive elements during their early delicate growing season and provides them with proper conditions for maximum maturity. At a given point the young plants reach a "graduation point" and they are ready for transplant. The end result is they are larger, stronger, more productive and better prepared to ward off plant diseases and stand on their own than their counterparts who had their start in the wild.
>
> The parallel is obvious. If young plants are better prepared to face the world having had their start in a greenhouse, then young children educated in a positive Christian school environment (which exposes students to the errors of the world but does not

teach them the ways of the world) will be significantly stronger than their secular counterparts.[2]

Everything Dr. Kienel said about the Christian school applies twice as much to the Christian home. The Bible teaches that the Christian home is *meant* to be a greenhouse for young plants. "Your sons will be like olive shoots around your table" (Psa. 128:3). "Then our sons in their youth will be like well-nurtured plants" (Psa. 144:12). Both of these Psalms which speak about children as young plants nurtured at home are Psalms of blessing. Psalm 128 is about a blessed *man*. Psalm 144 is about a blessed *nation*. The family and the nation God intends to bless will nurture their children at home.

Let's look again at this idea that we shouldn't protect children from the outside world. We protect our children in *other* ways. We don't feed them poison. We cover the electrical outlets. But say some expert came along and told us this was all wrong. "Children need to explore," he says. "Let 'em stick forks in the electrical outlets and eat in the medicine cabinet. Electricity and medicine are part of the real world, you know, and children should have an opportunity to be exposed to them." Does that sound smart? No? Then why should we believe that *spiritually* and *emotionally* our children don't need protection, while physically we feed them and guard them from all harm? Picture Junior telling Mommy in the middle of the winter, "I'd like to put on my bathing suit and go sleep in the snow." Now picture Mommy saying, "O.K., dear. You're a big boy. I trust your judgment. Far be it from me to smother you. Go ahead!" If Junior's so all-fired independent, why does he need so much protection from his own foolish ideas?

Day-Care and the Unprotected Child
Yet things have gotten to the point where parents who don't put their children in day-care are considered "overprotective." My friend Dot was practically crying as she told me of an experience she had in her church nursery. The other women, who are all working wives and who are all fully aware that Dot is staying home to be with her daughter, spent a whole hour loudly swapping stories of how "independent" their children were getting to be because of day-care and exclaiming how glad they were that they weren't smothering them by hovering over them all day. And Linda Burnett tells of a newspaper editorial that actually said, "Women who stay at home show a callous self-interest."[3]

Let's call a spade a spade. Putting a child in day-care is simply *handing over control of that child to another person who is not his mother*. If day-care is better for children than staying home with Mommy, this means that *total strangers make better mothers* than the natural mother. Or if we admit that being stuck in a room with 100 children and four workers is not quite as good as mother's care, then it becomes clear that the real issue is not what is best for Baby, but what does Mommy want? As for "overprotection," anyone who rejoices that she is not overprotecting her children at home is really admitting that *day-care is not as protected an environment as home*. She *knows* her baby or toddler won't be looked after as carefully in day-care, and has the nerve to glory in it!

What shall I say? Shall I point out that the only women the church considered worthy of financial support in New Testament times were widows who had "brought up children," which in the Greek has overtones of *personally cherishing* those children (1 Tim. 5:10)? Shall I mention that the whole concept of modern day-care was invented by a playboy type who wanted to free mothers for promiscuous sex?[4] Or that since then secularists, "free love" advocates, and atheists have been the driving force behind day-care in this country (until the church foolishly, foolishly decided it was respectable)? How about some true facts about those underprotective day-care centers that are saving children from the dread disease of overprotection?

> The *Washington Monthly* states, "Most day-care facilities do not meet the widely accepted standards of 'quality' because the government has never enforced the standards it adopted in 1968. A recent study by HEW of 607 federally funded day-care centers in 9 different states found that 70 percent failed to meet federal standards of health and safety and that children's lives were actually endangered in some of them."[5]

The Child Welfare League estimates that 77 percent of available child-care spaces are inadequate and should not be used at all.[6]

A newspaper article in our area several years ago told of a beautiful little girl who is now brain-damaged because of being beaten by her sitter. The mother came one day to pick her up and was handed an unconscious little bundle. The sitter said, "If she keeps behaving this way I won't sit her anymore." Investigation revealed the baby girl had been beaten on a regular basis in the past. Since she could not talk, nobody had known. The parents couldn't even stop this woman from continuing to sit children by state law—all they could do was sue her. The real point of the story was given by an official who said, "It's incredible, but we have trouble even following up on complaints like this because so many parents don't even know the exact street address or full name of their sitter." He was upset that people would so naively trust their baby with a stranger.

Abuse is becoming a common problem with sitters and other "caregivers." We should *expect* this when a child is turned over to someone who doesn't love him or her and the person in charge is burdened with the care of perhaps ten or twenty young children. A baby who screams and yells at the sitter, but who can't tell her parents what is going on, is the perfect victim for a sadist, or even a not-well-controlled person, who may prefer hitting to cuddling.

Even older children can become the victims of an unprincipled sitter. When we lived in Connecticut I remember reading in the paper about a kiddie-porn ring that was broken up when police discovered that a teenage girl had been taking the children she sat to a friend's house where the children were sexually abused, and all this was captured on film. Threats kept the children quiet until one discerning mother finally broke through to the root of her child's inexplicable distress.

A federal government report indicates that in 1983, more than 1.5 million youngsters under 16 were involved in pornography or prostitution. . . .

California medical researchers have discovered a shocking number of children under five with venereal disease, and a state official reports revoking ten times as many day-care licenses in 1983 as it did in 1978 because of sexual molestation.

Child abuse experts generally urge caution in leaving children with adults, even those familiar to the parents. Dr. Ronald Summit, a psychiatrist with the University of California at Los Angeles, noted that "there is no question, from all the research, that the risk of exploitation for a child increases directly as the child is removed further from the care of its biological mother."[7]

"But we put our son in a Christian day-care center!" "But we leave our baby with a Christian mother!" Let us assume, for the moment, that the day-care personnel or sitter in question are indeed earnest Christians. That still doesn't mean that God has given them your maternal hormones and instincts, or that your child will be equally as pleased to be left with them as he would be to be with you. In the case of day-care centers especially, there are inherent problems that no amount of doctrinal orthodoxy can solve. Quite apart from the emotional trauma of being placed at a tender age in a large group of unrelated children watched over by a small group of unrelated adults, there is your son or daughter's physical safety to consider. If the old woman who lived in a shoe had so many of her *own* children that she didn't know what to do, any day-care worker can sometimes say the same.[8] Nobody has eight eyes. Accidents can and do happen that would never occur when a mother's watchful eye is on her very own boy or girl.

Just this last summer a little boy died in our city who was being looked after in a church day-care center. On a 105° day the sitters, well-intentioned Christians all, took the children on an outing. This little boy was forgotten in the crowd and left asleep in a locked bus, where he suffocated.

I am sorry to frighten you with these tragic stories. But I think it's time that American parents woke up to reality. Day-care is not the rosy-painted picture we might like it to be. Children have been and continue to be abused, raped, and neglected by day-care personnel and other adults who gain access to the building. Did I forget to mention that even when the day-care personnel or sitter check out O.K., that is no guarantee that their friends and relatives, or even strangers off the streets, might not enter into the situation?

Washington state representative Dick Bond has given the best advice on this issue that a mother could hear. After a Washington couple's nineteen-month-old daughter had been molested by the *son* of the operator of a state licensed day-care center, they wrote to every one of their state legislators urging stronger licensing laws. Representative Bond wrote back, "All the licensing, rule, and regulations in the world cannot prevent what happened in your case. Raising your children at home can prevent it. Think about it."[9]

God gave your children to *you*, not to Suzy Surrogate. *You* are the one responsible to mother them. If they need mothering at all (and day-care is a tacit agreement that children do need some kind of care), they need it from you.

Mothers matter. Relationships matter. Think of it this way. How would you feel about taking home a different child every night? Would it make some slight difference that the child you were tubbing, reading to, and saying prayers with was not your own? Well, if you don't want any child but your own, why should he or she want any mother but you?

Even day-care workers can see that children want only their mothers. One such worker writes,

I am so concerned for children whose mothers work full time. You see, I've been working in a nursery school, Sunday school and afterschool program for K-6th grade for the past five years and I just want to cry sometimes. Some of the families need two bread-winners, but some don't. It is depressing. Those kids need love and attention (individually) so badly, but they don't get it. Most kids want to go home to be with Mommy right after school. They want to hug and kiss their moms. They want to talk and show off for their parents. But all they get is me. I try my best and I love those kids so; but I'm not Mommy.[10]

"God sets the lonely in families" (Psa. 68:6). He is not in the business of making family members lonely. As long as a child is young enough to need mothering, he needs his mother.

School as Baby-Sitter

Day-care is only one horn of the beast, though. Even mothers who are opposed to day-care have been trained to matter-of-factly hand their children over to surrogates whenever the children reach "school age." Linda Burnett, for example, who helped write *The Unwanted Generation,* a book which takes a strong stand against day-care, says, "As mothers we will have our children at home under our primary care for only four or five years."[11]

The day-care boom can be partly understood as an extension of the "hand 'em over to school" mentality. If we hand them over at four or five, why not at two or three?

I have already shown in a previous chapter how modern schools work to usurp the parents' right to shape their children's values. Now I'd like to look at the other side of the coin—the willingness of parents to dump responsibility for their children on poor, hapless, overworked schoolteachers.

The Bible makes it plain that the parents are responsible for train-ing their children. We are supposed to impress God's commands on our children at home at all hours of the day. This clearly bars us from handing their moral and spiritual training over to surrogates.

But today parents expect schoolteachers to raise their children. I recall an Erma Bombeck column about ten or fifteen years back in which she said that the *real* reason public education would never be abolished is that the mothers of America couldn't stand having their children home with them. Schools have become glorified day-care centers, to the detri-ment of parents, children, and teachers.

It was not always so. William McGuffey, the author of *McGuffey's Readers* and a champion of public education, insisted strenuously that parents ought not only to superintend but even to accompany their children in their school studies.[12] In his day children were commonly first sent to school at age eight or ten, having first learned to read and write and having already had their character well developed at home.

Today we are at a crossroads. The NEA and some public officials, along with the feminist lobby, are calling for *earlier* schooling with *longer* days and *longer* school years, in a move toward total control over our children. On the other hand, articles are beginning to appear in major magazines like *Fortune* and the *Mother Earth News* which label public education an experiment that has failed. Futurists like Alvin Toffler and John Naisbitt are predicting that home-based education will become more popular as we move into the computer and video age. We have, in short, to make a choice. Will we go back to raising our children *ourselves* until they are mature enough to be benefited by the instruction of a tutor or school that *we* choose, or will we surrender them to the State?

Some brave parents are now struggling to win back the right to educate their children as they see fit. But they cannot succeed alone. The baby-sitting mentality, which drops the kids off at school with a sigh of relief, actually welcomes more government intervention. Only if parents love their children enough to want to take responsibility for them can we persuade government to stop trying to be Big Mother.

The alternative to ever-earlier compulsory public education is *diversity*. Home schools. Tutors. Private schools. Apprenticeships. Computer-assisted instruction. Video tapes. Cassettes. Lecture series. Seminars. Charity schools. All these, and many more, are perfectly valid ways for people to learn.

Internationally-known economist Peter Drucker pointed out in a very stimulating interview in the March 26, 1984 issue of *U.S. News and World Report* that the economy of the future is in dire need of "technologists—people who are neither skilled workers nor, in the old sense, knowledge or white-collar workers. They take theoretical knowledge and combine it with the practical." The interviewer then asked, "Would you say that our schools are producing such technologists in enough number?" Professor Drucker's reply is most informative:

No—though so far, whenever we've needed them, they have appeared. Partly it is because they fit into the genius of the American people and partly it is because, thank God, we have no ministry of education. Any fly-by-night outfit can start a course, and five years later the state colleges take it over, and 20 years later Harvard has a department with a Ph.D. program—by which time it's obsolete.

So these people are appearing. Some learn their skills in the community colleges, but far more do so in free enterprise—places outside the official and approved and anointed educational system.[13]

We don't have to hand all control over our children to public education "experts" in order to prepare them for life. We can keep control of their educational influences and still produce productive men and women. The state as baby-sitter? It's not needed.

Peers and Pressure

Many Christian parents have made the sacrifice and either started up a home school or dug deep into their pockets for a Christian school. Our leaders have done a commendable job of alerting us to the public school's dangerous drift away from Christian values. But too few parents yet realize how much power they have to govern their children.

Remember that speech I told you about, given in a Christian school, where the speaker took it for granted that the teenage sons and daughters of his audience would date unsupervised, be hooked on trendy entertainment, and conform to their peers? His hearers were understandably worried about things like unwed motherhood for their daughters, and drunkenness and drugs. Yet nobody thought to mention that parents have the *right* and the *duty* to prevent their children from roaming unsupervised and to keep filthy books and TV shows out of their houses, which would effectually prevent all those catastrophes.

Let me take dating as an example. Dating is a recent invention of Western civilization. It has never before been practiced in the history of the world. For millennia people got married without it. The idea of sending an adolescent man and woman off to spend all evening in the close, unsupervised society of someone they find sexually attractive is almost too foolish to be believed. But anyone who dares to say so is labeled a smother mother. We are supposed to *trust* these young people as angels of virtue who are able to overcome all temptations and get home by curfew. The surprise is not that some 95 percent of boys and 80 percent of girls are no longer virgins by their last year in college, but that *anyone* remains pure in these circumstances. Parents should insist on *only chaperoned group outings*. If this sounds too restrictive, remember that this way to get acquainted has worked for generations.

The same principle applies to "hanging around" in general. If parents want their children to become drug addicts, drunkards, and degenerates, I can tell them how to do it: let the children go wherever they want with whomever they please. We have to take an active hand to make sure that our inexperienced offspring don't get themselves into serious trouble. "A companion of fools suffers harm," and "a companion of gluttons disgraces his father" (Prov. 13:20; 28:7). It is not open-minded and progressive to ignore your child's choice of companions; it's just plain stupid. In today's world, where even young children are involved in sex and drugs, we can't take it for granted that our children's friends will be a good influence. We have to check them out. As as for running around alone at all hours of the day and night, especially with money in their pockets, that's asking for trouble.

Mothering means making sure that our children are trustworthy at home *before* sending them out into the world. It means protecting even trustworthy children from the genuine dangers of a world they are not yet strong enough to fight. This takes time and concern. So in our selfish society, it is unpopular. But it is necessary.

College A La Mode

I really wonder why, when humanists have so plainly captured our higher educational institutions, parents think it is worthwhile to spend a small fortune to send their children into this sea of degeneracy. As James Fitzpatrick says,

> When this modern permissiveness is considered in perspective, it boggles the mind. Eighteen-year-olds being sent away from home for the first time by their own parents to live in a cluster of buildings filled with booze, drugs and "creative" sex, and New Left professors as dormitory advisors. We *paid* to send them there, and then we brood about their turning away from us. Occasions of sin? We purchased them for our children. Lead us not into temptation?
>
> But perhaps, we might say, God will not be too demanding on an eighteen-year-old who gives in after living for years with all that going on in the room next door. It could be. I've talked to those vacant-eyed, frizzy-haired, drug-aficionado, rock-poetry-spouting cretins. Maybe they are beyond morality. "It's what's happening, man." "Outta sight." "Outrageous, man." But what of those of us who, at the very least, did nothing to prevent the establishment of *public* places within our societal life for the inculcation and promulgation of their suicidal hedonism? Do they still make millstones?[14]

College is no place for boys and girls. If a child of mine ever goes there, he will have to be a full-grown man, not a boy who we call a man to flatter his ego. And he will *not* live in dormitory housing. I remember my college dorm. The Happy Hooker would have been right at home there.

No *responsibility for a job, an atmosphere that encourages sin, the company of hedonists, and no parental oversight spells a recipe for disaster.* Add to this rich brew the demand that your son or daughter "not get married until you graduate," and if he or she doesn't lose his or her chastity, it is a miracle.

And then there's the matter of *spiritual* purity. Dr. Francis Schaeffer tells us,

> In every academic discipline the temptation and pressure to accommodate is overwhelming. . . . Evangelicals were right in emphasizing the Lordship of Christ over all areas of culture—art, philosophy, society, government, academics, and so on. But then what happened? Many young evangelicals heard this message, went out into the academic world, and earned their undergraduate and graduate degrees from the finest secular schools. But something happened in the process. In the midst of totally humanistic colleges and universities, and a totally humanistic orientation in the academic disciplines, many of these young evangelicals began to be infiltrated by the anti-Christian world view which dominated the thinking of their colleges and professors. In the process, any distinctively evangelical Christian point of view was accommodated to the secularistic thinking in their discipline and to the surrounding world spirit of our age.[15]

Dr. Schaeffer knew what he was talking about: his major ministry consisted of trying to claim, and *re*claim, for Christ young intellectuals who had been spiritually destroyed in secular universities.

Nor are Christian colleges always the answer. In one school, well-regarded as a bastion of orthodox Christianity, a professor required his students to read *Playboy* "to get in touch with the culture." A fellow who lived with us for awhile told us that he left his college, which prides itself on its "Christian world view," because he was sick of how the students would go downtown to drink beer, which was against the rules, and the school administration made no attempt to discipline the offenders or even check up on them.

The fact is that many (not all) Christian colleges and universities have sold out their Christianity for academic recognition and accreditation. The very students who shucked off their Christianity in order to accommodate to the peer pressure of their secular colleges, in the words of Dr. Schaeffer, "make the cycle complete" when they "have now returned to teach at evangelical colleges where what they present in their classes has very little that is distinctively Christian."[16] As he says, and my experience leads me to agree with him, "The danger is present in the colleges which are thought of as the best Christian colleges."[17] Such a college may rejoice when it receives a major grant from the National Endowment for the Humanities in order to conduct workshops "from a Christian perspective" on sociology; however, the real joy may belong to the humanists who gave the grant, as they realize that a Christian institution has finally come around to repeating exactly the same things they have always said.

Obviously Christian parents who care are going to have to be more careful about their children's college education than most people are today. I would like to suggest, just to be radical, that you seriously consider *not sending them to college at all.* With the cost of college now averaging $10,000 a year, the price of four years of college and a year of grad school would pay for setting your son up in his own business. He could spend those five years working for free, getting trained in the line of work that interests him. At that price, *anyone* will hire him, no matter *what* the unemployment rate is. Consider it an unofficial apprenticeship, after which he can be his own boss for the rest of his life. As for "intellectual stimulation," there is always the public library and the Christian bookstore. Any young man who spends five years reading and studying the classic literature of our and other civilizations will be an educated man, whether he goes to college or not.

The Great God Entertainment
Plants in a hot house do better than plants outside, except under one condition. When pests or diseases are introduced *into the greenhouse environment,* they spread even faster than they do outside.

Marie Winn, a regular contributor to the *New York Times* magazine, points out that

> never in their wildest fantasies did parents in the past imagine that their ten- or eleven-year-olds might smoke dope or get involved in sexual activity or run away from home. . . . Today, parents are faced with the knowledge that their children *can* get involved in any number of dangerous, illegal, or merely unsuitable activities. Today kids *do* become potheads, *do* have sexual intercourse, *do* watch pornographic films on television.[18]

She traces how adults' view of children has changed, as shown by movies that feature children possessed by demons, are sexually precocious, or suddenly become uncontrollable teenage werewolves on entering adolescence. Mrs. Winn remarks that

> perhaps the teenage-werewolf myth is a projection of the parents' guilt at pursuing their own narcissistic aims of "self-fulfillment." Instead of being willing as a society to sacrifice for children, to consider their care a primary duty, adults have transformed the very image of childhood from one that deserves protection and nurture to one that justifies their own sometimes monstrous abandonment of children.[19]

Mrs. Winn further points out, and rightly so, that most of the change in children's behavior can be traced to

> this decline in child supervision . . . the rising divorce rate and the increase in two-career families. In each case the parents' attention is inevitably diverted from child supervision to adult matters.[20]

I have been stressing that the only way for parents to safeguard their children's moral and spiritual purity is to take charge of supervising it themselves. But even this is not enough. For, as Mrs. Winn goes on to point out,

> Even the most old-fashioned, protection-minded parents today recognize that no matter how cleverly they plan their children's lives, how cloisterlike a school they choose, how carefully they hide their own troubles, how self-sacrificingly they conduct their lives, nevertheless they have little chance of controlling their children's exposure to every variety of adult sexuality, every permutation and combination of human brutality and violence, every aspect of sickness, disease, and suffering, every frightening possibility for natural and man-made disaster that might impinge on an innocent and carefree childhood. There is always the television set waiting to undo all their careful plans.[21]

Television! That major influence allowed into 99 percent of American homes, where it is on for an average of eight hours a day—a figure that *increases* by two hours if there are children in the home. That obviously addictive medium which parents deplore, yet consistently fail to control. Can home be a greenhouse with an operating TV set?

It's not only the *contents* of TV shows—the anti-Christian morals, the sex, the drinking, the mockery, the glorified selfishness—that affects our children.

> Television's very presence in the home has worked to alter children's lives in ways that have nothing to do with *what* they might be watching. Parents' use of the medium as a child-rearing aid is one such way. . . . Before television, parents had to make sure that their kids could be relied upon to "mind" when necessary. . . . Television, however, provided an easy alternative to parental discipline.[22]

I still get upset every time I remember an article that a pastor's wife wrote for an evangelical magazine in which she tut-tutted the use of TV as a baby-sitter, but concluded that she and her friends would continue to use it as one anyway. This lady mocked a family she knew who had decided that TV was harming their lives, and who had taken their set out to the dump and stoned it. But I felt then, and still believe now, that their act was scripturally valid. Jesus said that we should "cut off" *anything* that causes us to sin, be it as dear to us as a right hand or eye (Matt. 5:29, 30). Why should it be unthinkable to ban the boob tube?

Facing facts, most TV owners are addicted to it, and virtually every one of their children is enslaved by it.

Marie Winn does not believe that banning the tube is the answer, because she says our children would still be exposed to heaven knows what TV shows in the schools and in their friends' homes. However, Christian parents aren't locked into sending their children to public school. Nor do we have to send our children into the homes of people who don't share our values. Let their friends come over to *your* house. Make them milk and cookies. Let them eat cake.

The answer to TV and other canned entertainment is active fun and games. Christians can use entertainment for recreation: to revive our worn-out minds and bodies and to cheer up depressed spirits. Making and eating a batch of gingersnaps, stringing popcorn for a Christmas tree, playing cooperative and low-stress games—all serve this purpose much better than TV. Recreation can and should *strengthen* our children, rather than throwing them into a depraved adult world on their own.

When parents admit that a certain form of entertainment is wrong for their children, or that they can't control it, banning it *is* the answer. Television's positive contribution is so minimal and its potential for misuse so alarming that Bill and I got rid of our set seven years ago. People warn us that our children won't grow up like everyone else's, but we don't *want* our children to turn out like everyone else's! We want their hero to be Jesus Christ, not some punk rocker.

Will people call you a smother mother if you seriously try to protect your sons and daughters until they are truly old enough to face temptation and danger? Perhaps so. But remember that "smother mother" putdowns are the defense women use to rationalize away the very real guilt they feel for neglecting their own children. Children are not born independent. They are full of folly and need our constant guidance. They need our time. All of which means, *they need our love.*

Kids today are growing up without natural affection because they have never received it. These are the selfish narcissists and psychopathic killers of tomorrow. All so their mothers can be "fulfilled"! It makes you want to cry.

An anonymous letter printed in *Welcome Home* magazine strips away the propaganda of "having it all":

> I am sure my main motivation [for staying home with the children] was that my mother was liberated long before it became fashionable. Everyone marvelled at how she could handle job, home, committees, hobbies, etc. Everyone, that is, except her children who were just in the way. . . .
>
> My mother is now a lonely old lady who can't understand why we don't come to visit more often. Heck, I don't even know her![23]

Weeds can grow up anywhere, but precious fruit has to be tended with care. Like everything else in the Christian life, motherhood takes hard work. But the results are worth it.

Firmly and lovingly, parents need to take back the care of our little plants. Mother needs to be home so her children can be home. Then, when they are ready to leave the greenhouse, they will be mature. They will be *really* independent. They will have strong characters formed by saturation in God's Word and the sight of it in your life. You will have given them *roots* and *wings!*

Part Four:

BACK TO HOMEWORKING

"train the younger women to . . . be busy at home . . ." (Titus 2:4, 5)

11 Would You, Could You, in the Home?

Slumped in a chair in the doctor's waiting room, I sat gloomily twiddling my pencil and staring at the little white box on the Patient's Form marked "Occupation."

I was tired of those little boxes.

What *can* a woman who doesn't have an outside job write down as her occupation? Housewife? The word conjures up a dull creature with her hair in curlers, addicted to soap operas, and possessing barely enough intelligence to wash the dishes. Homemaker? That sounds a little better—cheery inefficiency in a frilly apron and high heels. Homemakers are pretty white females who approach housekeeping with zest and enthusiasm—as a hobby. Homemakers are a decorative luxury only a few men can afford.

Only a Housewife

Are these caricatures of housewives and homemakers accurate? Of course not. But stage, screen, and television promote these images. To label oneself a housewife or homemaker is to label oneself a dud. Hear how women apologize for their profession: "I'm *only* a housewife." That word "only" speaks volumes.

But to be a "working wife" is a different story. What do you think of when a woman introduces herself to you as a "working wife"? Smart efficiency in a $200 business suit? Paychecks? Prestige? In the battle of words, feminists have mined the harbor. Mrs. Frumpy Housewife can't hold her own against Ms. Savvy Workingwife.

As I sat there eyeing that blank, unhelpful Occupation box I began to wonder, why aren't housewives considered working wives? The more I thought about it, the more unfair it seemed. To call *only* women who leave the home working wives amounts to saying that *women who stay home don't work!* This psychological word game is at the root of our modern career movement.

Careerism is based on an inferiority complex, as follows. (1) Only men's work has worth. Women's traditional work is useless. Therefore, (2) I must get a job to prove I am somebody. If all the action is out in the men's "economic-opportunity sphere," well then, we'll all have to crowd into that end of the bus.

But 'tis not so, not so at all. As I sat there that day in the doctor's office wondering what word would better express my career than "housewife," a word flashed into my head. *Homeworking.* That word is the center of the passage in Titus which tells young wives how to live a Christian life. Homeworking is what young wives are supposed to do. Homeworking is a *job.* "Why, I'm a working wife after all," I thought, and gleefully scribbled down my occupation as "Homeworker."

Why We Need Roles

The Bible teaches that the church is a body made up of many different parts (1 Cor. 12). Each part has a different function. Each Christian has a different job to fill that God has set aside especially for him or her.

Today we hear a lot of talk about the gifts of the Spirit, but not nearly as much about the "different kinds of service" (1 Cor. 12:6)—that is, the different *roles,* the different *jobs,* the different *positions* in the body that our Lord Jesus Christ has created. In this era the whole body wants to be the mouth! Scrambling and scuffling, people vie for public position. Even Christians are being pressured to feel dissatisfied with every role but that of Fearless Leader. Christian *women* especially are confused, as we're told on the one hand that it's our duty to get out there and make a name for ourselves, contending for men's leadership and business positions, and on the other hand we don't want to totally abandon our homes and families.

"The wisdom of the prudent is to give thought to their way," as Proverbs 14:8 declares. William Gurnall, an outstanding Puritan preacher and the author of the spiritual classic *The Christian in Complete Armour,* shares some thoughts on the value of knowing your own way, the path God has laid out for you.

It should be the care of every Christian, *to stand orderly in the particular place wherein God hath set him. . . .* The Christian may be considered as related to a threefold society—church, common-wealth, and family. . . . The welfare of these societies consisteth in the order that is kept—when every wheel moves in its place without clashing, when every one contributes by performing the duty of his place to the benefit of the whole society. . . .

A person then stands orderly in his place when he doth these three things—*First.* When he *understands the peculiar duty of his place and relation:* "The wisdom of the prudent is to understand his way," Pr. 14:8—*his* way, that is, the way which he in particular is to know. . . . Yet how prone are we to study another's way and work rather than our own. . . .

Second. When *knowing the duty of our place, we conscientiously attend to it.* . . . Religion, if not practiced in our several places and callings, becomes ridiculous and vanisheth into an empty notion that is next to nothing. Yet many there are that have nothing to prove themselves Christians but a naked profession, of whom we may say as they do of the cinnamon tree, that the bark is more worth than all they have besides. Such the apostle speaks of, "They profess that they know God, but in works they deny him, being abominable and disobedient, and unto every good work reprobate," Tit. 1:16. . . . In opposition to these, he presseth those duties which Christians in their particular places and relations . . . ought to perform. A good Christian and a disobedient wife, a godly man and an unfaithful servant, or undutiful child, is a contradiction that can never be reconciled.

Third. To *stand orderly,* it is requisite that we *keep the bounds of our place and calling.*

Gurnall then shares with us five thoughts which he hopes will encourage us to do our jobs instead of hankering after everyone else's.

1. Consider what thou doest out of thy place is *not acceptable to God* . . . it cannot be in faith, because thou hast no call. God will not thank thee for doing that which he did not set thee about. Possibly thou hast good intentions. So had Uzzah in staying the ark, yet how well God liked his zeal, see II Sam. 6:7. . . .

2. By going out of our proper place and calling, we *put ourselves from under God's protection.* The promise is, he will "keep us in all our ways," Ps. 41:11. When we go out of our way, we go from under his wing. . . . As the earth could not bear the usurpation of Korah and his company of what belonged not to

them, but swallowed them up, so the sea could not but bear witness against Jonah the runaway prophet, disdaining to waft him that fled from the place and work that God called him to. . . .

3. We shall *never be charged for not doing another's work.* . . . We are to pray for magistrates that they may rule in the fear of God, but if they do not, we may not step upon the bench and do his work for him. . . . He is a fruitful tree in God's orchard that "bringeth forth *his* fruit in his season," Ps. 1:3.

4. There is poor comfort in suffering for doing that which was not the work of our place and calling. . . . The apostle makes a vast difference between suffering "as a busy-body" and suffering "as a Christian," I Pet. 4:15, 16.

5. It is an erratic spirit that usually carries men out of their place and calling.

Gurnall systematically pins down the "erratic spirit" that causes men *and women* to flee their God-given callings. Let me quote him, substituting the word *women* for the generic term *men.* Gurnall's words then drip with relevance for our careerist age.

(1) Sometimes it is *idleness.* Women neglect what they should do and then are easily persuaded to meddle with what they have nothing to do. The apostle intimates this plainly, "They learn to be idle, wandering from house to house; and not only idle, but tattlers also and busy-bodies," I Tim. 5:13. . . .

(2) It is *pride and discontent* that makes persons go out of their place. Some women are in this very unhappy. Their spirits are too big and haughty for the place God hath set them in. . . . Shall they be hid in a crowd, lie in an obscure corner, and die before they let the world know their worth? No, they cannot brook it, and therefore they must get on the stage, and put forth themselves one way or another. . . .

(3) In a third it is *unbelief.* . . . God needs not our sins to shore up his glory, truth, or church.

(4) In some it is *misinformed zeal.* Many women think they may do a thing, because they can do it. They can preach, and therefore they may. Wherefore else have they gifts?

The private Christian hath a large field wherein she may be serviceable to her brethren. She need not break the hedge which God hath set, and thereby occasion such disorder as we see to be the consequence of this. . . . There are many in a kingdom to be found that could do the prince's errand, it is likely, as well as his ambassador, but none takes the place but he that is sent, and can show his letters credential.[1]

Wives today are saying, "I *can* hold down an outside job. I *want* to hold down an outside job." But *should* you? Are one's husband and children just *appendages* to a busy productive life of one's own? Are men and women really interchangeable parts?

This idea would never have taken hold like it has if there weren't *some* truth in it. As a matter of fact, some women can do almost anything any man can do, and some men can do almost anything any woman can do. True, I don't know too many women who are strong enough to toss around 100-pound bags of cement all day, and I don't know *any* men who are able to breastfeed, but these are really minor quibbles, since hardly anyone wants to trade roles at those points. The fact is that, broadly speaking, we women are capable of doing just about anything men can do if we put our minds to it.

But, as Gurnall reminds us, this tells us nothing about what we *ought* to do. Just because you *can* do something, it doesn't follow that you *should* do it. For example, Russia and America *could* bomb each other into oblivion, but not too many of us think they *should*. Neither does the ability to do something tell us *under what conditions,* if any, we should do it. The same gift can be used in many different ways. We can all see that keeping the household accounts is not the same as leaving each morning for an office clerk's job, even though it requires the same skills; nor is building the kiddies a sandbox the same as an outside career as a carpenter. The same ability can be used in different spheres; the ability alone does not tell us which sphere is *right*.

The feminist theory of interchangeable parts has been riding high for a decade or more, and its presuppositions have been in vogue for almost half a century (more, if you realize how influential the original feminist/suffragist movement was). One would reasonably expect that if this is the way God really intended people to live, society would have improved under its influence. But look around you, and what do you see? Broken homes. Moral decay. Expanding statism. Compare this to the state of family and society three or four generations ago, when women were still mostly homemakers. To put it another way, would you rather be Laura Ingalls Wilder of *Little House on the Prairie* fame, or Billie Jean King's aborted baby?

This new theory, that men and women are interchangeable, was never spawned from the Bible. Christians have farmed the Bible's teaching on lifestyle for the past 2000 years without discovering one speck of feminist theology. The nineteenth-century feminists were at least honest enough to recognize this, which is why Elizabeth Cady Stanton, one of their leaders, felt impelled to invent the *Women's Bible* in an effort to debunk the obviously nonfeminist teaching of the original.

Not only is role interchangeability a nonbiblical discovery that has produced no good fruit whatsoever, but it is *artificial. Exceedingly* artificial. Without its technological props, especially scientific birth control and abortion, role interchangeability falls to the ground. Without central heating, air conditioning, microwave ovens, and machines to do all the heavy work—and especially lots and lots of money to pay all the surrogates who are taking over Mommy's real jobs—modern feminism would curl up and die.

We in the church are confusing the issue by debating whether wives should work. These debates all miss the point. Scripture draws the line not at *whether* wives work, but *where* we work. The Bible says young wives should be trained to "love their husbands and children, to be self-controlled and pure, to be *busy at home,* to be kind, and to be subject to their husbands" (Titus 2:4, 5).

Let's look now at that Greek word the NIV translates "busy at home."

What's in a Word?

The word in question is *oikourgous,* a very rare Greek word. It's so rare, in fact, that more modern Greek manuscripts substitute the word *oikourous,* which was somewhat more familiar to the scribes who copied down the New Testament. God, in his providence, has seen to it that whichever word one believes is the original, it makes no difference to the teaching. I shall discuss *oikourgous* first, and I hope you'll bear with me, because this is a very important point.

Oikourgous is a compound word, formed from the word *oikos,* which means house or home, and *ergos,* which means work. Literally translated it would be "homeworking." A similar compound, *ampelourgous,* from *ampel* (vine) and *ergos* (work) means vinedresser. *Geourgous,* from·*ge* (earth) and *ergos,* means farmer. Vinedressers work in the vineyard, with the vines. Farmers work in the fields, with the earth. From these similar forms, one would expect *oikourgous* to mean "one whose calling is to work in the home at household tasks"—that is, a housewife. *And that is exactly what it means!*

Arndt and Gingrich's translation of Bauer's *Greek Lexicon* (a standard work) defines *oikourgous* as "working at home, domestic." Thayer's equally standard Greek lexicon defines it as "caring for the house, working at home."

Unhappily Susan Foh, in her otherwise excellent book *Women and the Word of God,* has confused the issue by claiming *oikourgous* does not mean domestic:

> Titus 2:4-5 lists some requirements for wives. Among them is οι-κουργους or literally home-workers [actually, it is literally home-work*ing,* since the word is an adjective]. By some this word is taken to be confirmation that the woman's work should be confined to the home. It is sometimes translated "domestic," a word that conjures up a woman whose delight is baking homemade bread, sewing all her family's clothes and making her pots and pans shine and whose dress is incomplete without an apron. Because of these connotations, "domestic" is a misleading translation. The verb form of οικουργους is translated by Arndt and Gingrich as "to fulfill one's household duties." . . . This understanding of the word is helpful in that it does not limit the women to working only at home.[2]

At the risk of entangling the reader in linguistic semantics, let me point out a few facts. (1) Arndt and Gingrich translate *the word oikourgous itself* as "domestic," the connotation Susan Foh wants us to "avoid." (2) It is against all sound principles of translation and scholarship to substitute the translation of another form (in this case, the verb form) for *the word itself.* That would be like saying, "The word 'box' means a container. But the verb form 'to box' means to fight. So we should not think boxes are containers. This is misleading, because it raises connotations of packages and brown paper and string. A box *really* means a fight."

Susan Foh's antihomeworking prejudices come out clearly. For some reason she doesn't like women who wear aprons, sew, and bake bread. In view of this, all we can say is that she saw what she wanted to see, ignoring the real meaning of *oikourgous* in preference for a seemingly plausible alternative. (Perhaps she didn't look up the word herself, but left this part of her research to someone else. I hope so.)

Oikourgous means homeworking. But what about the other word that appears in some less ancient Greek manuscripts—*oikourous,* which the King James Version renders "keepers at home"? Arndt and Gingrich say it means "staying at home, domestic." It could also be translated "guardian of the home," the one whose job it is night and day to patrol the home and make sure things are in order. Thayer says this is its literal meaning: "keeping at home and taking care of household affairs: domestic."

So whether you prefer *oikourgous* or *oikourous,* both say a wife's job is in the home.

Am I putting too much weight on one word? Well, *every* word in the Bible is true, and every word makes a difference. The Apostle Paul produces an entire case for justification by faith from the single word "credited" in the phrase from Genesis 15:6—"it was credited to him as righteousness"—(see Romans 4). Jesus rested a claim to Messiahship on the single word "Lord" from a Psalm of David (Luke 20:41-44). Writing to the Galatians, the Apostle Paul goes even further, proving Jesus is the Christ from a *single Hebrew letter* (Gal. 3:16)! Moreover, as I hope to show, the whole counsel of Scripture upholds the *oikourgous* teaching.

Today many people simply do not want to believe the Bible says what it says. So modern commentaries that discuss the word *oikourgous* either misdefine it or try to tie it to first-century culture. But absolutely nothing *in the context* suggests that Paul merely wanted us to conform to our society's idea of what makes a good wife (which in first-century Greece happened to be homeworking). Paul said, "Love your husbands and children, be self-controlled and pure." Does that mean that we shouldn't love our husbands and children any more since our society now encourages divorce and abortion? Does it mean that when immodest dress becomes fashionable we can forget modesty? By what standard can anyone pick *one word* out of this verse as "culturally bound," irrelevant to our modern age, and keep all the rest?

I agree that the Bible's teaching on homeworking raises cultural problems. But it's because our culture *has* problems, not because the Bible is out-of-date.

The Fulfillment Mistake

Modern women are used to being told we can do anything we want. So when God says to stay home and work there, it grates harshly on our ears. Stay home and be housewives? How legalistic and enslaving! Surely an intelligent woman has better things to do than wash dishes for the rest of her life!

This kind of argument arises because we misunderstand the Christian life. Much of the church is obsessed with success and fulfillment and is oblivious to God's commands. Because of this, we are conspicuously lacking in true success (the advance of Christ's Kingdom on earth) and real fulfillment (the peace of a conscience secure in its obedience to God).

Susan Foh states the true Christian position on fulfillment beautifully:

What is fulfillment and how does one find it? Generally, fulfillment involves feeling complete, content, useful, at peace; it means feeling that life has meaning, and you have a part in it. . . .

Friedan's answer is that meaningful work will bring fulfillment. There are other suggestions—love, one's children, the acquisition of material things, art. Those who advocate a shorter workweek must see personal fulfillment in leisure time.

From a Christian perspective, none of these goals is sufficient. . . .

Real fulfillment is possible only for those who know the God of the Scriptures; and to those, fulfillment is possible in whatever circumstances they find themselves. . . .

For the Christian, satisfaction is found in obedience to God. . . .

The Christian woman should not be deceived by feminist dreams and promises. Women will not automatically become immune to *anomie* [the feeling one's life is meaningless] when they are given equal opportunity in the work world. . . . The Christian who lacks fulfillment lacks it because he or she is sinning by not fixing his or her mind and trust on Christ, the only one who fulfils.[3]

Woman's chief end is to glorify God and enjoy him forever, not to glorify herself and grab for all the gusto she can get! This does not mean Christian women are unfulfilled. But fulfillment is a reward the Lord grants his sons and daughters for their unselfish service, not a prize to be grabbed from God's hand by force. Even Christ did not grab for fulfillment but sought it by the road to the Cross. "Let this mind be in you" which was in him.

The real question about homeworking, then, is not "Do I want to do it?" or "Will it fulfill me? or "What do I get out of it?" God has spoken, and we should only be asking, "*How* do I do it, Lord? Speak, Lord, for thy servant heareth."

Thank God—homeworking is *not* just washing dishes, as I feared when I first timidly laid aside my career plans and began to try to do what God said. But I didn't know that when I started! I thought having babies was a great sacrifice, that housework was drudgery (I still hate housework!), and that I was being a noble martyr. But I found out otherwise; and so will you, if you have enough of the Christian spirit of adventure which allows you to take a running jump into the blue, not knowing where you will land, but only that God told you to do it!

If you are that kind of woman (and I hope you are), then read on. For God has given us an adventure, sisters, and far more power to advance his Kingdom than we have been told. I'm just going to make one detour (in the next chapter) to show why the old warhorses that our feminist friends constantly trot out to bolster their cause—Deborah, the woman of Proverbs 31, and so on—are stuffed with straw. Then the rest of the book is about what homeworking *is* and the vast difference it makes to our families, churches, and nation.

12 The Good, the Bad, and the Irrelevant: Scriptural Examples of Working Wives

I met Pam at a home schoolers' meeting. We had been discussing parents, children, education, home businesses, the role of government, and so on, and I had shared some of the scriptural teaching on these matters. Pam kept saying, "You ought to write a book!" and I kept saying, "I *am* writing a book." Finally she saw that I wasn't kidding—I really was writing a book—and she asked for my phone number because she wanted to talk some more about women's role and hear why I said the things I did.

She got in touch with me the next day. After asking for the address of a foreign language program I had mentioned at the meeting, Pam got right to the point. "I mean, all that stuff about homeworking sounds pretty good, but what about the noble wife in Proverbs 31? Wasn't she a working wife? And what about Deborah and Priscilla?" Pam was sincere in asking these questions. A working wife herself, she cared enough about her son to be thinking of home schooling. But her husband was in seminary; they needed the money; she had a useful job in the public schools; and besides, didn't the Bible hold up working wives like the lady in Proverbs 31 as a good example?

Wherefore Art Thou, Working Wife?

I have found that invariably when the subject of homeworking comes up, someone will bring up the supposed scriptural examples of working wives. In most cases they have not carefully checked out the Scriptures to see whether the alleged example actually applies. It's a taken-for-granted sort of thing; surely all those Christian magazine articles can't be wrong!

Four hundred, three hundred, two hundred, or even one hundred years ago the church had not discovered how neatly certain female Bible characters fit into the working-wife mold. Somehow, in poring over these passages generations of Christians missed the obvious applications to day-care and office jobs. But now our society is running after these things, and suddenly there they are in the Bible! How convenient.

I believe that *none* of the women in the Bible who are used nowadays to support the careerist movement actually does. Typically a magazine article or sermon will make some casual reference to one of these ladies, just slap the label "working wife" on her, and then breeze on. I don't know who started this fashion, but apparently once *somebody* did it, everyone else thought there must be sound exegesis behind those examples and just copied them without inquiry. All one need do now is intone "Proverbs 31" and readers by the millions nod their heads. "Yeah, the wife in Proverbs 31. Everyone says she's a working wife."

Is this demonstrated logic? No; it is bald *assertion*. Someone *says*, "So and so is a working wife." But does the Bible say so?

Before we start checking out these "examples," let's review the basic principles of correct Bible interpretation. Then we can see if any of the "examples" actually are.

(1) Bible interpretation is not "you interpret your way, I interpret my way, nobody fish in the middle." The relativistic position that contradictory interpretations of a passage can be equally correct is exactly what the whole epistle to Titus is against. An elder must "hold firmly to the trustworthy message as it has been taught, so that he can encourage others by sound doctrine and refute those who oppose it. For there are many rebellious people, mere talkers and deceivers. . . . They must be silenced, because they are ruining whole households by teaching things they ought not to teach. . . . Therefore, rebuke them sharply, so that they will be sound in the faith" (Titus 1:9-13). Not a hint here of open-minded tolerance of opposing views. The Bible teaches only one truth—"sound doctrine"—and opposing views must be "refuted," "silenced," and "rebuked."

(2) When using Scripture to interpret Scripture, explicit teaching (such as Titus 2:5's insistence that young wives should be homeworkers) is used to interpret examples. Examples do not overrule specific teaching. For instance: Lot committed incest with his daughters; Lot was a righteous man; therefore incest is OK. No, it is not, because an explicit command of God forbids it (Lev. 18:6).

(3) We must ask two questions of every example:

(a) Is it *normative*? Does God endorse this behavior? Is the example *good* (like Jesus) or *bad* (like Lot's daughters)? We find this out by looking at any scriptural commands that apply to the person's behavior, and at God's comments about that person if there are any in the Bible.

(b) Does it *apply* to the subject we are discussing? Or is it irrelevant?

Here is my charge: those who push careers for wives *never base their position on the commands of God*. That is because there is no Bible verse that commands wives to be breadwinners. There *are* verses that tell women to bear children, to manage the household, and to be homeworkers (1 Tim. 5:10, 14; Titus 2:4, 5), but careerists ignore or slight these verses. Instead, they try to build their case on examples, hoping to overrule the clear commands of God by theological juggling.

Now let's take a look at the examples they commonly use.

Deborah

Deborah was a prophetess and a married woman. She was a leader in Israel during the time of the judges. "The Israelites came to her to have their disputes decided" (Judg. 4:5). The important thing to remember about Deborah's doings, and the activities of all the people in the Book of Judges, is that *they are not normative*. In that time "Israel had no king; everyone did as he saw fit" (Judg. 17:6; 21:25). The people were doing as they saw fit, not as God commanded. They worshiped idols. Oppression was rife. Women were gang raped and kidnapped as brides. I could go on, but why don't you just read the book for yourself? You will see that the theme of Judges is "what happens to people when they abandon God's law."

Elsewhere in Scripture God spells it out that it is not his plan for youths or women to govern a country. "Woe to the wicked. . . . Youths oppress my people, women rule over them. O my people, your guides lead you astray; they turn you from the path" (Isa. 3:11, 12). We should not, therefore, look to Deborah as a normative example of careers for women.

If you are still unconvinced, consider this: Samson was a judge who slept with prostitutes (Judg. 16:1). Do we then throw out 1 Corinthians 6:15, which forbids Christians to patronize prostitutes in the strongest terms, because of Samson's "good example"? Do we make vows to offer whatever comes out of our door as a sacrifice to the Lord, and then keep the vow even if it means burning our only daughter, like Jephthah (another leader of Israel in the time of the judges)? How about nailing a guest's head to the floor, like Jael did to Sisera? Isn't this ridiculous? No;

we judge the judges by the explicit commands of God, not vice versa.

In any case Deborah was not a nine-to-fiver. She was a ruler, and the people came *to her*. She could have been a widow or childless. The text does not tell us. (Deborah calls herself a "mother in Israel," which in Hebrew idiom could just as well mean a mother *of* Israel, since she was the "mother of the country" at that point.) Deborah was not anxious to venture forth into the "economic-opportunity sphere." When her big chance came to lead the army in battle she demurred, and only the commander Barak's cowardice forced her to go. Neither did God bless Barak for his nonsexist willingness to follow Deborah to the battle. Barak's punishment was that he would not get the glory for the victory; that fell to Jael, who nailed Sisera's head to the floor.

When the men are all dishrags incapable of leadership, a woman may end up leading a country. Thus, Deborah was a leader, not a working wife; her example is not normative. Nothing in Scripture says we should abandon homeworking and deliberatly try to recreate the atmosphere of moral and social decay in the time of the judges, when Deborah ruled.

Priscilla

Priscilla helped her husband Aquila with his tentmaking business (Acts 18:3). Priscilla is definitely normative—that is, a good example. She and Aquila were among the Apostle Paul's most intimate friends. He greeted them personally in his letters, lived with them, and traveled with them.

Here we must notice a few things.

(1) Tentmaking is a home crafts business. It is nothing like getting into the car, driving fifteen minutes across town, parking, walking into an office building, staying there for eight or nine hours, and then driving home. You don't go to the office to make tents. Not in first-century Europe.

(2) No children are ever mentioned. Because of Priscilla and Aquila's extreme mobility (they were in Corinth, in Ephesus, in Rome, back to Ephesus, etc.), some commentators assume they had no children. This is only an assumption, but it's worth mentioning.

(3) Aquila was a tentmaker, and Priscilla worked with him. Their business was not Priscilla's independent operation.

All that can be said from Priscilla's example is that it is certainly fine for married Christian women to help their husbands with their home businesses. No word here of day-care for tots or nine-to-five outside careers.

Lydia

This example is not commonly used, but some people are desperate. I saw an article in a leading conservative Christian magazine which used Lydia as an example of a wife with an outside career. Is she?

Lydia was a dealer in purple cloth (Acts 16:14). Nobody ever said she was married. No husband or children are ever mentioned. The opposite is more likely to be true. Lydia invited Paul *and* his companions to stay at her house (more probably her mansion, complete with servants) on her own authority after being converted (Acts 16:15). If Lydia had a husband, he just might perhaps frown on such proceedings. "Hi, honey! I just got saved, and here are all my new friends who are coming to live with us."

It is not logical to reason from an irrelevant example. Lydia a working wife? Nobody can prove she was even *married!* The evidence is actually *against* it! Nor, for that matter, do we know that her cloth dealing was an "outside career." Lydia could have transacted all business from her mansion, using slaves as her intermediaries.

We can glean one extremely interesting fact from Lydia's example, though. It was *not* unknown for a woman to have a business in those days! This fact is significant, because boosters of careerism are so fond of the "cultural" method of debunking homeworking. "Paul just told women to be stay-at-home wives because women couldn't get into business back then," they say. Not so. Paul spent a fair amount of time living in a Greek businesswoman's house, and he probably was alert enough to notice she existed.

Hannah

You may not believe this, but in a letter I received explaining why her magazine wouldn't print a prohomeworking article I had submitted, an editor mentioned Hannah as a justification for married women who put their children in day-care. Well, why not? Hannah has about as much to do with married women with careers as does Lydia.

Let's dispose of this quickly. (1) Hannah, the mother of the prophet Samuel, never had a career. (2) Hannah only brought Samuel to the High Priest Eli because of a vow she had made before the Lord. We no longer make those Nazirite vows under the new covenant. (3) Samuel was Eli's permanent guest. It would be like a mother dropping her son off at the day-care center and coming to see him once a year. (4) Therefore the example is irrelevant.

Hannah bringing Samuel to Eli more closely resembles a homeworking mother apprenticing her son to a minister than anything having to do with careerism. Hannah, if you recall, went back to her husband and dedicated herself to having as many more children as possible. She wound up with three more sons and two daughters, which was a sign that the Lord was being "gracious to Hannah" (1 Sam 2:21). Children were what Hannah wanted, not an outside job. Hannah's freedom after leaving Samuel with Eli was used to have *more* babies and raise them.

I am sure career-pushers can find more examples to twist. But you see my point. So far the examples they like to quote are either not normative or irrelevant. Such exegesis should make us suspicious. Why all this grasping at straws? Could it be they are seeing only what they want to see?

I want to look now at two *good* examples who are commonly overlooked when women talk about careers. Then we'll finish up with that poor lady in Proverbs 31 on whom the careerist movement has been forcibly begotten.

Sarah and Mary

Two wives in the Bible are excellent examples, except for the few concrete instances when God rebuked them. They are Sarah and Mary.

> Listen to me, you who pursue righteousness and who seek
>   the Lord:
> Look to the rock from which you were cut
>   and to the quarry from which you were hewn;
> look to Abraham, your father,
>   and to Sarah, who gave you birth. (Isa. 51:1, 2)

Sarah, our first good example (see also Heb. 11:11 and 1 Pet. 3:6), was a *rich* wife. Yet she found her greatest fulfillment in motherhood and helping her husband ("like Sarah, who obeyed Abraham and called him her master"). When the angels came looking for Sarah, she was "in the tent." She made food for these heavenly visitors with her own hands (Gen. 18: 5, 9). Sarah loved her son Isaac so much and spent so much time with him that it took him three years to get over her death (Gen. 24:67).

Mary, our second good example, was the wife of a *poor* man. The angel Gabriel, however, did not appear to her to offer her a job, but a son. Would anyone dare say that the mother of Jesus Christ missed out on fulfillment by mothering this Child?

If you were Mary, would *you* have left Jesus with a baby-sitter for ten hours a day while you went off to work in a market stall to "help Joseph out"? That doesn't sound like a good idea, does it? Well, *your* child is special too. Jesus said that when we welcome one of these little babies, we welcome him (Matt. 18:5; Mark 9:37; Luke 9:48). So in some sense *all* Christian mothers are Marys.

Rich wife, poor wife, tentmaker's wife, chief: so far we have found no scriptural support for careerism. Now comes the $1,000 question. What about the ideal wife of Proverbs 31?

The Ideal Wife of Proverbs 31

Here is the unfortunate victim the modern career movement has been fathered upon. She is extolled in the Christian press as a real estate salesman, office worker, factory worker, merchant, and who knows what else. Nobody can *prove* these assertions. If they are successful, it is because the general public is reluctant to look up Scripture references and examine them in context. We are going to be different and walk through the entire passage, so we can see for ourselves what it says.

> A wife of noble character who can find?
> She is worth far more than rubies.

This tells us that the woman who is about to be described is a good example for us to follow.

> Her husband has full confidence in her
> and lacks nothing of value.

She is not an autonomous feminist following "individualistic pursuits." Her husband's needs are her concern, and she works to satisfy them.

> She brings him good, not harm,
> all the days of her life.

By implication it is possible for a wife to bring her husband harm. The rest of the passage will tell us how to be good, not harmful, wives.

Notice how this woman's husband is emphasized. Feminists hate this. They don't want a woman to be identified in terms of her husband and children. But this woman's achievements are stated in just these terms.

> She selects wool and flax
>   and works with eager hands.

Wool and flax are the two raw ingredients of Mideastern clothing. Nothing careerist about this so far.

> She is like the merchant ships,
>   bringing her food from afar.

Now the chorus starts. "She's a merchant!" "A salesman!" "An able-bodied seaman!"

But *how* is she like the merchant ships? Does she bulge and sit low in the water? Is she covered with two coats of deck paint? This is a simile, not a definition. She is *like* the merchant ships in one particular respect, that of "bringing her food from afar."

Look at the following context (getting up while it is still dark, staying up late at night at home), and you will see that she does not go in person to Syria or Tarshish on business trips. She is bringing home food, literal food, not a paycheck. Like the merchants, she has scouted out her neighborhood for food offerings of quality and value, and like their ships she carries them home.

Picture a housewife coming home with bags of food, having stopped off at the supermarket first, then the health food store (because yeast and other bulk items are cheaper there), and the produce market (for fresh fruit and vegetables), and you've got it. This is the picture the passage is trying to convey. Wives who join food co-ops, who trek out monthly to a nearby farm to buy eggs, honey, and grains in bulk, who carefully sift over the radishes before putting any in their shopping basket, who have learned to stretch a dollar farther and buy better food with it—these are the women this passage commends.

> She gets up while it is still dark;
>   she provides food for her family
>   and portions for her servant girls.

This wife personally provides the household's food. She has servants for the housework, it seems. Housework is *not* what staying home is all about. We can do it, but we don't have to. It's scriptural for a homeworking wife to employ servants.

Today our servants are mostly mechanical: dishwashers, food processors, vacuum cleaners. Thus technology makes homeworking easier for those who can afford these tools, just as male and female servants did in the old days. Paul Hawken, author of *The Next Economy*, says that every man, woman, and child in America today employs the equivalent of 100 servants through the services of our energy-fueled technology.

> She considers a field and buys it;
>   out of her earnings she plants a vineyard.

Tell me how buying shoes for your family make you a shoe salesman, and I'll be able to explain to you how buying a vineyard makes this woman a real-estate dealer! Christian magazine articles and books commonly refer to her as such, but this makes no sense. She bought *one* field *for her family's use;* she didn't resell it, much less make a career out of buying fields here and there and tooling around on her donkey to show the properties to prospective buyers.

As for planting a vineyard: Some folks have gotten it into their heads that homeworking means nothing but dishes and diapers. So then, they reason, if Scripture shows a woman doing *anything* but inside-the-house tasks, that must give us all license to do *anything* we want to outside the house.

But homeworking means working on the home *estate,* not just within the four walls of a house. Housewives from time immemorial have planted gardens in their back yards, or tended truck patches on a portion of the family's forty acres. This was considered household work and rightly so, for the wife never strayed off the family property. Furthermore, she was producing goods under her own supervision, not that of an outside boss.

Here we see a wife putting her earnings to their best use—*permanently increasing the family capital.* She was not making money for "personal fulfillment" at all, but for the good of her family. In a minute we will see how she made her money, and why it was not an outside career.

> She sets about her work vigorously;
>   her arms are strong for her tasks.

A real hard worker.

> She sees that her trading is profitable,
>   and her lamp does not go out at night.

From this we see that (1) she was involved in trade. People bartered everything in those days. "Trade" is not international finance; it is the process of exchanging goods. This can be done at home, as housewives used to barter expertly with traveling peddlers for their products. See, for example, the example of Almanzo Wilder's mother in *Farmer Boy* by Laura Ingalls Wilder. (2) She did a good job of it. (3) Trading was her last priority. When does she inspect the accounts? At night, after all the other work is done.

> In her hand she holds the distaff
> and grasps the spindle with her fingers.

So much for all housework as "mindless, enslaving drudgery," as the feminists would have it. The ideal wife of Proverbs 31 positively *revels* in it. She doesn't mind spinning and weaving her family's clothes, or resent it because it takes her out of the "economic-opportunity sphere." As Matthew Henry says about this verse in his famous *Commentary on the Whole Bible:*

> She perceives that she can make things herself better and cheaper than she can buy them; and she does not reckon [sewing and spinning] either an abridgment of her liberty or a disparagement to her dignity, or at all inconsistent with her repose.

Moving back to our passage, we find that far from focusing on "individualistic pursuits," the ideal wife is known for this:

> She opens her arms to the poor
> and extends her hands to the needy.

Charity at home. We'll look at this in detail in Chapter 17.

> When it snows, she has no fear for her household;
> for all of them are dressed in scarlet.
> She makes coverings for her bed;
> she is clothed in fine linen and purple.

She makes garments both for function and for beauty. We will look at the homeworker as artist in Chapter 14.

> Her husband is respected at the city gate,
> where he takes his seat among the elders of the land.

The gates were where the business of government and society was dispatched. If ever there was a woman who could honestly say she was gifted for leadership, it was this one. But her husband, not her, had a seat in the gate.

> She makes linen garments and sells them,
>   and supplies the merchants with sashes.

Now the chorus starts again. "She's a merchant!" "A factory worker!" "A traveling salesman!" No, not quite. She *supplies* the merchants with sashes; she is not a merchant herself. She makes linen garments— where?—at home. Homeworking wives may make money, lots and lots of it, if they want to. No law of God says products may only be produced in a factory.

> She is clothed with strength and
>   dignity;
> She can laugh at the days to come.
> She speaks with wisdom,
>   and faithful instruction is on her tongue.

To whom does she speak with wisdom? Is she a preacher, a toastmaster, a politician? Not likely, in view of her other duties. She speaks with wisdom *whenever she opens her mouth.* It is her daily habit, not a professionally paid position.

> *She watches over the affairs of her household*
>   *and does not eat the bread of idleness.*

I emphasize this because it is the key verse of the entire passage. Is she out making a name for herself in the business world? No; her concern is for home and family. She is, in a word, "busy at home."

What is the fruit of the ideal wife's devotion to her family and home? Does everyone belittle her for isolating herself from the world, for being a "parasite on society," for neglecting her God-given talents? Here is God's verdict:

> Her children arise and call her blessed;
>   her husband also, and he praises her:
> "Many women do noble things,
>   but you surpass them all."

Charm is deceptive, and beauty is fleeting;
    but a woman who fears the Lord is to be praised.
Give her the reward she has earned,
    and let her works bring her praise at the city gates.

Her husband, her children, and ultimately the whole community praise her. Male patriarchal bias? This passage shows none of it. There is not one negative comment about women in this passage; instead we are told that many women do noble things.

The men who wrote the Bible weren't prejudiced against women. *They* didn't call housewives dull drudges and parasites. Who throws around those insults? The feminist movement, which claims to be on our side!

Scriptural endorsements of careerist wives? There's not a one.

Now let's see what we're really supposed to do at home.

13 Business at Home

Lisa, a college-age friend of mine, called me up one day in mild distress. Her parents were insisting that she pick a major that would lead to a useful job; but Lisa and I had talked about homeworking before, and she didn't want to get locked into a fast-track career that would unfit her for housewifely pursuits. How to please her parents and yet find a major that would be helpful in the home—this was Lisa's dilemma. After looking over the various options, we found one that was ideal. Lisa enrolled as a *business major!*

Maids and Managers

Feminists have long derided homeworking as mere maid work. But voices are being raised that challenge this assumption. A new magazine for women who choose to stay home, *Welcome Home,* was started recently (this in itself is a good sign). Janet Dittmer wrote an article for the March 1984 issue called "The Home Manager," which contrasts the homeworker as maid with the homeworker as manager.

> I picture a maid going about necessary tasks without much comprehension of how those tasks relate to the whole. A manager, on the other hand, keeps the long-range picture firmly in mind. Whatever the organization (in this case, the family) is hoping to achieve—happiness, cooperation, mutual love—the manager knows how today's activities relate to goals that may not be reached for quite some time. . . .
> Not only does a maid lack overall perspective, she also lacks control over what can be done about it. Basically she follows orders

based on what someone else thinks ought to be done. However, a manager is the one in charge. . . . She can choose which hour out of all twenty-four in a day and which day of the seven in a week to do any of her responsibilities, and only her imagination limits how she carries them out. The laundry can be an efficient routine done without a hitch at a regular time; it can be an opportunity to teach colors, sorting and matching to a young child; it can be whatever the homemaker wants it to be. . . .

A maid usually carries out her tasks alone . . . her major responsibility is over "things." By contrast, to a manager . . . people are her top priority. Household tasks are delegated at her discretion; she makes assignments, supervises when necessary, receives reports back on jobs completed. She teaches, trains and evaluates progress. She recognizes when a job is too difficult or dangerous for the rest of the team and handles it herself. Sensitivity to the team is a must.

Scripture goes along with what Mrs. Dittmer has just said, and pushes it even further. Young wives are supposed to have children and *"manage their homes"* (1 Tim. 5:14). We are supposed to be home-managers. The word in the Greek is literally "house-despots." So much for wives as the poor downtrodden victims of biblical patriarchal bias! Home *despots*—that's what we are, not household slaves!

And there's more to being a home despot than even homemaking. Mrs. Dittmer mentioned a homemaker's typical activities: training children, creating a pleasant home atmosphere, doing housework. These are very valuable and scriptural things to do, but our economic role goes *beyond* homemaking.

Homeworkers have an economic role that affects our families and an economic role that affects society. Both are vitally important, and both are little understood.

Let's talk first about our economic role in society.

Of Socialism and the Meal Hall
Economists understand that the fundamental difference between free enterprise (also called capitalism) and socialism (also called totalitarianism) is that in free enterprise *the home is a separate economic entity.* Each family not only consumes (which they could do under socialism) but *produces*. Socialism means family functions are sent outside to be performed by "society"—i.e., under the authority of those in power. Free enterprise means the family takes bids on how much it would cost to have a function performed by someone else, then either accepts the best bid or opts to do it themselves.

To bring this down to earth, let's take food as an example. If cooking were socialized, houses would no longer have kitchens. No longer would children gather in the kitchen come evening to watch Mommy make a batch of cookies and help her lick out the bowl. Instead of the "inefficient, traditional" method where each family either prepared its own food or voluntarily went out to a restaurant, we would have meal halls. All citizens would assemble at a particular time at the meal hall on their block, where they would be fed whatever government-appointed nutritionists thought was good for them.

Sounds far-fetched? Then listen to this:

> Before the end of the Civil War and the beginning of the Great Depression, three generations of material feminists raised fundamental questions about what was called "woman's sphere" and "woman's work." They challenged two characteristics of industrial capitalism: the physical separation of household space from public space [meaning private homes], and the economic separation of the domestic economy from the political economy. . . . They developed new forms of neighborhood organizations, including housewives' cooperatives, as well as new building types, including the kitchenless house, the day care center, the public kitchen, the community dining club. . . . For six decades they expounded one powerful idea: that women must create feminist houses with socialized housework and child care before they could truly become equal members of society. . . .
>
> Their theoretic position represented the logical extension of many ideas about women's autonomy. . . .[1]

Those turn-of-the-century feminist ladies were logical thinkers. They saw clearly that role obliteration would not be possible while families could operate independently of the economy. In other words, they saw that (1) *role obliteration is only possible under socialism,* and (2) *the stay-at-home wife is the single greatest deterrent to socialism.* Private houses, private kitchens, private children—all must go. As Dolores Hayden, who is trying to bring back the old-time feminist emphasis on meal halls and kitchenless houses, writes, "Any socialist, feminist society of the future will find socializing domestic work at the heart of its concerns."[2]

> Iona Gale concluded that "the private kitchen must go the way of the spinning wheel, of which it is the contemporary." In the same spirit, Ada May Krecher had written for Emma Goldman's anar-

chist journal, *Mother Earth*, of the consolidation of home on a large scale: "The same forces . . . will build the big dwelling places and playgrounds and nurseries for tomorrow's children and make them measurelessly better to our socialized ideals of tomorrow than could possibly be the private little homes of today."[3]

Would you believe that *Ladies' Home Journal* once devoted a series of articles to eulogizing the kitchenless house? Yes, they did, in 1918-19![4] So intensely did the feminists of that day desire to socialize American housing that they regarded "the development of 50 million low technology, single family homes housing three quarters of American families" as "a decisive ideological defeat."[5]

Ladies, please take note. You may not be going out to work in hopes of losing your house and your microwave, but if you go out you lend power to somebody who *does* have those goals. Constitutional attorney John Whitehead says,

> The feminists view women in the work force as a key to their movement. An interview in *Working Women* magazine of nine top corporate women revealed their belief that the basic method of breaking male dominance in the business world is having more women in the work force.[6]

But when nobody's home to run the house, who will? As Mr. Whitehead says,

> This raised a question of what to do with children of working mothers. The answer was state-financed day-care centers.[7]

"State-financed" *anything* means, of course, *more* power for government, and *more* money. Taxes must be raised to support government day-care, and more state employees recruited to run it. When a government has *total* power and controls *all* our money, we say it has become "totalitarian."

Feminists are forced into demanding that Uncle Sam take over our private·lives and property and children because of their own position. Every woman, they think, should have the right to a fulfilling life in the economic-opportunity sphere. But women can't eliminate childbearing altogether, or in one generation there will *be* no economic-opportunity sphere. Feminists don't think a woman should be "forced" to stay home with her own infant. Neither can they logically reason that the father should be forced to stay home. So somebody will have to be paid to watch Baby. But not all women can afford day-care costs. The solution? Tax us all to pay for their baby-sitting, then, to justify the program, *force* us all to participate.

This line of reasoning can be extended to all family functions, and *will* be extended to all family functions if feminism is allowed to remain unchallenged. Women shouldn't be "forced" to do housework. But not all women can afford to hire a maid; so start a federal Department of Housework. Women shouldn't be "forced" to do the family cooking; so let's have a meal hall at which we all will be forced to eat. Abolish the kitchen and the supermarket to make women "free," and we will abolish our freedom to feed ourselves. We must give up *all* of our freedom before feminists will consider us "free."

Remember this. *Feminism is barren and must inevitably die out unless imposed by force on the rest of us.* A generation of women who refuse to have babies, and who farm out the few they do have to day-care, will be swept away in twenty years by the children of those who stay at home and the resentful children of feminist mothers who remember what day-care did to them. *The only way feminism can survive is to impose its lifestyle on the culture by force.* That is why feminism and socialism go hand-in-hand. Socialism steals family functions, and feminism is only too glad to hand them over. Christian women who voluntarily give up their homeworking duties may find someday that they cannot take them back. The child put in day-care by choice may be kept there by force, subjected to virulent anti-Christian teaching and moral degradation, and it will be the mother's own fault.

Feminism and the Unfree Society

Feminism is a demand for *legislated* equality between the sexes. It *needs* legislative action to prop it up because it is unnatural. Normal biology tends to keep mothers at home and emphasizes various differences between men and women. Feminism, in an attempt to obliterate all that, depends on coercive laws to force people to behave in a way they don't want to.

The most basic example of feminist coercion is feminists' most basic demand: equal pay for equal work. Everyone I have read, feminist or not, agrees that this demand is fair and should be met. I am going to show that it *cannot* be met in the way feminists want without destroying economic freedom.

You can convince people to adopt your values in two ways: (1) persuasion, and (2) force. Force is not the only option. Women who want equal pay for their work could ask for it politely. Peer pressure could be brought on employers who pay women substandard wages. Women could demonstrate outstanding competence, thus motivating employers to pay them superior wages in fear of losing their services to a competitor. This would be *persuasion*. In the days before ERA was a gleam in Gloria Steinem's eye, I worked as a bookkeeper for a tiny publishing outfit. Upon learning that my male predecessor was paid $1.40 an hour more than me, I brought the fact to my employer's attention. He agreed to pay me the previous bookkeeper's wage, retroactively. He did this because I was a good bookkeeper and he would rather meet my fair demand than struggle with the books himself while trying to hire a replacement. Also, he saw that it was the fair thing to do. I was fifteen years old, personally unintimidating, without any union or government agency behind me. Yet I got the raise.

Minority after minority has entered this country, encountered tremendous prejudice, yet ended up in the middle- or upper-class after a generation or two, *without* coercive legislation forcing employers to hire them or pay them "fair" wages. In a free market people can demonstrate to their employers that their services are valuable. In a free market people can move to a more appealing job if their present employer is unfair. Of course, the opposite is also true. In a free market employers can downgrade the salaries of those they consider less-valuable employees. They can even exercise charity toward their employees by, say, paying a married man with a family more than his job is worth. Jesus endorses this kind of selective charity in his parable of the workers in the vineyard— the latecomers got a whole day's wages, and the early birds got no more. This was not unfair to the early birds, but rather an act of charity to those the vineyard's owner hired later in the day. Jesus specifically condemns the envy of the early-comers (Matt. 20:1-16).

Force is a different story. Feminists want to restrict the free market by forcing employers to be "fair" in how they assign salaries. No longer can the married man with four children be given a break. The wife with no children who is working for an unneeded second income, or the single man or woman, must be paid as much as he. This reduces employers' ability to apply Christian charity by employing those who need it most, or by helping them out once they are employed. More than this, *it puts the market in the hands of the government*. Government will now determine who employs whom for how much. An employer no longer owns his business, then; he is merely managing it for Uncle Sam, who *really* runs the personnel department.

Feminists' further demands are right in line with this. They want salaries administered by "comparable worth," meaning that employers must pay secretaries as much as truck drivers if some official decides they have "comparable" jobs. This means wage-fixing by the government. Feminists want the free market to be "fair" to them by treating them like men, or even better. (How many *men* can cow their bosses into promoting them or overlooking slipshod work for fear of a "sex discrimination" lawsuit?) Feminists don't want to *earn* this fairness by proving they are as competent as men, like my grandmother did, who became a medical doctor in 1925. Too many employers are "prejudiced" against, for example, married mothers of newborns who want to dump their babies in day-care.

The upshot of all this? *Uncle Sam dominating business decisions.* Business practice under feminism moves from *personal freedom*—the freedom of employer and employee to arrive at an uncoerced contract— to *government intervention.* Employers in effect are made the slaves of their feminist or minority employees. As Morgan O. Reynolds says,

> The current situation is a reversal of the relation between the "employers" and employee of a feudal society in which serfs were bound to landowners by a variety of restrictions. Employers now suffer a limited form of bondage to employees. . . . The courts reinstate employees for almost any reason, often with back pay. If the same principle were applied without regard to status, private citizens could no longer . . . quit an employer without due cause, and employees would be found guilty of unfair labor practices to their employers and forced to return to their original employer, and provide the employer with "back output." Mediators, conciliators, arbitrators, government boards, commissions, and courts would have to rule on the fairness of each proposed dismissal by employer or employee in the economy, currently averaging over 4 million separations per month.[8]

Mr. Reynolds was writing about labor unions, but his remarks apply equally well to feminists who want "equal pay." Are they willing to give "equal output"? Do they recognize the consequences of turning over business decision-making from the owners of the business to the government?

Personal prejudices cannot be eliminated by force. All that government can do is to force people to act against their prejudices. This may seem a good thing, at first. Blacks can now eat in formerly segregated restaurants and be hired at formerly all-white companies. (However,

Thomas Sowell points out that desegregation was already proceeding before the laws went into effect, because people had been *persuaded* of its rightness.[9]) But the price for forced fairness is *the elimination of private property.* Employers have less and less freedom to run their own businesses. And this same principle of fairness-by-force can be applied to *any* form of property—not just giant corporations—or to people themselves. Public policy then overrules God's command "Thou shalt not steal." "Fairness" can become the justification for the most outrageous *oppression,* like the IRS's attempt to close down all Christian schools in this country by declaring any school started after desegregation went into effect guilty until proven innocent and liable to lose its tax exemption *retroactively.* The measure failed, but the principle remains.

The same "fairness" principle is behind the child-care credit in the 1984 tax return. Working wives get subsidized (because the credit is *actual cash,* not just a deduction) by the husbands of those who stay home. This is confiscation without representation, to subsidize the feminist movement.

Feminists want to impose an artificial and unnecessary burden on society, on us all, to give them and their values preference. They want to make us participate in, and failing that, to *contribute* to, their movement. And they are willing to sacrifice our freedom to do it.

Careerism and the Coerced Wife

With all our modern talk of liberation, women fail to realize that the homeworking wife is actually the only liberated female! She is her own boss during the same nine or ten hours of the day that other women are doing what their supervisors say. She can make her own schedule, run her own budget, and dress as she likes, without having to meet company standards. A homeworking wife is generally free to pursue her own interests to a reasonable extent, whereas the "working wife" can't very well read a book she enjoys during working hours. A homeworker serves her "customers" directly instead of pushing paper or pushing buttons, and receives tangible rewards daily for her labors ("Yum! This cake is delicious, Mommy!").

In all the zeal for liberation a new form of slavery is being established—the coerced wife. I first became aware of this problem through a letter in a leading evangelical magazine about five years ago. A woman wrote in misery, asking for help because her husband had forced her to work for their entire marriage, and after many years of this she was tired of it. His reason had been that they needed the money, but now they had lots of money and he still wanted her to have a job. (I seem to remember that he had also forbidden her to have children.) The magazine's advice team replied with some syrupy comments about submission and sympathetic excuses for her husband's behavior. (This same magazine about this time was printing articles informing men that it was their *duty* to help a working wife with the housework, whether they wanted to or not. Force a husband to do the housework for you, but "submit" if he won't let you do yours.)

When Bill and I had first arrived at seminary years ago, we were very poor. I, however, was not looking for a job, partly because I could no longer drive due to poor eyesight, and partly because I was being convicted by God of the rightness of homeworking. In my first real experience with Christians I was surprised to find some insisting that it was my *duty* to get a job and put Bill through seminary. I considered this the work of a few cranks at the time. But the above article showed me I was wrong. Women today are being pushed, in some cases with the church's blessing, into working outside the home *whether they want to or not.*

The culprit, in most cases, is the husband. Suddenly all the articles about working wives click, and he gets dollar signs in his eyes. "$10,000 a year on the hoof! I could buy a vacation cabin with that!" So he brutally forces his wife to put the children in day-care, forbids her to become pregnant, and sends her out into a job she does not want. My obstetrician in New York told me it was common for him to have patients come to him in agony, whose husbands had threatened to divorce them if they didn't abort the baby they had discovered they were carrying. I am thankful that my doctor is prolife, and that most of the women he counseled had the courage to defy their husbands' immoral demands. But here is a clear case of husbands *enslaving* wives as a *direct result* of feminism.

Feminists have foolishly claimed that woman's role as a homeworker is the result of male patriarchal bias. The opposite is true. Non-Christian male patriarchal societies have always enslaved women *outside* the home; Christianity set us free. Who is that out in the fields in the hot sun or carrying heavy loads while the men of the tribe lounge around with their peace pipes? *Women.* Even our modern cartoon "Andy Capp" reflects this truth. Andy lies on the couch all day or goes out to the pub while Flo has a "liberated career in the economic-opportunity sphere" as a scrubmaid.

Men may be the basic culprits, pimping their wives for a few bucks, but evangelical feminism gives the poor victims no sympathy. After all, they are supposed to *want* to be working wives. This particular aspect of feminism has infected even staunch conservatives. One of the most orthodox and caring Christian women I know, upon hearing that a friend of mine had been divorced by her husband, suggested that I baby-sit the friend's baby so she could get a job. No suggestion here of charity, of helping a mother stay home. Why *should* the church help her? It's the widow's or divorcee's job to pay her own way! Thus withers and dies Christian charity.

Feminism's ultimate goal is to have all wives work at all the jobs men do. This goal has been realized in one place already—the prison camps of Soviet Russia. There mothers are permitted to nurse their babies three times a day for fifteen minutes each, and then the babies are taken away at the age of two. The female prisoners are very liberated— they have been seen cutting down trees with axes and carrying away the heavy trunks themselves, mining, working in radioactive areas (without protective clothing), and in short making great inroads into previously male-dominated fields.[10] The KGB would call this "liberation of the citizenry." I prefer to call it slavery.

When laying God's blessings and curses before the people in Deuteronomy 28, Moses told the people that the slavery they had been freed from upon leaving Egypt would come upon them again if they rebelled against the Lord.

> All these curses will come upon you. They will pursue you and overtake you until you are destroyed, because you did not obey the Lord your God and observe the commands and decrees he gave you. . . . *Because you did not serve the Lord your God joyfully and gladly in the time of prosperity,* therefore in hunger and thirst, in nakedness and dire poverty, you will serve the enemies the Lord sends against you. (Deut. 28:45-48)

You too can have the freedom of those prison workers in Soviet Russia. Christian women who voluntarily leave the home, refusing to serve the Lord "joyfully and gladly in the time of prosperity," are setting up the conditions for female enslavement in our own country. A generation who abused their privilege of homeworking by coffee klatsching and soap opera addiction begat a generation who is forsaking homeworking entirely.

God is not mocked. It's not our personal choice to decide whether a career or homeworking would be more fulfilling. It's our job to do what God *says*. And if we don't, he will punish. "The fear of the Lord is the beginning of wisdom" (Prov. 9:10).

Of Vines and Fig Trees

Let's turn from this dreary scene and see what Scripture has to say about the *ideal* economic order, and which fits better into it— homeworking, or meal halls and the ERA.

What happens when "the law will go out from Zion, the word of the Lord from Jerusalem?"

> Every man will sit under his own vine
>   and under his own fig tree,
> and no one will make them afraid,
>   for the Lord Almighty has spoken. (Mic. 4:4)

His own vine. *His* own fig tree. And no government program to take away his control over his own property. *The biblical economic ideal is self-sufficiency, not government control.*

Please understand that when I talk about self-sufficiency I don't mean that we don't have to depend on God. I mean that under God we are responsible for ourselves and able to take care of ourselves better than any government can.

More and more people today feel like life has gone out of control. They want to buy a house, but the price is out of sight. So they think of building a house, but then they must hire union laborers, get building permits, pass building codes, and so on, and the price is still out of sight. They'd be willing to live in even a mobile home, just to have a place of their own, but mobile homes are only allowed in sardinelike parks that are inconveniently situated outside the city. Or perhaps they'd like to start a little home business that turns out to be forbidden by the zoning regulations. Or perhaps they even just want to dry their laundry on a line out back instead of spending money on electricity to dry it in a machine, only to find that someone got a law passed forbidding that in their community. Laws have been passed in our area requiring that RV's be concealed from public view; that the grass in front lawns not exceed x inches; that no more than two children occupy one room, and no two of opposite sexes (which essentially makes it illegal for large families to own a house, except for the very rich). It seems like every time you turn around there is a new law restricting what used to be your freedom.

What we're seeing happen is self-sufficiency slowly being made illegal, while upper-class lifestyle is required. In housing this is particularly obvious, as the house you grew up in very likely would not pass a building inspection today, and the house your great-grandparents grew up in certainly would not. No indoor plumbing? No electricity? Outrageous! People shouldn't live like that . . . so we'll make sure they don't have the option to try it.

Since America is a democracy, this kind of thinking can only prevail if a majority of the voters are sold on it. By trying to make our families more self-reliant we are an inspiration to others, who then might be less inclined to support statist regulations restricting the use of our private property. The organic gardening movement, for example, has grown from a few lonely voices to millions. More and more people are discovering gardening, as they hear about the joy of gardening and taste their neighbor's fresh produce. As a result, the foolish regulations in some towns requiring grass in front of every house are being challenged. Because organic gardening depends among other things on an abundant supply of manure, organic gardeners tend to favor home raising of small livestock (rabbits, chickens, even goats). So the equally foolish regulations that forbid useful livestock in residential areas, while permitting large, noisy dogs, are also standing on increasingly shaky ground.

Homeworking is essentially independent and works against socialism. The homeworking wife's ultimate financial goal is to increase the family's self-sufficiency, as we saw in Proverbs 31. If she doesn't like store prices, she will make an item herself. If it is a luxury item, she has the character to do without it if necessary (young wives are supposed to be "self-controlled," Titus 2:4). Her labor and creativity buffer her family from whatever problems are agitating the country's economy. Also, by doing her job she protects everyone else from being drafted to do it for her.

God gave the woman to the man as his helper because he *needs* a helper. Two people doing exactly the same thing are both vulnerable to the same pressures. Two people doing different things in harmony can allocate their resources much more efficiently. This is what economists mean by "the division of labor." If the economy goes sour and wages aren't what they used to be, I can make pea soup and whole wheat bread instead of dishing up steak. On the other hand, if money is rolling into the house, as the household manager I can give more attention to managing it effectively for God than if I only had five minutes at the end of a weary day.

Homeworking and Home Business

I originally intended to present the case for home businesses in this chapter. It seems clear to me that the scriptural ideal is to be self-employed. It's OK to be a slave (or in more modern terms, an employee), but if you can get your freedom, you ought to (1 Cor. 7:21).

I still think home business is the ideal, but I don't have to say it anymore, because everyone else does. As Professor Drucker says,

> We have on our hands an entrepreneurial boom the like of which we have not seen in a century. The most important economic event of the last few years, in fact, is the emergence of this entrepreneurial trend. . . .
>
> Most of these 20 million additional jobs [started in the past decade] are in small, new enterprises.[11]

Extra Income magazine informs us that "More than 2 million Americans are home-based in their work."[12] This number is growing by leaps and bounds.

What is causing this new trend? I believe that God is having mercy on America. More and more women are beginning to see that day-care is *not* where they want their children, and they are starting businesses at home. Between 1972 and 1980, the female share of self-employment rose by 60 percent.[13] These ventures often become the family's business, liberating Daddy from the outside work force too.

Homeworking means *working* at home. We are not supposed to be the breadwinners—that's the man's job. But we *are* supposed to make an economic contribution. You probably *already* make more money for your family than you realize. Do you sew? That $15 of materials that you turned into a $100 creation saved much more than the $85 difference. I calculate that every dollar saved by a homeworking wife amounts to *three* earned, because you don't have to pay tax, tithe, day-care, transportation, and a whole host of other expenses on money you save. Do you bake whole wheat bread or make your own yogurt? The money saved on medical bills from proper nutrition is no small change, and the amount you save by cooking from scratch can also be quite substantial. It's not uncommon for a homeworking wife to save her family thousands of dollars a year on their food bills alone. And wives who teach their children at home instead of paying for Christian school can save $10,000 a year or more, depending on family size.

Homeworking goes beyond saving, through, to actually selling some item you create, or at least creating some items you *could* sell if you needed to. The ideal wife in Proverbs 31 sold sashes and linen garments. You could sell plants, or art, or piano lessons, or birthday cakes. I think it is wise to not enter a business where your customers rigidly determine your hours. Children and husband come first or it isn't homeworking at all. But wives need to be productive at home.

When women were stuck at home in the fifties with only their birth control pills and dishwashers for company, no wonder they went crazy! If God really wanted us to live that way, we could swallow our frustrations and do it. But since it was an abnormal lifestyle, frustration led to rebellion. When people abandon God's way, eventually their lifestyle collapses. Barrenness and idleness are no substitutes for fruitfulness and productivity. As Petie Maker, editor of *Extra Income,* says, lolling around reading trashy novels and munching bonbons begins to pall after awhile.[14] The answer? Not home-abandoning careerism, but home business!

How to start a home business? Step one is *character development*—more diligence, less frivolity. We need to relax, but not to spend hours in front of a TV. Step two is *child development.* A good manager takes the long-term view, and these are your trainees. Bright, cheerful assets are what every home business needs, not ill-tempered, destructive detriments. Step three is *skill development.* The library will give you ideas for a business. Look under "Business," "Management," "Entrepreneurship," and so on. Correspondence courses or apprenticeship to an older woman are preferred ways to gain a profitable skill. Institutional courses are expensive and take you out of the home.

Step four is *your husband's consent.* This could be Step One, but he's not likely to give his consent to a project you have not yet developed the character or the skill to bring off. All this requires is that he approve of your making money from something you are already doing for free (since you can only develop your skill through practice in producing the desired item for yourself, your family, and your friends). If your skill could be the beginning of a family business—like designing games that your husband could produce and sell—so much the better.

Step five is *complying with the law.* There are forms to fill out and fees to pay if you make any substantial amount of money from your work. Bernard Kamaroff's *Small Time Operator: How to Start Your Own Small Business, Keep Your Books, Pay Your Taxes and Stay Out of Trouble* will tell you what you need to know. It's available from Mother's Bookshelf (an arm of the *Mother Earth News*), 105 Stoney Mountain Road, Henderson, NC 28791 for less than $10.

Home business is not a way to get rich quick. But it *is* a way to stay free, for you, your family, and our country. Home business is part of busy-ness at home.

14   Art and the New Renaissance Woman

One very common objection to homeworking is that it is *dull.* Uncreative. Some would even say, ugly. That all-too-familiar picture of the lackluster housewife scrubbing listlessly at a stack of greasy dishes seems to stick in our minds.

But does homeworking really mean burying your talents?

In this chapter we will see how homeworking and art go hand in hand. Creativity and the personal dimension in life which is so missed today both flower in the home.

What Is Art?
I'm not going to answer this question. Experts have debated it for years, and no definition I come up with is likely to satisfy everyone. For our purposes I am just going to say that anything people design or create or arrange is art—whether it is good or bad, beautiful or very, very ugly.

Given this definition, it's convenient to break art down into two main categories, based on what seem to be the major scriptural uses of art. (There are other categories, but these are the ones I want to talk about.)

The first kind of art is statement, or mass, art. This art takes seriously the biblical injunction to "Have nothing to do with the fruitless deeds of darkness, but rather expose them" (Eph. 5:11). It is designed to make us aware of the fruit of wicked schemes which we are being asked to embrace or have been exploited by. It might poke fun at the inconsistencies of God's enemies. (Generally this art is not pretty.) Or it might tell us something about the human condition, either good or bad, to persuade us to act.

167

Heroic pictures (which expose evil by contrast) and straight exposés both fall in the category of statement art. In Reformation times, cartoons exposing the corrupt practices and doctrines of the Catholic hierarchy were an example of statement art. In our day a picture of a sad child staring through window bars after a mother who is heading out carrying a briefcase and wearing an "I Have It All" expression would be a useful statement. So would a film satire on feminism, or an architectural design for an inexpensive, livable house designed for children. A painting, sculpture, lithograph, or photograph of a mother and father enjoying the company of their six or seven children would also make a positive statement. (I am *so* sick of the endless book jackets, billboards, and cereal boxes where "family" is represented by Mom and Pop and two kids!)

Statement art is not necessarily overt propaganda, although it can be that. It can simply arise out of the artist's desire to say something that matters to him or her. Harlan Ellison, the science fiction writer, put this well in a speech he gave to a group of us sci-fi fans in my college when he said that an *author* writes because he likes to see his name on a book jacket, but a *writer* writes because he *must*. Statement art, in the hands of a real writer (or painter, or film-maker), is the outpouring of his insides—the "fire in his bones." For an author, it is self-seeking propaganda; he goes looking for a parade and *then* makes up his posters.

Statement art is mass art because it is designed to teach and influence *groups* of people, whether for "pure" motives or false. This art is, of course, not confined to painting: music, poetry, prose, sculpture, film, even architecture can all make a statement.

The second kind of art I call domestic, or personal, art. The Bible tells us, "Whatever is true, whatever is noble, whatever is right, whatever is pure, whatever is lovely, whatever is admirable—if anything is excellent or praiseworthy—think about such things" (Phil. 4:8). Domestic art is the daily art we keep before us to train our minds on the excellent and lovely.

Although the forms are fluid, and various works flow back and forth between them, in general statement art is what you see in museums and art galleries and in the mass media. Domestic art is for the home.

Soul Food

Domestic art is homeworker's art. It is our job to purchase and create art which makes the home environment an uplifting place to be. In order for us to "think about such things" as are true, noble, right, pure, lovely, and admirable, it helps to keep them before our eyes, ears, noses, tongues, and skin. Lovely sights, tastes, textures, sounds, and smells help us keep our vision of the world as it *should* be, and fortify us to take on the ugliness in the world outside.

One biblical example of a domestic artist is the ideal wife in Proverbs 31, who made coverings for her bed and lovely garments for her family. Back in my Socialist days this bothered me a lot. How could the Bible justify wasting extra effort and materials on items that have no *practical* reason to be beautiful? Now I know. Beauty *is* practical. It is soul food that both *relieves the stresses and strains* of this fallen world, allowing us to function better, and *refreshes those with whom we share it.*

Mary, the sister of Lazarus, shared the beautiful smell and feel of her precious ointment with Jesus, an act for which he commended her, overruling Judas' self-righteous insistence that the perfume should have been sold and the money given to the poor (John 12: 1-8). Elisha, when troubled in spirit, listened to beautiful music until he was calm enough to prophesy (2 Kings 3:14, 15). These biblical incidents show us the value of beauty in a person's life. And not mass-produced, supermarket-style "beauty" either, but *personal* beauty.

Edith Schaeffer, in her excellent book *Hidden Art,* which I hope you will buy, has chapters on music, painting, sketching and sculpting, interior decoration, gardens and gardening, flower arrangement, food, writing, drama, creative recreation, clothing, personal relationships, and environment. These are all areas where domestic art is desperately needed.

People today are hungry—really hungry—for personal contact with another human being who cares about them. Love means sharing with them, as we will see in another chapter, and domestic art makes that sharing beautiful.

Becoming an Artist

I am going to suggest that *praising God* through *serving people* is the only reason for domestic art. That may not sound very radical, until you look at the insides of most homes today.

The American home is being pulled in two nonbiblical ways. One is to become a mere *refueling stop.* Some authorities predict this; others consider it a *fait accompli* and almost rejoice in it. Says one such authority:

The home will become a filling station for people's needs, a place where parents and children can come and go and have their wants met, without having to depend so much on each other. It'll be a different lifestyle than in the past, but it won't necessarily mean that families are disintegrating.[1]

Obviously, such an environment does not boost art. Art does not thrive in gas stations.

The other nonbiblical direction home environments have taken is to become *shrines of materialism*. Look at any house-beautiful type of magazine and you will see what I mean. Read two or three of those, and one gets a suffocating feeling. So much thought is invested in making the house "perfect"; but where is the room for *people?* Page after page of flawless decorating schemes are systematically designed to exclude human beings, who become the jarring note in those monuments to perfect taste.

Seen against this background, domestic art as a service to *people* seems almost revolutionary. Messy beings who track in mud and smoke cigarettes are going to invade our domiciles, not just to settle for a moment and fly away, but to be refreshed. We are going to deliberately serve them, not so we can have the glory of exposing others to our marvelous decorating schemes, but out of love. What an amazing contrast to the whole spirit of feminism, which regards all uncompensated service done for others as "slavery"!

Art at the Sink
Let's get back to that sinkful of dirty dishes we started the chapter with. Feminists think housework, symbolized by dishwashing, is demeaning for a talented woman. I prefer to think of it as art. Is a sinkful of dirty dishes, after all, more beautiful than a cupboard full of clean ones? Because of our modern revolt against housework, doormats and aprons featuring the slogan "Dull Women Have Spotless Homes" have become popular. But are clean floors a proof of dullness, or of someone's desire to not be overcome by ugliness in her personal environment?

The TV show "Mary Hartman, Mary Hartman" satirized housewives who are interested in learning how to keep floors cleaner or brew a better cup of coffee. Supposedly such interests betray a narrow, ignorant mind. I would like to say that it befits *anyone* to learn to be excellent at all aspects of her profession, and that includes cleaning floors and brewing coffee. Careerists can only afford to ignore these things because they hire someone else, or train hubby to do it. Nobody *wants* a dirty floor, after all!

Beyond the Sink

But domestic art goes far beyond the sink. I am always amazed at how talented my homeworking friends are. Prudence, for example, is a first violin in the St. Louis Philharmonic. Martha is an artist. Sue makes marvelous creations out of dough. Other women cook beautifully, or sew lovely clothes. Some have beautifully laid out gardens. I don't know how my downstairs neighbor Christine does it, as a single mother with four children and no money, but her children are always clean and cheerful and her place is always friendly, clean, and inviting.

Homeworking wives have the time to *make* things. As a fundamental fact of life, careerists don't. They must rely on store-bought goods. Hence those perfect, plastic home environments with the abstract art painting bought at a department store hung over the mantelpiece. It's not that careerists don't like beauty too. But they are forced to either buy it or go without. And since careerism is the opposite of giving oneself to people, often the environments they create reflect that fact.

Uncreative? Homeworking wives play musical instruments, practice art of many different kinds, create new clothing designs and food recipes, decorate the house, garden, teach their children. Think of the farm wife of old, with her quilting and canning, her rag rugs and homemade clothes, if you want to see an artist at work. Reproductions of this "authentic, primitive" art can bring a very good price, as our generation vainly scrambles to grab a handful of the beauty of the past.

The New Renaissance Woman

I believe the homeworking wife is the new Renaissance woman. The Renaissance man, if you recall, was interested in everything. Leonardo da Vinci, for example, was a great painter, an outstanding mathematician, an anatomist, and a philosopher. Today's business world has whittled down a person's achievement opportunities into a narrow specialization. Specialization isn't bad; it's part of the division of labor which God instituted in Eden. But it needs a counterbalance, which the home provides. At home a woman has the opportunity to try her hand at anything that interests her, from making laboratory slides of the drinking water to building a room on the house to writing a book. I must say personally that my interests and abilities have expanded tenfold since I left engineering and began homeworking, and seem likely to continue expanding in the future. In the "economic-opportunity sphere" I would never have had an opportunity to pursue such diverse interests as education, architecture, economics, calligraphy, poetry, writing, clothes design, gardening theory and practice, piano teaching, and so forth, all at the same time. But at home I am being broadened almost without limit. Each new interest leads to another. I am finally beginning to see why Edith Schaeffer talks so much about the problem of being finite, as for the first time in my life I have more interesting and useful projects than I can do.

Is beauty a potted plant in the executive suite or a lovingly tended garden? Is it a TV dinner or delightfully fragrant loaves of homemade whole wheat bread? Is it canned Muzak or Mommy teaching her boys how to sing the Psalms? You tell me, and then tell me if art flowers in the home.

15 The Times, They Are A-Changing

One of my favorite pastimes as a youngster was reading science fiction. After school I would head for the library and take out every book I could find with the familiar rocket logo on the spine. Those were the days of heroes who cruised far-flung galaxies, meeting and defeating every obstacle from nefarious alien empires to the Law of Entropy. Sometimes the hero got married; more often he didn't. But if the hero had a wife, or if the book featured a couple with children, at least 50 percent of the time the wife was a homeworker. It didn't trouble the sci-fi writers of those days to place homeworkers in the middle of their most technological scenarios.

Then society began shifting its values to feminism and "alternative lifestyles," and along came a new wave of science fiction. Suddenly every woman was childless and sexually available. The genre's unwritten code began to specify women holding the same kind of jobs as men. Every female now was a potential "Star Trek" crewperson, and nobody was a mommy.

The Rumors of Our Death

As our lives move ever closer to the technological achievements of "Star Trek," and away from the Middle Eastern shepherding and farming culture portrayed in the Bible, many people have come to believe that homeworking is dead, extinct, passé. Not only homeworking, but *all* the Bible's rules for human behavior are being challenged by those who see biblical commands as "irrelevant" to today's society. Some glory in what they see as the inevitable extinction of biblical culture, like the self-confessed witch Naomi Goldenberg, a psychologist of religion, who says,

173

All feminists are making the world less and less like the one described in the Bible and are thus helping to lessen the influence of Christ and Yahweh on humanity. . . .

"God is going to change," I thought. "We women are going to bring an end to God. As we take positions in government, in medicine, in law, in business, in the arts and finally, in religion, we will be the end of Him. We will change the world so much that He won't fit in anymore."

I found this line of thought most satisfying.[1]

Others, like the traditional Catholic scholar Stephen Clark, gently bemoan the passing of a truly biblical role for women. While realizing that in scriptural times "there was a sense in which, occupationally speaking, 'the woman's place was in the home,' " Mr. Clark goes on to say,

On the other hand, however, the home was then a far different place than it is now, and it fulfilled many economic and social welfare functions that it no longer fulfills today.

A significant change has occurred in traditional family functions, with the result that the majority of a woman's traditional tasks (economic, social welfare, educational) for the most part no longer occur at home.[2]

Mr. Clark does realize that

As a Christian community develops, more of these important activities might return to their traditional place in the home.

But he sees us locked into semifeminist roles by modern technology:

Yet, short of a complete withdrawal of the Christian community from most modern social institutions, there will always be a significant need in technological society for women to work outside the home. . . .

For women to remain home under these circumstances would leave them underemployed and, in addition, underrepresented in some of the most vital areas of modern society.[3]

No matter how wonderful homeworking is as an ideal, or how scriptural, if women believe it is impossible, they will not try it. Stephen

Clark echoes a widespread belief that the kind of lifestyle the Bible commands, and that this book tries to picture, is impossible in modern technological society.

But is it?

The Myth of the Helpless Consumer

I am always tempted, when discussing the difficulties Christians face in modern society, to launch into a brimstone-and-fire routine, reminding myself and everyone else within earshot that Christians are supposed to *make* history, not just *react* to it! I am tempted to shout that if our modern society prevents us from obeying God, we will just have to change it, or else! But actually we don't need a call to revolution as much as we need to be taught to make use of what we already have. *Technology, you see, does not hinder homeworking. In fact, technology can be harnessed to aid it.*

As a former engineer and computer systems specialist, I am constantly amazed at how helpless people feel about technology. Parents worry, for example, about video games enslaving their children and about the ill effect television is having on their youngsters. "Modern life is so difficult for young people," they complain. Yet it never occurs to them to *pull the plug!* TV sets don't run themselves; they need electricity, willingly supplied by the customer who connects them to a power source. Video games require not only electricity, but an unfailing supply of quarters and dimes to keep on playing. Both the on-off switch and the money supply are in the control of *people.*

We are not the helpless victims of technology, but its masters. The movie *2001: A Space Odyssey* graphically illustrates this point. Hal, the overintelligent computer who runs the spaceship, starts developing a quirky personality, and goes so far as to try to murder his human crew. But the hero gets to the power source and unplugs Hal's brain. (The movie's mistake is in having Hal be intelligent enough to plan and carry out a scheme in the first place. It is mathematically impossible, as my computer professors kept proving to us in engineering school, for an electronic computer to think.)

If our present technology does not *promote* homeworking, neither can it *prevent* it.

Making the Old Ways Better

People say we can't go back to the old ways. The Bible says we *must* go back to the old ways, and technology says that we can make the old ways better!

Take gardening, for instance. Early in this century, technology was developed that produced inorganic fertilizers, chemical pesticides, and huge farm machinery. Many said this was the only way for the land to produce food—"the old ways were gone." But in 1941 J. I. Rodale moved onto sixty-three acres of eroded Pennsylvania land determined to prove them wrong. He began using old-fashioned farming methods, in the face of much skepticism and scorn. But he and his sons did it smarter and better than the old-style farmers. Today the 305-acre Rodale Research Center is just part of an organic gardening empire which includes (among other things) the 1.3 million-reader *Organic Gardening* magazine, several other magazines, and several book clubs.

Modern organic gardeners have gone back to the *philosophy* of old-fashioned farming, but not to its outmoded and inefficient *tools*. Thus the June 1984 issue of *Organic Gardening* (to pick an issue at random) contains ads for

a small diesel tractor
several types of powered tillers
"the world's first aluminum greenhouse"
a portable power sprayer
a power chipper-shredder for making compost scraps
plastic irrigation systems
factory-produced peat pots
steel-core garden stakes
laboratory-produced pest diseases, for biological insect control
an electric garden tractor specially designed for older or handi-
    capped gardeners,
and a home well-drilling kit.

Readers can buy a woven polypropylene net to block garden weeds, a special polypropylene tape that scares birds with vibrations, and black or clear plastic mulch. And of course gardening researchers are feverishly hybridizing strains of disease-resistant, better-producing vegetables and fruits while other researchers labor on new methods of natural insect control, compost production, irrigation, and you name it.

You don't have to be an organic gardener to admit that plastic seed-sowers which drop one miniscule lettuce seed at the click of a thumb-press make it easier than sowing said seeds by hand, or that Garden Way carts are superior to unwieldy wheelbarrows. Technology can and does make "old-fashioned" gardening *easier.*

Organic gardeners don't *have* to use all the innovative new technology—they could use old-fashioned tools as well as old-fashioned methods. But they *like* to use it; so there is a burgeoning market for "organic technology." If the demand for compost exceeds the demand for N-P-K chemical fertilizers (which it might some day), modern inorganic farming will become the "old" way! Technology flows to whoever is willing to pay for it. Technology alone does not dictate our future.

In the same way, technology can be home-based as easily as office-based or government-based. Microwave ovens, vacuum cleaners, food processors, water distillers, refrigerators, sewing machines, washing machines, and so on all testify to producers' willingness to supply homeworkers with modern technology. Again, none of this technology is *necessary;* but it *is* technology. If we stop seeing homeworking as maid work, but rather as a ministry to people, these tools will no longer masquerade as a threat to our work.

Technology only cripples us when it is (1) monopolistic, and (2) mandatory. When every new house *must* contain a certain amount of copper plumbing, this reduces one's freedom to build cheaply. When hopeful home-builders are allowed to substitute plastic pipe for copper, that relieves their wallets slightly, but they still are tied to the cost of an entire plumbing system. If we are forced to use a certain technology (like copper plumbing), that binds us by *monopoly.* If we are forced to meet outside standards, but allowed to choose how we will meet them (like the choice between plastic or copper plumbing), then the rope that binds us is the *mandatory* standard. Following our example, if we were not by law required to build houses that conform to someone's high-tech standard of living, we would be freer. Most people would still put in conventional plumbing; some would choose the equally high-tech option of modern composting toilets; others would choose the low-tech privy.

Where technology is not stifled by monopolistic or mandatory standards, it tends to conform to the individual user. Take television, for instance. First there was ABC, CBS, and NBC. Then there was UHF, with its reruns and late-late shows. Then there was cable. Now, with the advent of the video cassette recorder (VCR), television is almost in the hands of the people. With a VCR you can not only record TV programs to be viewed when *you* want to see them (in itself, no small gain, as it frees viewers from enslavement to a TV schedule), but you also can view programs *specifically designed* for home viewing. Ultimately you might be able to buy just the programs you want, whether entertainment, travelogue, talk show, or whatever, and dispense entirely with the channel knob. At that point I might consider buying a TV. TV tech would have arrived at the ultimate technology has to offer: individual selection.

Technology *can* make more possible for more people in more places—if that's what the people want.

Plastic Woman and the Law

Repressive laws *can* be enacted which prevent us from producing or buying home-based tech. Feminists are constantly pressing for such legislation. But they wanted many of the same things back in 1890 and never got them then. If they succeed in oppressing homeworkers legally, the difference is not technology (telephones, TV sets, personal computers), but *the moral climate of the country.* In 1890 there was more of a Christian consensus than there is today.

It could be argued that technology has *produced* feminism, and to that extent made homeworking difficult. With this I would agree. Feminism on a large scale has only become possible since the invention of effective birth control and abortion methods. However, *technology only sells if people want it.* If nobody *wanted* birth control and abortion, Upjohn Company wouldn't be trying to get a home abortion kit on the market. If people still felt about abortion today the way they used to 100 years ago (with disgust and abhorrence similar to the way people now feel about offshore oil spills), technology for producing abortions would meet with no more favor than technology for producing oil spills. Nobody has applied for a patent for a device to clog up oil rigs, whereas much effort and money has been expended to try to make offshore oil drilling spill-free.

Where Are We Going?

Let me turn the question around. Since homeworking is not widely practiced today, *could this be an area in which Christians are called to lead?* Since when, I ask, have Christians ever been called to accept the status quo of a pagan society? We are salt in the midst of corruption, light in the surrounding darkness, sheep among wolves, a lily among thorns. Such are the scriptural metaphors for Christians in the world; not one suggests we are meant to blend in.

I personally believe that there already are many fine Christian women who are never interviewed by the evangelical media or asked to speak at women's meetings, who are nevertheless already leading the way back to homeworking. For, in fact, our modern technological society is starting to take tentative steps back home. As Peter Drucker says,

> We are deinstitutionalizing. You see it in hospitals, where clinics now perform outpatient surgery. You see it in education, where the

huge consolidated high school is being judged a failure. And you see it in business, where the spotlight is shifting toward the smaller unit.[4]

I might add, you see it in home schooling, which according to the late Mary Bergman, a pioneer in the movement, is at least 90 percent composed of Christians. There are an estimated one million home school families, and the movement is growing daily.[5] You see it in the small-group movement in Christian churches. You see it most in the children. Babies are popping out all over, the pent-up result of a generation that is sick of planned barrenhood. There is a growing swell of home-based technology, too.

Home-Based Tech

Let's look for a minute at the personal computer, the symbol of the eighties. Did you ever stop to think how strange it is that the computer, a technological device which everyone expected to remain the sole property of massive corporations, has become available to Everyman? This particular technology has been tamed and brought home, for no other reason than that *people wanted it there*.

Believe it or not, the personal computer may help to bring back home-based living on an unprecedented scale.

According to Dr. Jack Nilles, a telecommunications expert at the University of Southern California's Center for Futures Research, 15 to 20 percent of all "knowledge workers" will be telecommuters by 1990. . . .

Just as it matters very little whether this writer produces columns at home or at a newspaper, the trend from paper to electronic media for the storage and transmission of information means that millions of clerical workers . . . can work at home. So can thousands of engineers, programmers, consultants, and others who work primarily with "information." Indeed, Nilles expects that home telecommuting will grow as workers *demand* it.[6]

Major futurists Alvin Toffler and John Naisbitt have both predicted that home computers will encourage an at least partial return to home schooling.[7] Since public opinion is molded by these predictions, making them in some sense self-fulfilling prophecies, we may very well see a return to the home *caused by* high technology that makes it easy to do things at home which since the Industrial Revolution were done in outside institutions.

Let's pursue this a little further. We now can do more things at home, with greater ease, than in ages past when homemaking was in vogue. Food can be sliced in a food processor, twirled in a blender, cooked in a microwave, and perhaps even graced with a swirl of freshly whipped cream from one's personal compressed-air dispenser. With a small-to-medium capital investment, more varieties of food can be prepared at home in less time than ever before. Does *this* technology make homeworking obsolete?

If there is an economic demand for home-tech items, someone will produce them. As home schooling is becoming a viable movement (in our area, an *exploding* movement) more and better curricula, books, games, and so on are now available that cater to home schooling parents. And the more parents who teach children at home, the harder it is for legislators to forbid it.

Homeworking creates its own market, as we have seen. Homeworking also does not depend for its lifeblood on technology that can be withdrawn, as careerism does. Wives were homeworkers *before* the Pill, the automobile, and the factory. Nor are homeworkers the victims of technology. We can always exercise veto power—pull the plug, learn to live without. Moreover, homeworking creates its own movement. The more women there are who homework, the more feasible it seems to others.

Stephen Clark in his book *Man and Woman in Christ* painstakingly lays down guidelines for

> the establishment or restoration of a Christian social structure within which the scriptural teaching on men's and women's roles can be lived.

He then admits that

> One reasonable response to these guidelines is the question: Is this approach really feasible?

That is the question we have been discussing. Homeworking is scripturally required—it is also feasible. But there is one more side to the question, which Mr. Clark goes on to reveal.

> Though it is admittedly very difficult to restore a fabric of Christian social relationships in a contemporary technological society, it is

still possible in most places. However, another way of raising the question reveals the heart of the issue: *How long can Christians in contemporary society continue to survive with any genuine faithfulness to Christian teaching if they do not create a new social structure?*[8] (emphasis mine)

Homeworking will not usher in the Millennium, but it will change society. And if homeworkers don't reconstruct society, the feminists will. The technology we will produce, and how we will use it, will be decided by the life we choose.

Technology as a tool for homeworking? Yes. In the next section, we will look at home as a "center of care and service" (Mr. Clark's phrase) and see how technology can actually enhance it.

Part Five:

FORWARD TO MINISTRY

"... train the younger women ... to be kind, and to be subject to their husbands ..." (Titus 2:4, 5)

16   Charity Belongs at Home

Little children growing up in pretelevision America had a whole folk culture of their own. There were special games and special sayings, passed from child to child. (What grown-up ever taught a boy or girl to play Engine, Engine Number Nine?) This folk culture was enriched by the wise sayings of one's parents, which they themselves had learned from their parents before them.

Such a saying is, "Charity begins at home."

When I was young, even though TV had exploded into every house, parents still told their sons and daughters that charity began at home. Those were the days before the Great Society and the War on Poverty, before it was discovered that charity begins in Washington. Americans had not yet learned to be ashamed of taking care of their families *first*, and *then* branching out to help other people. We did not yet feel responsible for solving the entire world's problems before solving our own.

But the family is now out of the running when it comes to charity. Private, personal charity has in our generation largely been replaced by institutions whose professional job it is to do good. The home is now seen as merely a channel of money for these professionals ("If you can't go yourself, at least give").

Coincidentally, the family now ranks seventeenth in the list of "Institutions That Affect The Nation," compiled by *U.S. News and World Report*. The family follows *after* government, television, federal bureaucracy, newspapers, advertising, and even public opinion polls in the thinking of those who responded to the survey![1]

In this chapter I'd like to take a look at the individual family's role in caring for and serving others, and particularly the homeworker's role as a servant to the needy. Is charitable ministry really just for those without outside careers in the "helping" fields, or is it for all wives? Does God have a ministry here for you and me?

Kindness and Respect

The passage we are studying in this book, Titus 2:4, 5, after saying that young wives should be trained to be homeworkers goes on to say we should be "kind." The word the NIV translates "kind" is *agathos*, a very common word in the New Testament, which is normally translated to mean "good." The Epistle to Titus, which we are studying, places great stress on good deeds, using both *agathos* and a similar word, *kalos*. An elder "loves what is good" (1:8, *agathos*). The rebellious people whose wicked lifestyle and doctrine Paul wrote the epistle to correct are "unfit for doing anything good" (1:16, *agathos*). Older women must "teach what is good" (2:3, *kalos*). Titus must set the younger men an example "by doing what is good" (2:7, *kalos*). Paul reminds us that Jesus Christ died to redeem a people who are "eager to do what is good" (2:14, *kalos*). Christians in general should "be ready to do whatever is good" (3:1, *agathos*). Those who trust in God must be "careful to devote themselves to doing what is good" (3:8, *kalos*). Finally Paul tells Titus, "Our people must learn to devote themselves to doing what is good" (3:14, *kalos*).

Agathos, as used in Titus 2:5 (where Paul says younger women should be trained to be kind), means more than good. It means "benevolent, kind, generous" (Thayer's *Greek Lexicon*). It means being the kind of woman who goes out of her way for others, who serves others, who lays down her life for others.

Feminists, evangelical or otherwise, have a real problem with the idea of serving others. Their entire position depends on the idea that servitude to others is "slavery," and if a woman enters into such service voluntarily she must be "brainwashed." This in turn rests on a massive inferiority complex—that only positions of "power" over others are worthwhile. Women have to grab for a hunk of masculine "power" in order not to feel left out.

So Scanzoni and Hardesty say,

> What are the basic issues of women's liberation? Do women want to become men? No, we simply want to be full human beings. In the minds of many, however, only men are human—women are their female relatives. Only men can participate in the full range of earth's activities—women have a "proper feminine sphere."[2]

Actually men can't participate in the "full range of earth's activities" either, since a proper masculine sphere does not include childbearing or breastfeeding. But Scanzoni and Hardesty, like others before them, are thinking in terms of power and respect—about being "full human beings" who nobody will put down. Their answer? Compete with men. *Force* them to show respect.

The Bible says wives are entitled to respect. But it gives entirely different reasons. First, our husbands should respect us because we are *weaker* than them (1 Pet. 3:7). I don't think this is so much a reference to muscular weakness—some women are pretty strong and their husbands are pretty scrawny—as it is to our need of support as the "vessel" that bears the stress and strain of carrying children into the world. Husbands should respect our role, and not disdain our feminine contribution because it is different from theirs. Second, we gain respect through our *kindness*. "A kindhearted woman gains respect," says Proverbs 11:16, whereas "ruthless men gain only wealth." (Men have no monopoly on respect, either!) Romans 5:7 tells us that though "Very rarely will anyone die for a righteous man," yet "for a good man someone might possibly dare to die." The word "good" here is *agathos* and refers to a benefactor, a kind person who has helped you. For a kind woman, someone might risk death—the ultimate sign of respect.

Wives are entitled to respect; God says so. But that respect is based on our *role* as the "weaker vessel" and on our *kindness*. Respect is not something we fight for; it is something we earn.

We are getting a pretty good idea of our biblical role. But what does it mean for a young wife to be "kind"? First Timothy 5:10 gives the answer. This verse lists the qualifications required of a widow before she would be put on the list of those authorized to serve the church and receive its support. She had to be "well-known for her good deeds [*kalos*], such as bringing up children, showing hospitality, washing the feet of the saints, helping those in trouble and devoting herself to all kinds of good deeds [*agathos*]."

Any woman who didn't meet those qualifications was not considered worthy of church support. Think about that for a minute. The verse strongly implies that any Christian wife worthy of the name would get a reputation for doing the above-mentioned good deeds. For a widow to be known for these good deeds at the age of sixty (when she was eligible to be considered for church support) she must have been doing them when she was young. And by these acts of kindness, she earned the respect and support of the church.

So let's take a closer look at the good deeds that separate the wheat from the chaff.

Bringing Up Children

The first good deed on the list is "bringing up children." Paul wasn't talking about merely handing children over to a day-care center either. The Greek word he used has overtones of cherishing, of nurture, of personal attention.

So right at the start God wants us to be sure that charity begins with our own families. Good deeds done inside the home count as much as good deeds done outside. In fact, they must come first. Our families have to be strong and healthy before we can invite others into them with profit.

Showing Hospitality

Hospitality is *house*-pitality. It means sharing your family life with another person. This can be as simple as a friendly meal together, or as big a commitment as Priscilla and Aquila taking in the Apostle Paul while he was in Corinth.

The Bible really stresses hospitality to our fellow-Christians who for some reason are lonely or in need. "Offer hospitality *to one another,*" says Peter (1 Pet. 4:9). Some consider good deeds done for our fellow-Christians unimportant since they are already saved, and believe all our efforts should be thrown into outreach. The Bible, however, puts fellow-believers immediately after one's own family in the order of priorities: "Therefore, as we have opportunity, let us do good to all people, *especially to those who belong to the family of believers*" (Gal. 6:10).

Hospitality to our needy fellow-Christians is Step One in convincing the world that Christianity is for real. Jesus said, "All men will know that you are my disciples if you love *one another*" (John 13:35).

Hospitality to our fellow-believers is not necessarily smug coffee klatsching, either. The word for "showing hospitality" comes from the root *xenos,* which means "stranger." "God sets the lonely in families" (Psa. 68:6). Christian hospitality means inviting poor, blind, lame, and otherwise needy believers to our feasts, not just those who are already our bosom pals (Luke 14:13, 14). By showing hospitality to our fellow-Christians, who God has commanded to love us, we get the training and confidence we need to successfully minister to non-Christians in their difficult circumstances.

And in some special way we are inviting Jesus over when we invite one of his needy brothers. When the Judgment comes,

The King will say to those on his right, "Come, you who are blessed by my Father; take your inheritance, the kingdom prepared for you since the creation of the world. For I was hungry and you gave me something to eat, I was thirsty and you gave me something to drink, I was a stranger and you invited me in." . . . Then the righteous will answer him, "Lord, when did we see you hungry and feed you, or thirsty and give you something to drink? When did we see you a stranger and invite you in. . . ?" The King will reply, "I tell you the truth, whatever you did for one of the least of *these brothers of mine,* you did for me." (Matt. 25:34-40)

Personal Comfort in an Impersonal World
Homeworking wives have a monopoly on a highly prized commodity—*personal hospitality.* This is how one woman's homeworking mother shows kindness in an increasingly impersonal world:

> When I come home there is always one of my mother's flower arrangements about. . . . The house is neat, almost always, and the kitchen generally has evidence of the beginnings of the next meal—something thawing in the sink, simmering on the stove, or marinating in the refrigerator.
>
> The sheets in my old bedroom are turned down and some additional comfort like a nightgown on the pillow or a turned-on electric blanket has been added for the night. . . .
>
> My mother sets the stage for talk better than anyone I know. If there has been anything visibly wrong with me before the all-important "talk," my mother has already set her arsenal of Vaseline Intensive Care, Amino-Pon, Aloe Vera plants, Neosporin and Vitamin B complex to work. She sends me to bed with a kiss and 60 recorded minutes of a waterfall.
>
> In my parents' house, I feel good the minute I walk in the door.[3]

As Linda Burton began, inspired by her mother's example, to make the extra effort to create a hospitable home she

> began to notice that when the table was nicely set, when fresh flowers were out and centerpieces completed, everyone's voice level would sink to half and people who ordinarily only argued together would make a special extra effort to be sensitive and conciliatory. When my immediate environment comforted me and responded to my individual needs, I was able to function at my very best.[4]

Linda Burton is not speaking from an explicitly Christian viewpoint. She doesn't have to. *Everyone* needs hospitality! Christians and non-Christians alike will respond to this ministry. As Mrs. Burton says,

> More than anything else, I think this is the secret of successful homemaking: creating a place that makes people feel good. And that is the reason I think the work is so rewarding. It means creating a home where people will want to talk with each other; where they will want to linger over dinner; where they will want to snuggle up with a quilt or a book on a rainy day instead of escaping to the shopping mall. . . .
>
> There is not much, after all, that lies between us and the complete indifference of the rest of the universe—other than our family, our friends, and our homes.[5]

Homeworkers who *love* their husbands and children, instead of trying to escape into a career or becoming gadabouts, are building the precious resource of a home where people will be attracted to the Lord, and where the hurts of God's people can be healed and they can find new strength. We build up our homes not just for ourselves, not even just for our families, but for the church, and after that for the world.

Getting Dirty for God

The next item on the young wife's list of good deeds is "washing the feet of the saints." What does it mean for a young wife to wash the feet of the saints in twentieth-century America?

First, foot-washing is part of hospitality. When a Middle Eastern hostess of New Testament times greeted a guest, she offered him water to wash his feet. Jesus took this one step farther, by washing his disciples' feet himself. Following his example, we invite our fellow-Christians over to serve them, as I already mentioned.

Secondly, foot-washing stands for *all dirty work done for our fellow-Christians.* Thus we remember that ministry is not all glamour, and we should not expect it to be. Those who stress "women as ministers" have contempt for our humble work at home simply because it *is* humble. However, ministry that doesn't include foot-washing is mere pride and arrogance. As Jesus said, "The greatest among you will be your servant. For whoever exalts himself will be humbled, and whoever humbles himself will be exalted" (Matt. 23: 11, 12).

Even the most exciting, world-shaking ministries are based on hard, dirty work. Edith Schaeffer, who together with her husband Francis founded the L'Abri ministry, says of their early days,

> Life wasn't easy by any means. There seemed to be constant stacks of dishes to wash, a tremendous succession of meals to prepare, endless sheets to hang out, countless letters to write, hours on end of conversation which took precedence over all other work—because these were people sent to us for a purpose. . . .
>
> Sometimes when difficult times are being lived through it seems as though the difficulties are simply too mundane to be the least bit worthwhile. Martyrs being tortured or persecuted for their faith at least sounds dramatic. Having to cook, serve meals to two sittings at times without ever sitting down to eat in between yourself, having constantly to clean up spilled and broken things, to empty mounds of garbage, and to scrub a stove that things have boiled over on, or an oven in which things have spilled over and baked to a black crust is neither dramatic or glamorous! . . . The Lord was sending people and amazing things were "springing forth," but the prayer answers brought with them the need to be willing to accept *all* that the answers meant, in the way of work, as well as excitement.[6]

I feel certain that Mrs. Schaeffer could never have handled the L'Abri ministry if she had not first gone through the midnight feedings, the cooking, cleaning, and picking up spills with her own children. L'Abri was and is family life intensified and shared with seeking non-Christians and hurting Christians. It also just happens to be a ministry that has influenced millions of people and led thousands to the Lord.

Homeworking is more than a dirty chore. It is a ministry. Humble, yes. But she who humbles herself *will* be exalted.

Sociable Security

Moving on to the next good deed, we come to "helping those in trouble." The great Greek scholar A. T. Robertson defines this phrase as "relieving the afflicted . . . to give sufficient aid."[7] The word "to help" is only used twice in the Bible: in this list of good deeds, and six verses later when Paul tells young women to "help" the widows in their families so the church can devote its funds to helping widows who have no possible source of support (1 Tim. 5:16). So its most obvious meaning is *taking care of dependent relatives*.

But Americans increasingly expect government to do this job. Temple University demographer Joseph McFalls remarks, "It's really not so unusual for one institution, such as the family, to give up some of its functions to another, such as the government. Families used to be responsible for the education of children and the care of the aged; the government does both now."[8] He uses this argument to justify possible future government intervention in the area of reproduction: test-tube babies, surrogate mothers, financial rewards (or penalties) for childbearing. This summarizes the situation neatly. The family has given up three of its God-given jobs: motherhood, education, and care of the aged. Now it's time to think about taking them back.

We've already looked at the importance of motherhood and of parents personally controlling their children's education. Homeworking has been debased because women have been cut out of these areas. What about the care of the aged or other dependent relatives? Can we do this? *Should* we do this?

To answer the question, "Can we do this?" let's return to the example of a woman who has. Edith Schaeffer had a daughter with chronic rheumatic fever, and a son with polio, both of whom she cared for personally. Sometimes visitors got sick; sometimes even her helpers got sick, and she had to nurse them. Then for years Dr. Schaeffer's aged mother lived with them. Mrs. Schaeffer literally nursed her mother-in-law back to life after the doctors had given her only a brief time to live. Dr. Schaeffer developed cancer in his old age, and again Mrs. Schaeffer helped relieve his pain by her ministrations.

When the time came for Dr. Schaeffer to die, Mrs. Schaeffer and her children brought him home. Dr. Schaeffer, like so many of us, didn't want to die in a noisy, neon-lit intensive care unit, sedated to the point of imbecility. He got his wish. The family made up a bed for him in the living room, where he could look out the front window and see the sky, and nursed him themselves in his last days. He died right there, in front of his own fireplace, in the arms of his wife.

Could you do this? Could I do this? Edith Schaeffer *did* do this, and she had (and has) a worldwide ministry too.

Or, if Edith Schaeffer seems like too hard an act to follow, how about my friend Peggy? Peggy is the mother of four healthy sons and a daughter with Down's syndrome. Back when Jennifer was born, doctors were still telling mothers to put their Down's syndrome babies in an institution because they were "bound to be vegetables for life." Disregarding this august advice, Peggy began developing her own therapy program for Jennifer. Jennifer is now in the sixth grade in a "normal" classroom at the age of thirteen, can read and write, and leads her class in Bible memory work! Peggy's mother also lives with her, confined to a wheelchair from which Peggy must lift her to her bed, to the toilet, to her chair, and so on. Peggy is active in her church, extends hospitality to all who show the slightest signs of needing it (including me on occasion!), and is the ever-willing grandmother of a flock of beautiful young girls.

God intends that children should care for their parents when the parents grow old and feeble. Jesus sharply rebuked the Pharisees for trying to wiggle out of this duty (Matt. 15:3-9). Now government has been called into action to replace homeworking wives, but again has failed. The Social Security system is an actuarial disaster ticking away, just waiting to go off and bring the entire economy down with it. Medicare isn't doing much better. Both systems are outstripping both the GNP and inflation in rising costs, and thanks to the feminist- and ZPG-fueled baby bust, there is no way for the few workers in the coming generation to support the enormous crowd of barren old people, which will include you and me.

The alternative? Home-based care. Don't say it can't be done, because

> By 1981 home health care was a $2.5-billion-a-year business, up from a $500-million-a-year business in 1970. And its future looks bright. By 1990, sales should reach $10 billion.[9]

This business includes sales of home diagnostic kits ($100 million of the market), but the bulk of sales are for home health technology. Business and insurance companies are starting to notice how inefficient institutional health care is for noncrisis cases as compared to home care. Why, even *government* is catching on!

> With self-care on the increase, the health care focus has shifted from medical facilities to the home. One of the major reasons, of course, is cost. A pilot project in New Jersey sponsored by the Veterans Administration is fostering home care, contrasting the high costs of hospital care with $15 per day for home care. In Connecticut, Blue Cross/Blue Shield will offer home care for the terminally ill. Again, because it is cheaper.[10]

As the VA goes, so might go the country. Harry Walters, chief of the Veterans Administration, recently said in an interview,

How we care for the aging veteran will serve as the model for the care for the aged in America, because the crescendo of aging veterans is preceding the aging of America by about 10 years. The Cabinet Council on Human Resources this year is discussing health policy, with the VA's aging plan as the focus for all of the aging of America. . . .

We must learn how to treat patients—all patients, but predominately those over age 65—as outpatients. . . . we want to learn how to treat people at home.[11]

It costs a whole bunch less to put Mom in the spare bedroom than to pay for her apartment in a nursing home. And there is equipment available on a rental or purchase basis which will answer all of Mom's noncrisis health care needs. From hospital beds to portable oxygen tents, you can rent it or buy it. It's also a lot easier to become an expert on the specific health problems of one person than you might think. I have known several women who took over advanced nursing tasks when it was their own dear ones who needed help, and who did well even without being R.N.s.

Can you imagine what a blessing it would be to the economy if this kind of family responsibility spread? And it would show true Christian charity to the world as well.

Sociable Welfare

Relieving the afflicted does not stop with our own families. The ideal wife in Proverbs 31 was the family deaconess. "She opens her arms to the poor and extends her hands to the needy" (Prov. 31:20). Being at home, she has a better chance to evaluate who needs what kind of help than her husband. A fellow-Christian might need food, or clothes, or baby-sitting for her children while she tackles some particularly nasty piece of housework. The neighbors might need assistance with their food budget—perhaps a gift of vegetables from the garden would be in order. Dealing with people all day, serving them in practical ways, makes a homeworking wife a charity expert.

The welfare state is a poor substitute for the personalized ministry of Christian wives. As Stephen Clark says,

An approach which makes the family a center of care and service has two particularly significant benefits. First, it will usually *improve the quality of the service.* Childrearing, charitable works, hospitality, evangelism, and many other services are best performed within a network of committed personal relationships rather than through special institutions. Secondly, *the woman's domestic role will become more significant* in the community as the responsibilities of the household increase. This frees the woman from the typical modern female dilemma: Whether primarily to take responsibility for the household and thereby assume a role that has less and less importance and interest, or to primarily pursue a career and thereby abdicate domestic responsibility.[12] (emphasis mine)

God intended women to spend their whole lives serving other people. Young women serve their children, their mothers, their husbands, and the community at large. Older women train and assist the younger women, and in some cases become church helpers. Women are not called to pursue motherhood for five years, get a career, and thereafter live for themselves. We are responsible for keeping society healthy and human. And for this, we get respect.
Charity at home?
What an opportunity!
What a *ministry!*

17   The Church in Your Home

Before I became a Christian, the Bible doctrine which was most like waving a red flag in front of a peevish bull as far as I (the bull) was concerned was wifely submission. It says in Titus 2:5 that young wives should be trained to be "subject to their husbands," and this note is echoed in several other places (Eph. 5:22-24; Col 3:18; 1 Pet. 3:1-6). How I *hated* that doctrine! Reading the Bible through for the first time, every time I saw a passage that taught wifely submission I flung the Bible on the floor.

In God's providence both my Bible and I survived, but not until I had explored every possible way of cutting that doctrine out. In the end I saw that if I was going to believe the Bible at all, I was going to have to be a submissive wife; so with loud screeches of protest I gave in.

My attitude was all wrong, of course. I was thinking of leadership and submission as if they were a hammer and a nail. The husband got to be that hammer and the poor wife was the nail. I hadn't seen that the issue is not power and force, but *structure* and *roles*.

In the beginning God created marriage with a division of labor and responsibility. Man was to subdue the earth, woman was to help him, and together they were supposed to be fruitful and multiply.

Feminism and its ugly daughter careerism are in rebellion against our God-given role. This rebellion, grabbing at power while attacking God's role structure, has serious consequences for the work of God's Kingdom.

Christians have said for years, "God's work done in God's way will never lack God's provision." This is true. But what happens when God's work is *not* done in God's way? What if the work being done is *not God's work at all?* Will God bless it then?

We've already looked at marriage, children, economics, and service to others. In this chapter I would like us to finally look at the ministry of women in the church. I am going to show how homeworking and being subject to your husband combine to form a fantastic ministry. Why arm-wrestle the preacher for his pulpit when you can have a *church in your home?*

Body Life

Why did God tell us to be subject to our husbands in the first place? There are many ways to answer that question, but I prefer to come at it from the angle of the husband's headship. If you are subject to your husband, *you relate to him as your head.* Paul tells us, "Now I want you to realize that the head of every man is Christ, and the head of the woman is man, and the head of Christ is God" (1 Cor. 11:3). Again, "Wives, submit to your husbands as to the Lord. For the husband is the head of the wife as Christ is the head of the church, his body, of which he is the Savior. Now as the church submits to Christ, so also wives should submit to their husbands in everything" (Eph. 5:22-24).

It is true that this doctrine has sometimes been preached in a tyrannical way. Feminists often become feminists because they are reacting against sermons and books that make the husband a little god to be unquestioningly obeyed no matter what. Virginia Mollenkott voices a typical complaint when she says, "The husband is often lifted to the level of an absolute norm, as if he were God, while the wife is reduced to the worst kind of self-sacrificing idolatry."[1]

However, God is not teaching tyranny here. He is presenting us with a *metaphor* and an *analogy.* The metaphor is that of *marriage as an organism.* Head and body are connected; neither can survive without the other. The analogy is that *marriage is like the relationship between Christ and the church.*

The problem comes when we fit our picture of Christ and the church into our modern ideas of marriage, instead of the other way around. Modern marriage is seen as an end in itself, for the happiness of the couple alone. The Bible, however, shows us Christ at work *with* his church and *through* his church. Christ, the divine Head, directs the body in her task of bringing his gospel to the world and discipling the nations. Both work together for a single end: the advancement of the glory of God. "Thy kingdom come, thy will be done."

In the same way, husband and wife are meant to work together for the sake of God's Kingdom.

An evangelical feminist might say, "I see that husband and wife are supposed to work together, but why does the wife have to submit to her husband? Why can't everything be 50/50?" This line of questioning (which is tied up with women seeking ordination) winds up obliterating the role differences between men and women.[2] It makes head and body interchangeable—which they never are in real life. I can think of no better answer to it than that great Bible passage which explains how the spiritual body works—not by everyone doing everyone else's job, or even the job he or she chooses, but rather the job God assigns.

> Now the body is not made up of one part but of many. If the foot should say, "Because I am not a hand, I do not belong to the body," it would not for that reason cease to be part of the body. . . . If the whole body were an eye, where would the sense of hearing be? If the whole body were an ear, where would the sense of smell be? But in fact God has arranged the parts in the body, every one of them, just as he wanted them to be. (1 Cor. 12:14-18)

Many other human relationships require one to submit to a head. The employee has to submit to his boss (1 Pet. 2:18). The child has to submit to his mother and father (Luke 2:51). The citizen has to submit to the governing authorities (Rom. 13:1; 1 Pet. 2:13). Younger men in the church have to submit to the elders (1 Pet. 5:5). Wifely submission is *not* the only kind of submission. It means we recognize that the family is an authority structure, in which different members have different roles and responsibilities.

Submission is not exactly the same thing as obedience, either. Though Christians are supposed to submit to the government, the very Apostle Peter who gave us that rule told his Jewish rulers when they tried to stifle his preaching, "We must obey God rather than men" (Acts 5:29). Christians are supposed to obey God's commands in *every* relationship, even if our "heads" overstep their authority and persecute us for it. That is why slaves are exhorted to do what is right even if they must suffer for it, and wives are told to do what is right and not give way to fear when dealing with a non-Christian husband (1 Pet. 2:20; 3:6).

The Church at War

Submission, as the late great Greek expert A. T. Robertson says, "has a military air."[3] For the greater good, the soldier is subject to his commanding officer, even if he disagrees with him. In wartime we don't have the luxury of round-table discussions for every field operation. Nor does this mean the soldier is inferior to his officer. He may be taller, stronger, smarter, and better educated, but as long as he is a private and not a sergeant, he has to follow orders. There is no daily evaluation of personal capabilities to determine who will lead the unit today, and no coin toss-up for who will make the military decisions. Right or wrong, the sergeant has been assigned his role, as the private has his, and it is his military duty to fill it.

This generation is in danger of forgetting that *the Christian life is still a war.* We have strong enemies—the world, the flesh, and the devil. We also have a Commander-in-Chief, Jesus Christ, who has created a winning battle strategy. Jesus is the one who assigns roles and goals in his own army. And Jesus, through the Holy Spirit, has said that wives are to willingly subject themselves to their husbands.

The private's job is to make the C.O.'s plans work, as long as those plans don't mutinously defy the higher directives of the Commander-in-Chief. If the C.O. should go mad and order a massacre of civilians (as happened at My Lai in Vietnam) the private is not obliged to obey him, since the C.O. is overstepping his own role by rebelling against the Army's rules. But this limitation on obedience does not give the private license to rebel against every decision he dislikes. When the private is committed to winning the war, and is willing to subject his personal desires to the goal of winning, and is willing to follow the leader his Commander has put over him, that Army stands a good chance of winning

The private/sergeant analogy breaks down, of course, because privates get promoted to sergeant, whereas family roles stay constant. Wives are not "promoted" to husband, and a child is never "promoted" above his parents. Each role is worthwhile in itself, and not just as a stepping-stone to a higher rank with more pay and power. But the analogy of a body engaged in work, or an army engaged in war, remains.

Submission, then, is dedication to God's interests (the war). You work for your head's best interests in obedience to God. Submission is *active*—you don't sit around waiting for orders, but look around to see what you can do for your family. Submission is *responsible.* You have your assigned area of work in which you are a manager. Like any other managerial position, the job demands *initiative* and *creativity.* It means *respecting* your head. It requires a *courageous* (not a groveling) spirit. Above all, submission requires *godliness.*

Virginia Mollenkott introduces the evangelical feminist Paul

Jewett's book *Man as Male and Female* by saying, "To my knowlege he is the first evangelical theologian to face squarely the fact that if woman must of necessity be subordinate, she must of necessity be inferior."[4] Mr. Jewett himself has "rejected the argument for female subordination as being incompatible with [among other things] the revelation which is given us in the life of Jesus."[5] Yet *Jesus is the ultimate example of submission!* As the Son of God, he constantly repeated that he came not to do his own will, but that of the Father (John 5:30; 6:38; 7:28; 8:28, 42; 12:49, 50; and so on). In Gethsemane he cried, "Not my will, but thine be done." Always Jesus subordinated his own desires. Does that mean Jesus is inferior to the Father, or even inferior to *us*, because we are the people he came to serve? Or does it mean, as Christians have always held, that Jesus had a special role to fill that required submission for our sakes and for the sake of the "joy set before him" (Heb 12:2)?[6]

The Apostle Paul warned us, "Each of you should look not only to your own interests, but also to the interests of others" (Phil. 2:4). Our "attitude should be the same as that of"—who? A feminist fighting for equality? No, "Christ Jesus: Who, being in very nature God, did not consider equality with God something to be grasped . . ." (Phil 2:5, 6). Paul was worried, seeing that "everyone looks out for his own interests, not those of Jesus Christ" (Phil. 2:21). When we stop looking out for our own interests (which is what feminism and careerism are all about) and start looking out for those of Jesus Christ (which is what biblical submission is all about), then his Kingdom will start making some progress.

Thy Kingdom Come

What kind of progress can we expect in God's Kingdom when women wake up to the tremendous possibilities of our own role?

We have looked at the role of the younger woman: art, home business, hospitality, charity, bearing and raising children, and so forth. Now let's look at her reward. What kind of ministry does God have in store for those who have faithfully followed him all their younger days?

She has spent years learning how to teach children. Now she will teach adults. If you can explain God's sovereignty to a two-year-old, you can explain anything to anybody. And the older woman has a *duty* to explain things, since God has called her to teach the younger women (Titus 2:3-5).

Women today harm themselves terribly by expecting their husband, or male counselor, or male pastor to do for them what other women are meant to do. No man can meet all of a woman's needs. No man ought to have to try! How much less of a strain modern marriage would be if every wife had an understanding and experienced older woman to answer her hard questions and give her support.

Having trouble with the children? Ask the older woman. Don't know how to boil water? Ask the older woman. Your interior decoration efforts are turning into interior desecration? Ask the older woman!

The younger woman is supposed to grow into the older woman's job. Toward this end, she needs help which only the older woman can supply. The older woman gets respect and attention; the younger gets wisdom. Can anyone improve on this?

The older woman is also able to offer nitty-gritty help, since her children are no longer small. When your mother is a thousand miles away, it is more than comforting to have a trustworthy older woman volunteer to help with the house and kids when you and the new baby come home. An older woman has dozens of opportunities to show kindness to an inexperienced and perhaps overworked young mother.

But perhaps the most exciting ministry the older woman can have is her ministry of evangelism and hospitality. Her youngest children are old enough to help, or perhaps are grown and on their own. Now her years of learning how to create a gracious home for her own family can be put to use for a wider flock. She knows the Bible and how to answer serious questions. She knows how to create a warm and loving atmosphere and is sensitive to people's needs in the way only a mother learns to be. She has, in short, been trained to be an evangelist.

I often wondered, as I read the New Testament, what those frequent references to "the church in your home" meant. It seemed that quite a few people in New Testament times had something dynamic and exciting going on in their own living rooms. Now I think I know what it was.

When God calls a man and equips him to be an elder or a deacon, the Bible insists that his wife must be qualified in a special way too (1 Tim. 3:11). The reason? God wants them to form a *team*. Church growth is not the job of some superman of a pastor, or of the visitation teams alone. As I see the Scriptures, much church growth is supposed to come through quiet discussions over a cup of coffee. The early disciples chatted about the Good News everywhere, and the most natural setting for that chatting to occur is the Christian home. Husband and wife combine their talents of teaching, parenting, and home management to surround the visitor with the evidence of the power of God.

The most widely-known example of this kind of team, where both husband and wife played an equally important part, is in the ministry of L'Abri. The work of Dr. and Mrs. Francis Schaeffer has become internationally known, not because of any publicity-seeking on the Schaeffers' part, but because of the unending stream of converts from their house to all parts of the earth. This work started when the Schaeffers opened up their house for hospitality (and preaching the gospel) to the people whom the Lord brought them. The first contacts were made without any design at all, by the Schaeffers' own daughters. Soon the word spread, and with it the Schaeffers' ministry. People came to live near them; they got married and had families; they began sharing the Schaeffers' work. People moved to different countries to do similar work. The Schaeffers' children now have ministries of their own in different parts of the world. Franky, their son, is a film-maker and author who under God has helped his parents to move modern evangelical Christians to repentance and action. The daughters, Susan, Debby, and Priscilla, all have L'Abri work in their homes. Grandchildren are now coming into the ministry. I can't possibly describe how great an impact this one familiy has had on the world, through turning on Christians to the arts and to working for God in everyday life, as well as through bringing literally thousands to the Lord. I myself became a Christian partly through reading two books the Schaeffers wrote (*L'Abri* by Edith and *Escape from Reason* by Francis) though I never was at L'Abri itself. And I'm not the only one who can say that.

Why did the Schaeffers have such great success? *For the same reasons you and I can.* They obeyed God and tried to really live by the Bible. Their two great assets were sound biblical doctrine and a family.

In today's broken world, a genuinely loving family shines like a bonfire in the night. Human beings desperately need a family, and at the moment anyone who can give them one will find people eager to find them. People came to the Schaeffers for various reasons, but the reason they stayed long enough to hear Dr. Schaeffer's carefully reasoned arguments was that they already were experiencing Mrs. Schaeffer's home. A friend of ours who has been at L'Abri told us seriously that, as he saw it, as many people were brought to the Lord through Mrs. Schaeffer's cinnamon buns as through Dr. Schaeffer's sermons!

In an age when any group that offers family life (like the Mormons) is growing by leaps and bounds, and even counterfeit "families" like the Moonies draw converts, Christians have a wide-open market for the genuine, unadulterated product of a truly Christian home. Those agitating for ordination for women are throwing away with both hands the biggest ministry we could ever have in favor of a mere second-rate shadow. Two Dr. Schaeffers would not have been nearly as appealing as one Dr. and one Mrs.

The Schaeffers "fell into" their ministry, not through consciously deciding to return to biblical church structure, but through being sensitive to God's leading in their lives. I am asking you to consciously do what God gave Mrs. Schaeffer by accident. Be a homeworker. Work to build up your husband, and help him attain an elder's qualities. Exercise hospitality. Serve people in your home. Be creative. Worship and praise the Lord, first with your family, then with others the Lord will bring. Seek further knowledge and the example of older women who have successfully raised godly children. Become the kind of woman who is now more rare than diamonds, and who has always been more precious than rubies (Prov. 31:10).

Do you have a non-Christian husband? Then your first priority is to win him to the Lord, so you can begin Kingdom work together. If anything will win him, submission will, as Peter points out:

> Wives, in the same way be submissive to your husbands so that, if any of them do not believe the word, they may be won over without talk by the behavior of their wives, when they see the purity and reverence of your lives. (1 Pet. 3:1, 2)

Submission to a non-Christian husband is also excellent training for a future fruitful ministry, just as the gold is always purer when tried in the fire.

If you have a Christian husband, what are you waiting for? You don't have to search for a ministry, you *have* a ministry!

What a day it will be when all God's women return to homeworking and every wife has a church in her home.

Part Six:

CONCLUSION

"... train the younger women ... so that no one will malign the word of God." (Titus 2:4, 5)

18 Homeworking or Homeleaving: The Consequences

Women today are on the move. But will we like where we are going when we get there?

Homeworking, as we have seen, is based on the Scriptures. Homeleaving, its opposite, is not. Homeleaving includes careerism, day-care, and outright feminism, as well as old-fashioned gadding about and neglecting home duties while coffee klatsching with the neighbors. Scripture draws the line between these two roles for women. Now it's time to see where *we* will draw the line.

Consequences to God's Name

We have been looking at Titus 2: 4, 5, which says young wives should be trained to "love their husbands and children, to be self-controlled and pure, to be busy at home, to be kind, and to be subject to their husbands . . ." This is what God tells us to do. But then he tacks on a consequence: ". . . so that no one will malign the word of God."

Homeleaving causes people to malign the Word of God. It makes them question God's *truth, holiness,* and *power.*

Those in the world outside who know what the Bible says question the Bible's *truth* when they see professing Christians denying it themselves. Every Christian wife who refuses to be a homeworker (or to care for her children, or to submit to her husband) in the face of the biblical text is encouraging the world to reject God's Word entirely. She further can be an influence in leading the church away from the Bible's authority. As Naomi Goldenberg, a self-confessed witch who has studied at length the attempts of feminists to impose their teaching on Christianity and Judaism, says,

> Many feminists recommend ignoring parts of the Bible, but still claim that the book as a whole is God-given. It is hard to deny that an eventual consequence of criticizing the correctness of any sacred text or tradition is to question why that text or tradition should be considered a divine authority at all.[1]

So those who know what the Bible says, but see us denying it, will question its truth. Those outside the church who *don't* know what the Bible says, if they see us living a lifestyle that is self-centered and greedy, will question God's *holiness*. All they know of God and his Word is what they see in our lives. If we are no better than they are, why should they think God's standard is any higher than theirs?

And of course the *power* of God is totally invisible when Christians allow themselves to be swept along by worldly trends. When every little obstacle becomes an excuse for giving in to the current lifestyle, who can see God's power in us?

Wouldn't it be something if we were standing on the threshold of the greatest revival in history—and *the only thing holding it back was the sin of God's people?* There is so much more to one's life than "feeling good" or "being fulfilled" or all the other pink cocktails the world has to offer. What about the expansion of God's Kingdom? What about God's Name being honored instead of blasphemed and ignored? What about thousands of new churches and millions of new Christians? Can you get excited about this? Do you want to be a part of it?

For us young wives, it boils down to this: *are we willing to obey God,* to love our husbands and children, to be self-controlled and pure, to work *at home* (not the office), to be kind, and to be subject to our husbands, so that no one will blaspheme the Word of God? Are we out to nurture our families, putting others first, or to destroy our churches and country, putting ourselves first? Will we rock the cradle, or cradle the rock?

I have real hopes that God *is* going to send revival and bless the efforts of those faithful ones who have all along been living the lifestyle this book sets forth.

Homeworking will not automatically solve every problem. But it will get us on the right track. "The wise woman builds her house, but with her own hands the foolish one tears hers down" (Prov. 14:1). Women have helped tear down down the home; women can rebuild it.

We have seen enough torn-down houses: broken marriages, rebellious children, barren churches.

Now it's time to be wise.

It's time for homeworking.

It's time to see what the *true* God can do.

Appendix:
First Steps to
Homeworking

For revival to come, God's people must humble themselves and pray and seek God's face and turn from their wicked ways (2 Chron. 7:14).

Individually we must repent of our proud and arrogant ways. This includes, in the case of young wives, admitting you were wrong if you abandoned homeworking or if you had not been actively seeking out the Bible's teaching. Anyone who has offended God in this or any other respect must pray and seek his favor.

Next, we have to turn from our "wicked ways" to *good* ways. This means coming back to homeworking.

But there may be obstacles in the path of a woman who sincerely desires to return home. Let's look at these obstacles, and how to overcome them.

Goals First

You want to nurture your children, help your husband, have a nome business, create objects for beauty, and have a fruitful ministry at home The point is not just to be home, but to be accomplishing at least some of these goals, and growing into the others.

Winning Your Husband

So the very first step is to *win your huband's consent*. Most husbands would be thrilled to have an old-fashioned wife who cooks their favorite meals and keeps the shirt buttons sewed on. But some are counting heavily on your paycheck to meet their financial commitments, and need to be persuaded.

A submissive wife doesn't just force her will on her husband. She explains to him how what she is asking fits into *his* goals. If a Christian husband's goals are un-Christian and materialistic, a Christian wife can gently point this out, since his *basic* goal is the same as hers—to be godly and fruitful. Even better, she can encourage him with the vision of fruitful ministry for the Lord which I have tried to share in this book.

A non-Christian husband may put his foot down and insist that his wife retain her job. In this case she can try to discern his *real* goal. Does he want the money, or does he have some other reason for wanting her to work outside the home? She can explain how homeworking is financially feasible. She can reassure him that his goals will be met this way (assuming they are not directly anti-Christian). If he still is obstinate and fearful of the change, she can offer (like Daniel—see Daniel 1:11-16) to try God's way for a set time, and then to return to the office if it doesn't work out (praying like crazy that it *will* work out). A totally obstinate non-Christian should not be argued with at all, but served with such gentleness and respect that he might be won to the Lord (1 Pet. 3:1, 2). All other things being equal, the non-Christian's wife's first duty is to win her husband. No Christian husband, no Christian ministry.

Quitting Your Job

You may have an important job. People may be depending on you. Nonetheless, God still wants you at home.

If your job is a strong temptation to you, and you think that if you hesitate you will never leave, you have to quit. Flat. All idols must be cut off. Nobody will understand, but they'll survive. If you had died of a heart attack, they would have had to carry on without you and they would have muddled through somehow.

If the job is not a temptation, but people are depending on you, it might be reasonable to give them time to find a replacement for you. In the meantime, however, please make sure that your children are as well-cared for as possible, even if it means spending extra money. Should the replacement not show signs of ever showing up (within a reasonable period, like the standard two weeks to a month), I'd just go ahead and quit. Or should the Lord convict you that your children need you, right away, recognize that they are more important than your adult colleagues. Work can and will go on without you.

Sometimes you can help out your former boss from your home until he or she has things running smoothly. Being gracious to all people is certainly Christian; you want to help your former employer achieve his or her goals, as long as this doesn't interfere with more important responsibilities.

The Wolf at the Door

Some families are so overextended that there seems no way for Mommy to come home. Here the solution could be a cheaper lifestyle, or immediately starting up a home business.

In the very worst situation, God can always help. At the very least, you can be planning for and studying out a home business even while you continue at your old job. Plan together with your children! Then comes the difficult period of moonlighting—retaining your old job while you try to start up a new one. Finally you can quit the office job and stay home at your new business.

Absolutely nothing is gained if the new business soaks up all your time. Take this into consideration while planning it.

My experience is that any employed husband can provide for his family without sending the wife out to work, *as long as they are willing to live within his means*. Biblically, he should take two jobs before looking to you for support.

Not Giving the Devil a Foothold

Part of the reason homeworking is out of fashion is the flood of degenerate anti-Christian propaganda disguised as "entertainment." To keep God in our homes, we at least should not unnecessarily invite the devil in.

Homeworking is a million times easier when the family provides their own entertainment. You couldn't do yourself a better favor than to get rid of the TV, cancel your subscriptions to *Time, Newsweek,* and the other humanistic news organs, and throw out any accomodating "Christian" literature that plugs for humanistic values in the name of the Lord. For news, you could subscribe to *Commentary* and the *National Review;* for books, you could join Puritan-Reformed Book Club. With the TV no longer on six or eight hours a day, you will have time to develop a ministry that matters for eternity, and to play with and read to the children.

Support

"He who walks with the wise grows wise, but a companion of fools suffers harm" (Prov. 13:20). Search out like-minded women. Find a reliable older woman, if possible, who can be your mentor. I don't particularly favor official "support" organizations with their narcissism and endless meetings without children, but a network of homeworking wives will keep you from feeling isolated. More than that, we can learn from each other.

Welcome Home magazine just recently started up as a forum for homeworking wives (although it only presents homeworking as a valid *choice*, not a *rule*). I expect other magazines will follow, and there quite possibly are already good magazines for us that I don't know about. Latch on to as many networks as help you.

Homeworking is a fantastic career—maybe *too* fantastic for some of us to handle all at once. I myself did not know how to cook decently, sew respectably, or do the laundry when I started. I had never been a hostess or taught a child. All I was good at was writing computer programs and passing tests! I've been at it five years now, and I'm still not Edith Schaeffer. You will probably do better than me. Just take one thing at a time (children coming first), be willing to grow, and praise the Lord for the progress you make.

Notes

Introduction

1. John W. Whitehead, *The Stealing of America* (Westchester, IL: Crossway Books, 1983), p. 64.
2. Some critics blame isolation of the modern housewife on the rigid pattern of men's and women's roles which rigidly restricts her to domestic family-related tasks. However, such attacks on a "traditional" approach to the female role are not really attacking a fully "traditional" approach at all. Instead, they are attacking a remnant of an old order, a fragment that has lost much meaning as a result of being severed from its natural context. The domestic role of women in a technological society where the household has lost much of its strength and significance means something quite different from the domestic role of women in a society where the household is central to the corporate life of the entire society. It is important to understand that the full traditional approach to men's and women's roles passed away with the breakdown of the traditional social system.

So says Stephen Clark, author of *Man and Woman in Christ: An Examination of the Roles of Men and Women in the Light of Scripture and the Social Sciences* (Ann Arbor, MI: Servant Books, 1980), p. 499. Mr. Clark says the traditional social system (i.e., the biblical one) has passed away; I think it is alive, but suppressed.

Chapter 1: The Great Con Game

1. "Industry Must 'Automate, Emigrate, or Evaporate,' " an interview with James Baker, executive vice-president of General Electric, *U.S. News and World Report*. January 16, 1984, p. 44. Mr. Baker, answering the question of whether displaced low-tech workers will lose income as they try to switch to high-tech jobs, says,

Yes, many blue and white-collar workers are going to make less money. But when a man makes less money, his wife often goes to work to preserve their standard of living. I think you'll see virtually every family with two people working to buy that car and that house.

My point is not that high tech, or big business, is *bad* in itself, but that business is becoming callous to the desire of a man to provide for his family.

2. "Why Not Deaconesses?" *Presbyterian Journal.* April 16, 1980.

3. Mary Daly, *Beyond God the Father: Toward a Philosophy of Women's Liberation* (Boston: Beacon Press, 1973), p. 96.

4. Naomi Goldenberg, *Changing of the Gods: Feminism and the End of Traditional Religions* (Boston: Beacon Press, 1979), p. 92.

5. *Ibid.,* pp. 93, 94.

6. *Ibid.,* p. 4.

7. *Ibid.,* p. 8.

8. "Theology After the Demise of God the Father: A Call for the Castration of Sexist Religion," *Sexist Religion and Women in the Church.* Alice Hageman, ed. (New York: Association Press, 1974), pp. 132, 138, 139.

9. Daly, *Beyond God the Father,* p. 96.

10. Daly, "Theology After the Demise of God the Father," in Hageman, *Sexist Religion,* p. 130.

11. *Ibid.,* p. 133.

12. "No More Silence," in Hageman, *Sexist Religion,* p. 25.

13. *Ibid.*

14. *Bulletin of Washington University* (St. Louis, Missouri), 1984.

15. *Ibid.*

16. Susan Foh, *Women and the Word of God* (Phillipsburg, NJ: Presbyterian and Reformed Publishing Company, 1979), pp. 2, 3, 6, 7.

17. Letha Scanzoni and Nancy Hardesty, *All We're Meant to Be* (Waco, TX: Word Books, 1974), p. 143.

18. *Ibid.,* p. 141.

19. (Westchester, IL: Crossway Books, 1984), p. 136.

20. *Ibid.*

21. (San Francisco: Harper & Row, 1978), p. 135.

22. *Ibid.,* p. 121.

23. *Ibid.,* p. 120.

24. P. 196.

25. *Ibid.,* p. 97.

26. *Women, Men and the Bible* (Nashville: Abingdon Press, 1977), pp. 136, 137.

27. *Ibid.,* pp. 32, 33.

28. (Harrison, NY: Roman Catholic Books, 1977), p. 41.

29. Scanzoni and Hardesty, *All We're Meant to Be,* pp. 205, 206.

30. Gayle Yates, *What Women Want: The Ideas of the Movement* (Cambridge, MA: Harvard University Press, 1975), p. 171.

31. Dolores Hayden, *The Grand Domestic Revolution: A History of Feminist Designs for American Homes, Neighborhoods, and Cities* (Cambridge, MA: MIT Press, 1981), p. 1, 5.

32. *Ibid.*

Chapter 2: Beyond the "Me" Marriage

1. "When 'Family' Will Have a New Definition," *What the Next Fifty Years Will Bring: A Special Report to Mark the Golden Anniversary of U.S. News and World Report* (1984), pp. A3, A4.

2. Jay Adams, *Marriage, Divorce and Remarriage in the Bible* (Phillipsburg, NJ: Presbyterian and Reformed Publishing Company, 1980), p. 8.
3. *Ibid.*, p. 11.
4. Charles M. Sell, *Family Ministry* (Grand Rapids: Zondervan, 1981), pp. 23, 43.
5. *Ibid.*, pp. 54, 55.
6. *Ibid.*, p. 43.
7. Letha Dawson Scanzoni and John Scanzoni, *Men, Women, and Change* (New York: McGraw-Hill, 1976), pp. 235, 236.
8. *Ibid.*, p. 383.
9. *Ibid.*, p. 236.

Chapter 3: The Joy of Unkinky Sex

1. *Statistical Abstract of the United States* (Washington, D.C.: U.S. Bureau of the Census, 1983), p. 60.
2. Sell, *Family Ministry*, p. 109.
3. Scanzoni, *Men, Women, and Change*, p. 377.

Chapter 4: God's Least-Wanted Blessing

1. Even non-Christians are beginning to notice and comment negatively on the antichild prejudice of our day. Noted feminist author and lecturer Germaine Greer has devoted the entire first chapter of her new book *Sex and Destiny: The Politics of Human Fertility* (New York: Harper and Row, 1984) to lamenting and satirizing our modern lack of affection for children and lack of support for their mothers. As she says, "Historically, human societies have been pro-child; modern society is unique in that it is profoundly hostile to children. We in the West do not refrain from childbirth because we are concerned about the population explosion or because we feel we cannot afford children, but because we do not like children" (p. 2). The entire chapter is a trenchant analysis of why we find ourselves in this situation, and is well worth reading.
2. *Kitto's Daily Bible Illustrations*, Volume I (Grand Rapids: Kregel Publications, 1981), p. 560.
3. *Ibid.*
4. Sue Remmus, "Acquirers vs. Nurturers," *Unschooler's Project* (now *Family-Centered Learning: The Homeschooling Quarterly*), Fall 1983, pp. 2, 5.
5. *Ibid.*
6. *The Book of Psalms for Singing* (Pittsburgh: Board of Education and Publication of the Reformed Presbyterian Church of North America, 1980).
7. *Ibid.*
8. (Grand Rapids: Zondervan, 1981), pp. 222, 223.
9. *Word Pictures in the New Testament*, Volume IV (Grand Rapids: Baker, n.d; reprint of 1931 version), pp. 570, 571.
10. Susan Moller Okin, "Plato on Women and the Family," *The Family in Political Thought*, Jean Bethke Elshtain, ed. (Amherst, MA: University of Massachusetts Press, 1982), pp. 39, 40.
11. *Ibid.*, p. 41.
12. *Ibid.*, p. 48.

Chapter 5: Who's Afraid of the Big Bad Baby?

1. Scanzoni, *Men, Woman, and Change*, p. 399.
2. Bob Sheehan, "The Problem of Birth Control," *Reformation Today* November-December 1981, p. 22.
3. Scanzoni, *Men, Women, and Change*, p. 377.
4. *Ibid.*, p. 374.
5. *Ibid.*, p. 377.
6. *Ibid.*, pp. 449-452.
7. *Ibid.*, p. 378.
8. *Ibid.*, pp. 393, 396, 397.
9. Scanzoni and Hardesty, *All We're Meant to Be*, p. 143.
10. Germaine Greer, *Sex and Destiny: The Politics of Human Fertility* (New York: Harper and Row, 1984), p. 185.
11. *Ibid.*, p. 186.
12. *Ibid.*, p. 168.
13. *Ibid.*, p. 171.
14. *Ibid.*, p. 171, 172.
15. *Ibid.*, p. 172.
16. *Ibid.*, p. 172, 173.
17. *Ibid.*, p. 173.
18. *Ibid.*, p. 193, 194, 204:

> Because it is *in situ* continually, it is not immediately obvious that it is not a contraceptive at all. A device inserted in the uterus prevents intrauterine pregnancy, and intraurterine pregnancy only, by transforming the welcoming environment for the blastocyst [fertilized egg] into a toxic sink. . . .
> The fact that "if an I.U.D. is inserted after unprotected coitus it prevents pregnancy occurring," or, translated from Family Planningese, it "prevents pregnancy continuing" or "prevents implantation," seems proof positive that it does not work principally by preventing the encounter of live sperm and live egg. The insertion of an IUD as a form of preemptive abortion is now routinely practiced at the Marie Stopes Memorial Clinic and at Pregnancy Advisory Services clinics in London. . . .
> One thing is certain; the IUD prevents implantation, not conception.

19. *Ibid.*, p. 193-195, 197, 199.
20. *Ibid.*, p. 200.
21. *Ibid.*, p. 158.
22. *Ibid.*, p. 155-157.
23. *Ibid.*, p. 155, 156.
24. *Ibid.*, p. 128-143, 149-151.
25. Scanzoni and Hardesty, *All We're Meant to Be*, p. 138.
26. James Weber, *Grow or Die!* (New Rochelle, NY: Arlington House Publishers, 1977), p. 184.
27. *Ibid.*
28. *Ibid.*, pp. 15-149, especially pages 15, 16.
29. *Ibid.*, pp. 412-414.
30. *Ibid.*, p. 163.

31. *Ibid.*, p. 170.
32. *Ibid.*, p. 183.
33. "The Life of Mr. Philip Henry," *The Complete Works of Matthew Henry*, Volume II (Grand Rapids: Baker Book House, 1979), p. 678.

Chapter 6: Family Banning and Planned Barrenhood

1. They also present the rewards of having children, but in a mocking way that shows *they* don't believe in the rewards themselves. It comes across that only ignorant, blue-collar, lower-class Catholics really want children, and that all reasons for desiring a large family are either selfish or out-of-date.
2. Scanzoni, *Men, Woman, and Change*, p. 364.
3. "101 Uses for a Dead (or Alive) Baby," *A.L.L. About Issues*. January 1984, p. 6.
4. *Ibid.*, p. 7.
5 *Ibid.*, pp. 8, 9.
6. Donald DeMarco, "On Human Experimentation," *Human Life Review*. Fall 1983.
7. "101 Uses," p. 9.
8. "On Human Experimentation."
9. "Students Defend Abortion For 'High' Social Reasons," *Rutherford Institute*. January-February 1984, p. 8.
10. *Ibid.*, p. 8.
11. "Reflections After a Pro-Life Talk" (editorial), *Christian Statesman*, January-February 1984, pp. 5, 7.
12. Dean R. Smith, "Abortion: Doing Justice and Preaching Peace," *Christian Statesman*. March-April 1984, p. 6.
13. *Ibid.*, pp. 6, 7, 15.
14. "Family Violence Emerges from the Shadows," *U.S. News and World Report*. January 23, 1984, p. 66 (quote from psychologist Henry Giarretto of Parents United, a California group working with incest victims and offenders). Giarretto says incest occurs in one out of every six *families*, but a mother, daughter or sister is seldom the aggressor. The entertainment media play up female-initiated incest, not because it is really more widespread, but in order to deaden our disgust and prepare us for the real, male-initiated thing.

    Keep in mind that Dr. Giarretto works in California, and that this crime is *much* more common among stepfamilies, where the offender is not actually related by blood to the victim. Still, *any* amount of incest is loathsome, and all the more so if it increases to the point where these perverts will follow the "gays," lesbians, and fornicators out of the closet, demanding their right to commit perversion, which all the media coverage seems designed to accomplish.
15. "Speak of the Devil," *Commentary*. April 1971, p. 6. Cited in *Grow or Die!*, pp. 194, 195.
16. Weber, *Grow or Die!*, p. 179.
17. *U.S. Population Growth and Family Planning: A Review of the Literature* (New York: Planned Parenthood-World Population), p. viii. Cited in *Grow or Die!*, p. 180.

Chapter 7: Who Owns Our Kids?

1. The name of a book by Rael Jean and Erich Isaac, which exposes almost every utopian movement in our country except, unhappily, feminism.
2. Weber, *Grow or Die!*, p. 179.

3. (Old Greenwich, CT: Devin-Adair, 1981), pp. ix, x, l.
4. "2,000 Attend Wisconsin Legislative Hearing," *Parent Educator and Family Report.* March 1984, p. 5.
5. *Ibid.*
6. A Wisconsin update, from the *Parent Educator and Family Report* ("Victory in Home-Based Educational Statutes," June-July 1984, p. 5).

On April 5, 1984, the Wisconsin State Legislature overwhelmingly passed legislation protecting the rights of home schoolers and private schools. This victory was the result of prayer, diligent effort, and sacrifice by numerous individuals and organizations throughout the state. . . .

In retrospect this victory was a real surprise to all of us, especially when considering the powerful organizations (including the two largest parochial school systems in the state) with money, influence, and paid lobbyists arrayed against us.

The Wisconsin fight is not yet over, as apparently public educators are attempting "to develop Administrative Rules that would result in greater restrictions than the new law allows on its face." Nonetheless, a victory has been won that, realistically speaking, could not have happened through human effort alone.

A similar situation is developing in Nebraska. After the much publicized persecution of Nebraska church schools, including the famous padlocking of Faith Baptist Church and subsequent imprisonment of its pastor, the Rev. Everett Sileven, and seven of the schoolchildren's fathers, would you believe that the Nebraska State Department of Education has granted *all* parents with biblical convictions the freedom to home school this year (1984-85)? ("New Legislation in Nebraska," *Parent Educator and Family Report,* August-September 1984, p. 4.)

The moral? We absolutely can't afford to be apathetic about our children's freedom of education, but we don't need to be discouraged either. Christian parents *can* fight these battles and *win!*

7. *Parent Educator and Family Report.* March 1984, p. 4.
8. *Grow or Die!,* p. 180.
9. William H. Nault, *Typical Course of Study: Kindergarten Through Grade 12* (New York: World Book, 1982).
10. Cal Thomas, *Book Burning* (Westchester, IL: Crossway Books, 1983), pp. 63, 64, 67.
11. *Competent to Counsel* (Philippsburg, NJ: Presbyterian and Reformed Publishing Company, 1970), p. 253. Much else in this book is valuable, however.
12. *Ibid.,* p. 255, 256.
13. *The Abolition of Man* (New York: Macmillan, 1947), p. 23.
14. Kenneth O. Gangel and Warren S. Benson, *Christian Education: Its History and Philosophy* (Chicago: Moody Press, 1983), p. 358.
15. Those interested in the legality of home schooling should read John Whitehead, *Home Education and Constitutional Liberties* (Westchester, IL.: Crossway Books, 1984).
16. John H. Westerhoff III, *McGuffey and His Readers* (Milford, MI: Mott Media, 1982), pp. 182, 185-187.
17. The King James Version translated Romans 13:4 correctly: "For he is the minister of God to thee for good." Even more literally, the passage reads, "For he is the servant of God to you on behalf of *the* good." It is a tragedy that the NIV translates this verse as,

"For he is God's servant to do you good." The verse says nothing whatever about the ruler doing good, neither in the words themselves or in the context. The previous verse tells us the ruler will commend *us* if *we* do what is good (τὸ ἀγαϕόν). Why? Because he is God's servant to us on behalf of the good (τὸ ἀγαϕόν again). It is his job to provide an atmosphere in which private good works are encouraged and evil deeds are suppressed. Obviously, if the ruler begins to feel it is *his* job to do all the good deeds, he will not only fail to commend the good deeds of the citizens, but actively work to suppress them, as being in competition with his own projects and usurping his authority. This is exactly the situation in Soviet Russia today, where all private charity is forbidden by law. To say, then, that the ruler is God's servant to do us good, in the sense of the multiple welfare functions of the modern state, does not follow at all from the scriptural reasoning that he will commend *us* for doing good deeds. It contradicts both the text and the context.

18. Suggested reading for those who do want to investigate the facts:

BOOKS ON THE PUBLIC SCHOOL SYSTEM

Child Abuse in the Classroom by Phyllis Schlafly, Pere Marquette Press, P. O. Box 495, Alton, IL 62002. A shocking collection of the testimonies of hundreds of parents, teachers, and other concerned citizens at seven all-day hearings conducted by the U.S. Department of Education during March 1984. Deals with the psychological abuse—or to put it plainly, brainwashing—practiced in our federally-funded curricula.

Why Are They Lying to Our Children? by Herbert I. London, Stein and Day, Scarborough House, Briarcliff Manor, NY 10510. The author analyzes sixty-eight major textbooks and compares them with reality.

BOOKS ON EDUCATION IN GENERAL AND HOME EDUCATION
IN PARTICULAR

Teach Your Own by John Holt. Published by Dell Publishing Co., New York, NY. Available from Holt Associates, 729 Boylston St., Boston, MA 02116. Easy to read, well-researched, and logical. I also recommend *How Children Learn* and *How Children Fail*, both available from the above address. For anyone interested in education, or who wants to home school, I strongly recommend subscribing to John Holt's newsletter/magazine *Growing Without Schooling*. Mr. Holt is not a Christian, but that shouldn't stop you from enjoying *GWS*, the best home schooling resource around.

For the Children's Sake by Susan Schaeffer Macaulay, Crossway Books, 9825 W. Roosevelt Rd., Westchester, IL 60153. Excellent, inspiring, thought-provoking Christian look at education in general and the parents' role in particular.

Home-Style Teaching by Dorothy and Raymond Moore. Published by Word Books, Waco, TX. Available from Hewitt-Moore, P. O. Box 3200, Waco, TX 76707. The Moores are Christians, long-time advocates of home schooling, and believers in delayed formal education. This is their "how-to" book. Other books and materials, including a newsletter, the *Parent Educator and Family Report*, are available. Address for the *PEFR* is P. O. Box 9, Washougal, WA 98671.

Home Education and Constitutional Liberties by constitutional attorney John Whitehead. Published by Crossway Books. A look at the legality of home schooling, including the major cases.

"Must" books are *Teach Your Own* and *For the Children's Sake*. The "must" newsletter is *Growing Without Schooling.* There are many more fine books out there, but you will have no trouble finding them if you start with the list above.

HOME EDUCATION MATERIALS, CURRICULA, AND RESOURCES
Believe it or not, Holt Associates (address above) can tell you anything you need to know on any of these subjects. There are pamphlets, book lists, curricula lists, reviews of materials, and so on, enough to stagger the imagination.

PRIVATE SCHOOL MATERIALS
Alpha Omega Publications not only has a full set of curricula for the Christian school (their LIFEPACs) but also a full training program for everyone from the principal to the teachers to the parents. Alpha Omega has also recently started a program whereby they will train a home education liaison from your school to assist parents by setting up and supervising a home education satellite program for your school or church. You need not use Alpha Omega material to buy this training. Contact Alpha Omega Publications, P. O. Box 3153, Tempe, AZ 85281; phone (602) 438-8253.
I apologize if I have left out anyone's favorite book or resource. Space requires that I be selective. I plan on publishing a much larger resource list in my next book, which will be about how to do all the things I wrote about in this book!

Chapter 9: Raising Kids Without Confusion

1. "Expert Failures," *Pink and Brown People, and Other Controversial Essays* (Stanford, CA: Hoover Institution Press, 1981), p. 35.
2. William Kirk Kilpatrick, *Psychological Seduction: The Failure of Modern Psychology* (Nashville: Thomas Nelson Publishers, 1983), p. 29.
3. *Ibid.,* p. 30.
4. Of course in David's case he was speaking as a prophet and God did use David's experience to deliver an infallible oracle. But it's ridiculous to place a *Parent's* magazine contributor on the same level as a prophet of God.

Chapter 10: Home as a Greenhouse for Young Plants

1. Scanzoni, *Men, Women, and Change,* p. 364.
2. "Are Christian School Students Sheltered From the World?" *Christian School Comment,* n.d. Obtained from Christian Liberty Academy, 205 E. McDonald Rd., Prospect Heights, IL 60070, as part of their introductory literature.
3. Paul D. Meier and Linda Burnett, *The Unwanted Generation: A Guide to Responsible Parenting* (Grand Rapids: Baker Book House, 1980), p. 17.
4. Stephen Pearl Andrews, writing in the 1850s and 60s, pumped for the "baby world" which he defined as "nurseries for fifty to one hundred children, under the direction of 'scientific and professional nurses, matrons, and physiologists.'" Mr. Andrews operated a "free love" club which was finally raided by the police and closed down. *Grand Domestic Revolution,* p. 93.
5. Meier and Burnett, *Unwanted Generation,* p. 51.
6. *Ibid.*
7. "Child Abuse Rising Nationwide," *Focus On The Family,* June 1984, p. 12.
8. As a matter of fact, the most fiery speech my husband Bill reports ever hearing on the subject of day-care was given at his Toastmasters club (a public speaking organization)

by a day-care worker. The burden of her speecn was, "I'd *never* put any child of *mine* in day-care, and I hope I can persuade you that *you* shouldn't either!"

9. "Washington State Legislator Says Keep Children Home," *Parent Educator and Family Report.* August-September 1984, p. 3.
10. Shirin Razoni, "Letter of the Month," *Welcome Home.* March 1984, back cover.
11. *Ibid.*, p. 15.
12. *McGuffey and His Readers,* pp. 189-192.
13. "How New Entrepreneurs Are Changing U.S. Business," p. 69.
14. James Fitzpatrick, *Jesus Christ Before He Became a Superstar* (Harrison, NY: Roman Catholic Books, 1977), p. 186.
15. Francis Schaeffer, *The Great Evangelical Disaster,* 'Westchester, IL: Crossway Books, 1984), p. 119.
16. *Ibid.*, p. 119.
17. *Ibid.*, p. 120.
18. *Children Without Childhood* (New York: Pantheon Books, 1983), cover.
19. *Ibid.*, p. 18.
20. *Ibid.*, p. 23.
21. *Ibid.*, p. 42.
22. *Ibid.*, p. 45.
23. "Letters," *Welcome Home.* March 1984, p. 23.

Chapter 11: Would You, Could You, in the Home?

1. (Edinburgh: Banner of Truth Trust, 1979; orig. pub. 1662), pp. 279-285.
2. Foh, *Women and the Word of God,* p. 190.
3. *Ibid.*, pp. 227-230.

Chapter 13: Business at Home

1. Dolores Hayden, *Grand Domestic Revolution,* pp. 1, 5.
2. *Ibid.*, p. 28.
3. *Ibid.*, p. 17.
4. *Ibid.*, p. 226.

> The *Ladies Home Journal* was only one of several popular women's magazines to elaborate this theme enthusiastically in 1918 and 1919, with articles about new ways of living involving community kitchens, laundries, and day care centers, as well as kitchenless houses. Zona Gale, a playwright and well-known feminist, produced the most polemical of the pieces in the *Journal's* series on community kitchens.

> Thus have "women's " magazines ever paved the way for the obliteration of the female province.

5. *Ibid.*, p. 10.
6. Whitehead, *The Stealing of America,* p. 65.
7. *Ibid.*
8. *Power and Privilege: Labor Unions in America* (New York: Universe Books, 1984), p. 252.
9. He says,

Segregation in public places in Washington, D.C. ended by voluntary agreement two years before the Supreme Court decision, and was starting to erode in the border states and to be questioned even in the Deep South. Desegregation was an idea whose time had come. How, and through which mechanisms, did not seem to matter at the time. Now we know that this decision was only the first step toward an unprecedented expansion of the power of judges that went way beyond questions of race.

From his essay, "Government by Snobs" in *Pink and Brown People*, p. 21.
10. Shifrin Avraham, *The First Guidebook to Prisons and Concentration Camps of the Soviet Union* (New York: Bantam Books, 1982). See especially the photos on page 99 of women unloading heavy asbestos plates from a freight train, on page 177 of a woman carrying a huge tree trunk all by herself, and on page 180 of women cutting down and sawing up trees. This last picture carries the caption, "Women at work in Krasnoyarsk Territory, a logging region (Siberia, on the Enisei River). Equal rights for women, a dream that women in the free world are struggling for."
11. "New Entrepreneurs . . ."
12. January-February 1984, p. 31.
13. Census Bureau figures, quoted in *ibid.*
14. March-April 1984, p. 2.

Chapter 14: Art and the New Renaissance Woman

1. William Lazer, professor of marketing and future environments at Michigan State University, interviewed in "Challenges of the 80's," *U.S. News and World Report.* October 15, 1979, p. 51.

Chapter 15: The Times, They Are A-Changing

1. Goldenberg, *Changing of the Gods*, p. 10, 3.
2. Clark, *Man and Woman in Christ*, pp. 659-661.
3. *Ibid.*
4. "New Entrepreneurs . . ."
5. John Naisbitt, *Megatrends: Ten New Directions Transforming Our Lives* (New York: Warner, 1982) p. 144.
6. Scott Burns, "Your Electronic Home Office," Rodale's *New Shelter.* September 1983, p. 74.
7. Toffler, *Future Shock* (New York: Random House, 1970), p. 349; Naisbitt, *Megatrends*, p. 144.
8. Clark, *Man and Woman in Christ*, pp. 617, 618.

Chapter 16: Charity Belongs at Home

1. May 14, 1984, p. 50.
2. Scanzoni and Hardesty, *All We're Meant to Be*, p. 206.
3. Linda Burton, "A Place to Come Home To," *Welcome Home.* March 1984, pp. 4, 5.
4. *Ibid.*
5. *Ibid.*
6. *L'Abri* (Wheaton, IL: Tyndale House, 1969), pp. 149, 155, 156.
7. *Word Pictures in the New Testament*, Volume IV, p. 585.

8. "When 'Family' Will Have a New Definition," p. A-4.
9. Naisbitt, *Megatrends,* p. 136.
10. *Ibid.*
11. "VA's Goal: 'Model Care' for 9 Million Older Veterans," *U.S. News and World Report.* June 4, 1984, p. 93.
12. Clark, *Man and Woman in Christ,* p. 600.

Chapter 17: The Church in Your Home

1. *Women, Men and the Bible,* p. 40.
2. Naomi Goldenberg says,

> "The clergy will have to accept women," I thought. The feminist revolution will not leave religion untouched. Eventually, all religious hierarchies would be peopled with women. I imagined women functioning as rabbis, priests and ministers. I pictured women wearing clerical garb and performing clerical duties and suddenly *I saw a problem.* How could women represent a male god?
>
> Everything I knew about Judaism and Christianity involved accepting God as the ultimate in male authority figures. If enough women claimed to represent "His" authority—to embody "His" presence in synagogues and on pulpits—congregations would have to stop seeing God as male. God would begin to look like "His" female officials. . . .
>
> As a psychologist of religion, I do not agree that improving the position of women is a minor alteration in Judaeo-Christian doctrine. . . . When feminists succeed in changing the positions of women in Christianity and Judaism, they will shake these religions at their roots. The nature of a religion lies in the nature of the symbols and images it exalts in ritual and doctrine. . . . The psychology of the Jewish and Christian religions depends on the masculine image that these religions have of their God. Feminists change the major psychological impact of Judaism and Christianity when they recognize women as religious leaders and as images of divinity. . . .
>
> The images of Christ and Yahweh will be questioned because of the very basic quality of maleness. All of the roles that men and women have been taught to consider as God-given will be re-evaluated. . . . These changes will not be restricted to small numbers of individuals practicing nonsexist religions within a sexist society. Society itself will be transformed to the point that it will no longer be a patriarchy. For if men are no longer supreme rulers on earth, how could one expect them to retain sovereignty in heaven?

Changing of the Gods, pp. 3, 4, 8.
3. *Word Pictures,* Volume IV, p. 506.
4. (Grand Rapids: Eerdmans, 1975), p. 8.
5. *Man as Male and Female,* p. 134.
6. Not surprisingly, since our present-day feminists can't understand that women can be equal to men in *essence* but subordinate to them in *function,* the similar question of Jesus' relation to the Father caused perhaps the severest crisis the church has ever faced: the Arian controversy in the fourth century. Despite clear biblical teaching that Jesus and the Father are the same in *essence* (John 1:1; 8:58), but that Jesus is subordinate in *function* (John 4:34: 5:30), Arius and his followers were unable to hold

these two things in mind and insisted that if Jesus is subordinate in function, he *must* be subordinate in essence—that is, inferior. The church, of course, decided against Arius, and the universal, received teaching (Catholic, Orthodox, and Protestant) is that Jesus is equal to the Father in essence ("of one being with the Father," as the Nicene Creed says) but subordinate to him in function. If this kind of relationship can exist between Jesus and the Father, certainly it can exist between women and men.

Chapter 18: Homeworking or Homeleaving: The Consequences

1. Goldenberg, *Changing of the Gods,* p. 13.

Bibliography

Adams, Jay. *Competent to Counsel*. Phillipsburg, NJ: Presbyterian and Reformed Publishing Company, 1970.

————. *Marriage, Divorce and Remarriage in the Bible*. Phillipsburg, NJ: Presbyterian and Reformed Publishing Company, 1980.

Aland, Kurt, et. al. (ed.) *The Greek New Testament*, third edition. New York: American Bible Society, 1975.

Allen, Roland. *The Spontaneous Expansion of the Church and the Causes Which Hinder It*. Grand Rapids: Eerdmans, 1963.

Avraham, Shifrin. *The First Guidebook to Prisons and Concentration Camps of the Soviet Union*. New York: Bantam Books, 1982.

Bauer, Walter. *A Greek-English Lexicon of the New Testament and Other Early Christian Literature*. Translated by William F. Arndt and F. Wilbur Gingrich from Bauer's 5th edition. 2d ed. revised. Chicago: Univeristy of Chicago Press, 1979.

Blumenfeld, Samuel. *Is Public Education Necessary?* Old Greenwich, CT: Devin-Adair, 1981.

The Book of Psalms for Singing. Pittsburgh: Board of Education and Publication of the Reformed Presbyterian Church of North America, 1980.

Bulletin of Washington University. St. Louis: Washington University, 1984.

Burns, Scott. "Your Electronic Home Office." Rodale's *New Shelter,* September 1983.

Burton, Linda. "A Place to Come Home To." *Welcome Home,* March 1984.

"Challenges of the 80's." *U.S. News and World Report,* October 15, 1979.

"Child Abuse Rising Nationwide." *Focus on the Family,* June 1984.

Clark, Stephen. *Man and Woman in Christ: An Examination of the Roles of Men and Women in the Light of Scripture and the Social Sciences.* Ann Arbor, MI: Servant Books, 1980.

Daly, Mary. *Beyond God the Father: Toward a Philosophy of Women's Liberation.* Boston: Beacon Press, 1973.

DeMarco, Donald. "On Human Experimentation." *Human Life Review,* Fall 1983.

Dittmer, Janet. "The Home Manager." *Welcome Home,* March 1984.

Elshtain, Jean Bethke (ed.) *The Family in Political Thought.* Amherst, MA: University of Massachusetts Press, 1982.

Extra Income, January/February 1984.

_____. March/April 1984.

Fairfax, Olga. "101 Uses for a Dead (or Alive) Baby." *A. L. L. About Issues,* January 1984.

"Family Violence Emerges From the Shadows." *U.S. News and World Report,* January 23, 1984.

Fitzpatrick, James. *Jesus Christ Before He Became A Superstar.* Harrison, NY: Roman Catholic Books, 1977.

Foh, Susan. *Women and the Word of God.* Philippsburg, NJ: Presbyterian and Reformed Publishing Company, 1979.

Gangel, Kenneth O. and Benson, Warren S. *Christian Education: Its History and Philosophy.* Chicago: Moody Press, 1983.

Goldenberg, Naomi. *Changing of the Gods: Feminism and the End of Traditional Religions.* Boston: Beacon Press, 1979.

Greer, Germaine. *Sex and Destiny: The Politics of Human Fertility.* New York: Harper and Row, 1984.

Gurnall, William. *The Christian in Complete Armour.* Edinburgh: Banner of Truth Trust, 1979.

Hageman, Alice L. (ed.) *Sexist Religion and Women in the Church.* New York: Association Press, 1974.

Hayden, Dolores. *The Grand Domestic Revolution: A History of Feminist Designs for American Homes, Neighborhoods and Cities.* Cambridge, MA: MIT Press, 1981.

"How New Entrepreneurs Are Changing U.S. Business." *U.S. News and World Report,* March 26, 1984.

Hurley, James B. *Man and Woman in Biblical Perspective.* Grand Rapids: Zondervan, 1981.

"Industry Must 'Automate, Emigrate, or Evaporate.'" *U.S. News and World Report,* January 16, 1984.

"Institutions That Affect The Nation." *U.S. News and World Report,* May 14, 1984.

Jewett, Paul. *Man as Male and Female.* Grand Rapids: Eerdmans, 1975.

Joseph, Ray. "Reflections After a Pro-Life Talk." *Christian Statesman,* January/February 1984.

Kasun, Jacqueline. "The Population Bomb Threat: A Look at the Facts." *Intellect,* June 1977.

Kienel, Paul A. "Are Christian School Students Sheltered from the World?" *Christian School Comment.* Prospect Heights, IL: Christian Liberty Academy, n.d.

Kilpatrick, William Kirk. *Psychological Seduction: The Failure of Modern Psychology.* Nashville: Thomas Nelson Publishers, 1983.

Kitto, John. *Kitto's Daily Bible Illustrations.* Grand Rapids: Kregel Publications, 1981.

Lewis, C. S. *The Abolition of Man.* New York: Macmillan, 1947.

"The Life of Mr. Philip Henry." *The Complete Works of Matthew Henry,* Volume II. Grand Rapids: Baker Book House, 1979.

Meier, Paul D. and Burnett, Linda. *The Unwanted Generation: A Guide to Responsible Parenting.* Grand Rapids: Baker Book House, 1980.

Mollenkott, Virginia Ramsey. *Women, Men and the Bible.* Nashville: Abingdon Press, 1977.

Naisbitt, John. *Megatrends: Ten New Directions Transforming Our Lives.* New York: Warner Books, 1982.

Nault, William H. *Typical Course of Study: Kindergarten through Grade 12.* New York: World Book, 1982.

"New Legislation in Nebraska." *Parent Educator and Family Report,* August-September 1984.

Organic Gardening, June 1984.

Razoni, Shirin. "Letter of the Month." *Welcome Home,* March 1984.

Remmus, Sue. "Acquirers vs. Nurturers." *Unschooler's Project,* Fall 1983.

Reynolds, Morgan O. *Power and Privilege: Labor Unions in America.* New York: Universe Books, 1984.

Robertson, A. T. *Word Pictures in the New Testament,* Vol. IV: *The Epistles of Paul.* Grand Rapids: Baker Book House, 1979.

Scanzoni, Letha Dawson and Hardesty, Nancy. *All We're Meant to Be.* Waco, TX: Word Books, 1974.

Scanzoni, Letha Dawson and Mollenkott, Virginia Ramsey, *Is the Homosexual My Neighbor? Another Christian View.* San Francisco: Harper & Row, 1978.

Scanzoni, Letha Dawson and Scanzoni, John. *Men, Women, and Change.* New York: McGraw-Hill, 1976.

Schaeffer, Edith. *Hidden Art.* Wheaton, IL: Tyndale House, 1975.
―――――. *L'Abri.* Wheaton, IL: Tyndale House, 1969.
Schaeffer, Francis. *The Great Evangelical Disaster.* Westchester, IL: Crossway Books, 1984.
Sell, Charles M. *Family Ministry.* Grand Rapids: Zondervan, 1981.
Shaw, Jean. "Why Not Deaconesses?" *Presbyterian Journal,* April 16, 1980.
Sheehan, Bob. "The Problem of Birth Control." *Reformation Today,* November/December 1981.
Simon, Julian L. *The Ultimate Resource.* Princeton: Princeton University Press, 1977.
Simon, Julian L. and Herman Kahn (eds.) *The Resourceful Earth: A Response to 'Global 2000.'* New York: Basil Blackwell, 1984.
Smith, Dean R. "Abortion: Doing Justice and Preaching Peace." *Christian Statesman,* March/April 1984.
Sowell, Thomas. *Pink and Brown People and Other Controversial Essays.* Stanford, CA: Hoover Institution Press, 1981.
Statistical Abstract of the United States. Washington, DC: U.S. Bureau of the Census, 1983.
"Students Defend Abortion for 'High' Social Reasons." *Rutherford Institute,* January/February 1984.
Thayer, Joseph Henry. *A Greek-English Lexicon of the New Testament.* Grand Rapids: Baker Book House, 1977.
Thomas, Cal. *Book Burning.* Westchester, IL: Crossway Books, 1983.
Toffler, Alvin. *Future Shock.* New York: Random House, 1970.
"VA's Goal: 'Model Care' for 9 Million Older Veterans." *U.S. News and World Report.* June 4, 1984.
"Victory in Home-Based Education Statutes." *Parent Educator and Family Report,* June-July 1984.
"Washington State Legislator Says Keep Children Home." *Parent Educator and Family Report,* August-September 1984.
Weber, James. *Grow or Die!* New York: Arlington House Publishers, 1977.
Westerhoff, John H. III. *McGuffey and His Readers.* Milford, MI: Mott Media, 1982.
"When 'Family' Will Have a New Definition." *What the Next Fifty Years Will Bring: A Special Report to Mark the Golden Anniversary of U.S. News and World Report.* 1984.
Whitehead, John. *The Stealing of America.* Westchester, IL: Crossway Books, 1983.

Winn, Marie, *Children Without Childhood.* New York: Pantheon Books, 1983.

Yates, Gayle. *What Women Want: The Ideas of the Movement.* Cambridge, MA: Harvard University Press, 1975.

"2,000 Attend Wisconsin Legislative Hearing." *Parent Educator and Family Report,* March 1984.

INDEX